D0324146

TURNAROUND

The New Ford Motor Company

ROBERT L. SHOOK

PRENTICE
HALL
PRESS

New York • London • Toronto • Sydney • Tokyo • Singapore

PRENTICE HALL PRESS
15 Columbus Circle
New York, New York 10023

Copyright © 1990 by Robert L. Shook

All rights reserved,
including the right of reproduction
in whole or in part in any form.

PRENTICE HALL PRESS and colophons are registered trademarks
of Simon & Schuster Inc.

Library of Congress Cataloging-in-Publication Data

Shook, Robert L., 1938–
  Turnaround : the new Ford Motor Company / by Robert L. Shook.
    p.   cm.
  Includes index.
  ISBN 0-13-932062-8
  1. Ford Motor Company.   2. Automobile industry and trade—United States.
3. Corporate turnarounds—United States.   I. Title.
HD9710.U54F687 1991
338.7'6292'0973—dc20   90-36088
                                                         CIP

Manufactured in the United States of America

10 9 8 7 6 5 4 3 2 1

First Edition

This book is dedicated to Elinor
With love—RLS

CONTENTS

INTRODUCTION

During a three-year period beginning in 1980, Ford Motor Company lost a staggering $3.3 billion, an amount equaling 43 percent of its net worth—a net worth that took more than three-quarters of a century to accumulate. At the time, these losses were the most severe ever suffered by a corporation, yet few Americans were aware of the company's immense problems. Chrysler's near bankruptcy and its ensuing billion-dollar bailout by the U.S. government made national headlines. But, if the truth were known, Ford might easily have been the first to throw itself on the mercy of the government.

Only Ford's profitable overseas operations kept the company from incurring greater losses. Doomsayers had gone as far as to propose a plan that called for splitting the European operation from the North American Automotive Operations. Then, if the U.S. entity failed, a respectable relic of the Ford Motor Company could still have survived.

For years, Ford was considered an American institution, hailed as one of the world's leading industrial firms. Since 1903, when Henry Ford founded the company, the name *Ford* had been synonymous with automobiles. Henry Ford was the father of the mass production of cars, and there are still many Americans who erroneously believe he invented the automobile. At the company's peak in 1923, an estimated half of all car sales throughout the world were Fords as were 57 percent of all cars sold in the United States.

During the first 60 years or so of the twentieth century, America remained unchallenged as the dominant and most-productive nation in the world. Throughout this period, the heart of the U.S. economy was the automobile industry. Huge industries, including steel, glass, and rubber, were dependent on the production of automobiles. The good or bad fortune of General Motors, Ford, and Chrysler strongly influenced the welfare of every industrial nation. By the 1920s, General Motors became the world's largest automaker, while Ford has remained in the number two spot. And although Ford is not the largest automotive manufacturer, few American corporations have ever had the same impact on this nation.

Turnaround: The New Ford Motor Company is the story of how a giant multinational corporation was down for the ten count. It provides a stark lesson about what happens when a colossal company becomes complacent. To many, it appeared that Ford had reached the point of no return—the enormous bleeding organization, governed by a huge centralized bureaucracy, appeared incapable of being revived.

But this is also an inspirational story about what is now acclaimed the greatest turnaround in the history of American industry. Ford did not suffer a knockout after all; instead, it was a nine count. And after having lifted itself to its feet, Ford showed the stuff that true champions are made of—the ability to come back. Not only did Ford survive, the company emerged as the most profitable in what is perhaps the most competitive industry in the world. To do so, extreme discipline was essential. Ford's management team cut excessive layers of fat to become a lean, healthy enterprise. And while billions of dollars of unnecessary costs were cut, billions more were put into capital spending. Never were expenditure cuts made at the sacrifice of quality and productivity. Remarkably, while its work force was reduced from 500,000 to 370,000—a trauma that normally has a devastating effect on morale—the opposite happened. During the early 1980s, a reversal of Ford's long history of adversarial relations between management and labor occurred. And, for the first time in decades, a spirit of teamwork prevailed, in part due to a renovation of the management style that invited employees at every level to participate in rebuilding the company.

What Ford did to turn around from near disaster to become the world's most profitable automaker offers an important message that American business must heed. And Ford's success during the 1980s contains a message that should provide encouragement to all Americans. Ford workers have demonstrated that their productivity and workmanship does not take a back seat to that of any nation's people, in particular, the Japanese. While it is true there are more Americans employed today in the fast-food industry than the automotive industry, America need not resign itself to becoming a server of hamburgers to the rest of the world. In fact, if the United States is to enter the twenty-first century as the world's economic leader, it is essential that its manufacturing sector remains strong and capable of turning out quality products at competitive prices.

Finally, *Turnaround* is a story about change. Incredible change was made in a staid and mature industry that many thought was incapable of change. Still more turbulent times face the fiercely competitive automotive industry during the 1990s. What follows is a behind-the-scenes, step-by-step account of how Ford made its spectacular comeback and geared itself for the challenging final decade of the twentieth century.

A SEA OF RED INK

In the post–World War II era, America enjoyed unprecedented prosperity. No single nation had ever possessed such enormous wealth or so dominated the world's economy. So great was this dominion that in the 1950s, a comfortable assumption made by many was that American industry had indeed solved the problem of production. With their vast resources, America's powerful multinational corporations were viewed as invulnerable. And no others equaled the affluence and prominence of the elite members of the domestic automobile industry.

America's love affair with the auto industry dates back to Henry Ford's first mass production–assembly lines. Ford's initial automotive sovereignty was soon to be shared by General Motors and later Chrysler in the 1920s.

While hundreds of automakers have come and gone since the turn of the century, it was this trio, affectionately known as the Big Three, that not only survived the fierce early competition but, in the process, became the dominating force within American industry as a whole. By the 1950s, the well-being of the U.S. economy rested on the good fortune of these three corporations. The prosperity of mighty industries such as iron, steel, zinc, aluminum, rubber, and glass revolved around the production of Detroit-made automobiles and trucks. Nearly one out of five jobs in America was directly or indirectly dependent on either the production or sale of the products made by these three companies. In short, the manufacturing of automobiles was indispensable to the welfare of the entire nation. And as the American economy went, so went the world economy.

The automobile provided Americans with a luxury that was never before available to the general population—the freedom of mobility. By the post–World War II era, most working Americans could afford a car. The dream of driving from Boston to Los Angeles without encountering a stoplight became a reality in 1956 when the federal government authorized the interstate highway system. These superhighways reshaped the cities and suburbs, and, in doing so, the lives of millions of Americans. This freedom had an immense impact on our society—it offered many never-before-available options of where to live and where to work. People could commute daily from suburbs and communities located 50 miles or more away from their jobs.

The automobile offered an extraordinary convenience, and by the 1950s, practically every family owned one. In the 1960s, two-car families were commonplace. In time, merely owning a car was no longer the status symbol; instead it was the kind of car that counted. It was a period when bigger meant better in America, and bigger cars provided more prestige. They were heavy and bulky. Many even came equipped with "fins" to add a few inches to their already excessive length. As car sizes increased, so did fuel consumption. But during the 1950s and 1960s it did not matter that Detroit produced gas-guzzlers—energy was cheap.

By the early 1970s, Americans, an estimated 5 percent of the world's population, drove nearly 40 percent of the world's motor vehicles with 120 million cars on the road. There was practically a car for every licensed driver (140 million Americans possessed a driver's license). The car had become a necessity. Making one's car payment took priority over the mortgage payment.

As far as the public was concerned, there was a bottomless oil well beneath America's soil. The government artificially kept the price of energy low, so there was no reason for anyone to think differently. Washington had no real energy policy. The federal government spent $77.8 billion to construct an interstate highway system on which Americans could travel at 70 miles per hour (MPH) from coast to coast. The Big Three continued to produce oversize behemoths that were purchased as quickly as they rolled off assembly lines.

Even when it became known that there was a limit to the American oil supply, it had no appreciable effect on the production of gas-guzzlers. Americans still wanted their big cars, and the domestic automakers delighted in accommodating them. There was an added incentive: Big cars generated big profits.

On October 6, 1973, on the eve of Yom Kippur, the most holy day in the Jewish religion, Egypt attacked Israel. Israel struck back, and, for the third time since World War II, the small Jewish state whipped an enemy who greatly outnumbered her. The defeat humiliated the entire Arab world, and it retaliated with its most powerful weapon: an oil boycott, aimed primarily at the United States, Israel's supporter. It took the Yom Kippur War to create an awareness in America that the well did indeed have a bottom. The boycott began in November 1973, and lasted until the following March. For many Americans, it was traumatic to learn that one out of every three gallons of fuel poured into their gas tanks came from faraway, volatile countries. For the first time in memory, Americans were forced to do with less. Some of our smugness vanished, particularly when, by early January 1974, we found ourselves bumper-to-bumper in long lines to purchase gasoline. Long lines also appeared at the showrooms of automobile dealerships selling subcompacts and, in particular, fuel-efficient models equipped with stick shifts.

The gas shortages across America resulted in forecasts of small-car sales capturing 50 percent of the market by the end of the year. Big Three headquarters' predictions said this figure could reach 60 percent by 1980. Executives at American Motors, which only manufactured small cars, were patting themselves on the back for having anticipated the trend as they enjoyed an immediate 28 percent increase in sales by the end of 1973. In the meantime, Detroit was busy reducing the weight of its 1975 domestic models, which led to a 13.5 percent improvement in fuel economy. Automobile executives started gearing up to build small cars to accommodate the public demand.

Gas prices, however, leveled off at 60 cents a gallon by the spring of 1974, and a fickle America abruptly became disenchanted with little cars. By the end of the third quarter in 1974, huge inventories of small cars began to pile up. Ford had a 96-day supply of Pintos while the demand for Lincoln Mark IVs was so great that its employees were working two shifts to assemble them. General Motors (GM) was sitting on a 105-day supply of Vegas, yet its Cadillac plants were working overtime with an inventory down to 26 days. Chrysler accumulated a 105-day supply of Plymouth Valiants, and the inventory of its Japanese-made minicar, the Dodge Colt, was up to a 113-day supply.

The demand for small cars was suddenly so light that major rebate programs were implemented so automakers could rid themselves of their large inventories. Chrysler was the first to rebate, offering discounts on its entire line, the highest rebates offered on its small cars. GM and Ford gave rebates only on their subcompacts. Meanwhile, American Motors, which had enjoyed record sales on its hot-selling Gremlin only six months previously, was now forced to sell that model at a substantial discount.

Even with their bargain-basement prices, the huge inventories of small cars did not go away. Henry Ford II went to Washington to persuade the federal government to place a 10 percent tax on the price of gasoline, which would make small cars more appealing. President Gerald Ford's new energy czar, John Sawhill, went so far as to propose a $1 per gallon tax in an effort to induce the nation to conserve energy. By this time, a high percentage of the American public was seriously questioning whether there had ever been a gas shortage in 1973, calling the whole thing a hoax engineered by profit-hungry oil companies.

There was good reason for the average American to reach such a conclusion. The profits the oil companies realized when the oil embargo ended were huge. When it was over, the price of crude oil had quadrupled from $2 to $8 a barrel, which doubled the price of gas at the pump in the United States from about 30 cents to 60 cents. With a barrel containing 42 gallons, each $1 increase amounted to 2.38 cents per gallon. So while the increase from 30 to 60 cents was a big one, it was quite modest in view of the frightening predictions of the $2 and $3 per gallon costs rumored only months before. At 60 cents a gallon, the fuel cost of running an American car in 1973 was less than 4 cents a mile, or about $1 a day, small potatoes for the average worker who put in less than five minutes at his job to pay for the gasoline consumed in a ten-mile trip.

Consumer advocate Ralph Nader was one of the first to insist that vast oil reserves existed throughout the world and there was no real need to worry about shortages. Before long, the media had convinced the public that greedy oil companies were exploiting the consumer for obscene profits. A Democratic Congress disregarded President Ford's plea to abolish price controls on oil and actually voted to lower the price for the election year of 1976. Hence, in early December 1975, the Federal Energy Administration was ordered to roll back the price of oil by one dollar a barrel by February 1976. Although the legislation did permit the price of oil to increase with the rate of inflation, the increase was limited to no more than 10 percent annually. In effect, the government told its citizens loudly and clearly that cheap gas was here to stay. Energy analysts estimated that under the worst scenario, the price of a gallon of gasoline would remain below 70 cents through 1980.

There was no incentive for consumers to conserve oil, nor, for that matter, were domestic oil companies motivated to extract the precious substance from the ground. This prompted the government, under the auspices of the 1975 Energy Policy and Conservation Act, to establish Corporate Average Fuel Economy (CAFE). In doing so, the burden of energy conservation was placed on those manufacturers that built cars. Under CAFE, each automobile company's fleet of cars was required to be improved to achieve an average of 18 MPG by 1978, with this number increasing to 20 MPG by 1980 and to 27.5 MPG by 1985.

The year 1978 was selected as the first year for mandatory improvement in fuel efficiency, giving Detroit a three-year lead time to come up with the technology to meet CAFE requirements. However, imported cars, especially those made in Japan, were already small and had adequate fuel efficiency. The mandatory government regulations worked in their favor, providing them a strong competitive advantage over American automakers. This created a real dilemma in Detroit. The demand in America was for big cars, and while eager to offer what the public wanted, car manufacturers also had to comply with federal regulations.

The nation's two biggest automakers had the staying power to begin extensive retooling programs to "downsize," which appeared to be an adequate solution. GM announced that it would invest $15 billion by 1985 to downsize its entire line of cars. Following GM's lead, number two and much smaller Ford would make a more modest investment focusing on the immediate market. When Ford brought out its 1977 LTD, it was advertised as "big as a Cadillac, but priced like a Chevrolet," and it sold well. Both companies' full-size cars, such as the Mercury, Buicks, and Oldsmobiles, were built to give the appearance of being big, but actually were greatly reduced in length and weight. The public thought it was buying big cars and was satisfied.

Meanwhile American Motors, which had prospered during the oil embargo, had by the spring of 1975 begun the tailspin that eventually led to its demise. By 1978, American Motors had retained only about half the number of workers on its 1962 payroll. Only the sale of Jeeps kept the ailing company afloat. Chrysler was also in considerable trouble. It did not have the financial strength to keep up with Ford and GM. When the demand for big cars accelerated in 1976, the number three automaker began to flounder. Although 1978 was a big year for Ford and GM, Chrysler was operating in the red. In spite of having the best corporate average fuel economy of the Big Three, the company could not weather the demands of a market that teetered back and forth between small cars and big cars.

In addition to fuel efficiency regulations, the government saddled the domestic carmakers with another burden. The growing concern with the nation's environment created a public awareness of air pollution. Shortly after the publication of Rachel Carson's provocative book, *The Silent Spring,* April 22, 1970, was declared Earth Day, a symbolic event with millions of Americans demonstrating their sentiments for a cleaner environment. Public opinion placed the blame on those companies that made certain products, among which the automobile manufacturers were denounced as the most flagrant villains. It was the same year that the Clean Air Act was passed. Under the jurisdiction of the U.S. Environmental Protection Agency, the law declared that by 1975 federal standards would require hydrocarbon emissions to be no greater than 0.41 gram per mile. Carbon monoxide was limited to 3.4 grams per mile, and nitrogen oxide emission had a ceiling of 3.1 grams per mile. Meeting these standards would reduce by 96 percent the pollutants in the air caused by automobiles. To achieve this objective, all cars with a conventional internal combustion engine that did not meet these standards would be required to have a catalytic converter to suppress the production of the unwanted pollutants. The catalytic converter and other add-ons increased the cost of a car by an estimated $350.

There is no doubt that the needs for improved fuel efficiency and air free of automobile engine pollutants were crucial to the well-being of the nation. From the automobile industry's viewpoint, however, the government had taken the wrong approach. As Ford's Helen Petrauskas, vice-president of environmental and safety engineering and the company's highest-ranking woman, explains, "The government insisted that non-existing technology be invented according to a specific schedule it had legislated. The industry was forced to develop technology by 1975 that had never before been done. To make matters worse, we were asked to meet certain requirements piecemeal—do this by this date, so much by this year, and then do this, and so on, meaning that every year, we had to regroup and come up with more changes. It would have been more reasonable if each specific requirement was set with a long-term goal for which the industry was responsible. To do so would have been more reasonable and certainly more efficient. It's unfortunate but the government bureaucrats who didn't understand automotive technology had the power to set unattainable standards."

Henry Nichol, general manager of Ford's Powertrain Operations, puts it more bluntly, "It simply was not in the cards for the industry to meet the emission control regulations set by the government in the allotted time frame."

Thus the late 1970s were frustrating years for automobile executives.

Ford's chairman, Henry Ford II, had good reason to declare, "They [the government] took the fun out of the business."

To make matters worse, Washington's goals were conflicting. The improvement of engines that would result in less air pollution would also result in less fuel efficiency. Frustrated automotive executives stated their position at a series of Washington hearings, but for the most part government officials turned a deaf ear, frequently accusing the industry of dragging its feet. The public was unsympathetic to the industry's problems.

Honda's 1973 introduction of the compound vortex controlled combustion (CVCC) engine made the formerly minor automaker one of the major players in the U.S. market. Prior to the CVCC, Honda was considered a motorcycle manufacturer that also happened to sell cars. With its breakthrough technology, Honda was the only car company that eliminated the need for a catalytic converter, and by 1975, Honda was selling 10,000 Civics a month. When an article appeared in the December 1975 issue of *Reader's Digest*, titled "From Japan—A 'Clean Car' That Saves Gas," Honda quickly gained credibility. The following year, Honda brought out its larger Accord, which was named *Motor Trend* magazine's Import Car of the Year. This was a major turning point for Honda, Japan's third largest automobile manufacturer. By the 1980s, Honda became the fourth largest seller of cars in the United States, right on the heels of Chrysler.

So while the American automakers were concentrating on meeting government regulations, Honda and other Japanese automakers were able to gain a competitive edge. Although every manufacturer selling cars in the United States was governed by the same regulations, the Japanese companies sold mainly small cars, and were already capable of meeting CAFE standards. The Big Three sold a broad range of cars that included large sedans and station wagons, and this forced them to come up with improved technology so that their entire product line would *average* those required standards, as established by 1975 Energy Policy and Conservation Act.

The Japanese automakers took full advantage of their opportunity to gain ground. While Detroit executives were racking their brains to come up with the new technology, the Japanese were engaged in an all-out effort to improve the overall quality of their cars. In particular, they focused on adding deluxe features generally earmarked for big cars, such as automatic transmission and power steering. They also intensified their efforts to include extras as standard equipment.

In spite of the difficulties facing the domestic automobile industry,

Ford and General Motors continued to sell their big, expensive cars and enjoyed big profits. It was as though the 1973 oil embargo had never happened. The U.S. automobile industry realized $3 billion in profits during 1978, having its third best year in history (although this was when Chrysler started losing money). Ironically, it was a year in which Detroit was fearful that it would be unable to fulfill the strong consumer demand for big V-8-powered sedans. Not only did the domestic automakers produce more V-8-powered, full-sized cars, they also built longer and heavier compacts, many loaded to the hilt with options.

In 1978, when the American economy appeared to have fully recovered from the 1973 oil embargo, more troubles in the Middle East were brewing. The Ayatollah Khomeini's eventual overthrow of the Iranian government was underway, and the Shah of Iran, who had ruled since 1953, was about to lose power. Since the 1950s, the United States had centered its Middle East economic policy around its support of the Shah. Billions of U.S. dollars in military and economic aid had gone his way. But in the end, the Shah could not appease the mullahs, the holy men. Knowing he could not win what had become a holy war, the Shah and his family escaped from Tehran on January 16, 1979, taking a sizable fortune with them. The handwriting was now plainly on the wall; the world must brace itself for another energy crunch.

Once the Ayatollah seized control of Iran, he showed his contempt for the United States by denouncing anything connected with the Western world. Khomeini turned off the spigot and created a second oil crisis. In a matter of weeks the price of gasoline doubled. Once again, America was caught off guard. As Allan Gilmour, who then served as Ford's executive director of Corporate North American Analysis, explains, "On the surface, the business of Ford Motor Company was going very well. The company was enjoying a series of consecutive record quarterly profits. Then, along comes a second oil embargo, and the critics started to shout, 'But you damn fools, why didn't the company anticipate another oil crisis?' To them, my stock reply is we didn't hear anyone on the outside saying that the Shah of Iran was going to be thrown out." A valid point for the public to remember is that the U.S. government, even with its vast network of intelligence, was not aware of what was happening in Iran. So why should the nation's business community be expected to have been prepared for a second oil crisis?

In 1974, Henry Ford II vetoed a decision to spend $2 billion to build a U.S.-made, front-wheel-drive subcompact, instead opting to downsize the LTD and other models, and save money. In 1978, it was obvious

that the Ford chief executive officer (CEO) had made the wrong decision. The redone LTD had weak sales when it came out in the fall, and
Ford had no new domestically built subcompacts in its inventory. "We
misread where the market would be today," Henry Ford confessed. "We
were not as well prepared for it as we should have been. It was a big
mistake."

At the time of the Shah's fall there had been waiting lists for the Big
Three's full-size cars, so much so that Ford was actually rationing V-8
engines. By the spring of 1979, however, Americans across the country
were waiting in long lines for gas. A few weeks later, service stations
were working banker's hours and drivers were hard pressed to find gas
on the weekends. Americans began forming car pools, and in some areas,
most notably Los Angeles, cars on the freeways with no passengers were
confined to nonpassing lanes. Not only was gasoline hard to buy but the
price continued to rise. Once again the general consensus was that the
cost of a gallon of gasoline would hit the $2.50 mark within a few years.

History repeated itself. There was an overnight demand for small cars,
and once again, the domestic automobile industry did not have them. As
early as January 1979, Datsuns, Toyotas, and Hondas were packed into
dealers' showrooms and lots. Suddenly, there was enormous demand for
Japanese fuel-efficient cars and there were plenty of them to meet the
demand. According to *Ward's Automotive Reports,* by March 1, a total of
529,703 unsold Japanese cars and light trucks had accumulated at the
docks and dealer lots and showrooms across the country. Thousands
more were sitting on idle ships anchored in bays, waiting for somewhere
to unload their cargo. The Japanese had made practically nothing but
small cars for three decades, so whenever the demand changed, they
were ready.

Lines of customers formed at Japanese automobile dealer showrooms
throughout America. Suddenly, the American consumer was sickened by
the thought of purchasing a U.S.-made gas-guzzler. Japanese cars offered excellent fuel efficiency and improved quality, and they now contained many of the features of the big cars. At the same time, the quality
of American automobiles had actually slipped a few notches in the late
1970s as domestic manufacturers struggled to meet new fuel economy
and emission standards.

It was no contest. The Japanese cars sold like hotcakes, and, to the
delightful surprise of their purchasers, *they were good cars,* with far fewer
problems than those made in the United States. *Made in Japan* was no
longer synonymous with shoddy merchandise. The American public quickly

forgot that, as recently as 1970, imported cars accounted for only 15 percent of the market but amounted to 45 percent of the total recalls that year. By May 1979, there were waiting lists of up to a year for some Japanese models.

To add to Detroit's woes, interest rates soared to an all-time high, climbing well over the 20 percent mark. The prime lending rate, the interest banks charge their best customers, rose to a record 21.5 percent. High interest rates hurt big-ticket automobile sales more than less-expensive products. The high cost of money added to the cost of manufacturing, and this, in turn, increased the monthly payments of a financed car in the early 1980s. For the buyer with the ability to pay cash, it was obvious that his or her money could generate a double-digit return in a money fund or savings account if it wasn't tied up in a high-priced automobile.

The dollar was strong compared to the yen, giving the Japanese yet another edge. American manufacturers were also faced with labor costs in Japan that were about half of those paid in the United States.

By the first quarter of 1980, the U.S. market share of the Japanese automakers surpassed 21 percent. Sales would have been higher had they been able to satisfy the demand. The total of all small imports sold in the United States was more than 30 percent of the market for the year. This figure had been less than 15 percent as recently as 1972. The actual number of U.S.-made cars fell from 9.3 million in 1978 to 7 million in 1980.

It has been said that with its very expensive product line, the automobile industry tends to climb higher during good times and dives lower during bad times. As David Scott, vice-president of Ford's external affairs, explains, "In recessionary times, people are still going to eat cornflakes. They're going to buy the staples, and perhaps even semiluxury items. It's the sale of the high-ticket products like automobiles that get hurt the most." Car sales have always been among the first to suffer in a recession, and because there were 105 million cars on the roads in the United States, it was entirely possible for Americans to continue using them.

With the nation in the midst of one of its worst recessions in years, the domestic automakers were burdened with immense overhead in plants and equipment, so it is no wonder that the abrupt fall in sales caused the American automobile industry to come crashing to its knees. Chrysler was hit the hardest. The cash-poor company could not afford to build its own four-cylinder engines and was forced to contract Volkswagen to manufacture 300,000 engines for its cars in Germany. Had Chrysler possessed the inventory of small cars to meet the demand it might have survived the troubled times on its own. In 1978, when its other models failed to sell, the company's market share slid from 12.2 to 11.1 percent, a huge drop for one year's time. Then conditions worsened. By the middle of 1980, Chrysler had lost $2 billion in an 18-month period, at the time, a record amount for a U.S. firm. The company was able to stay afloat, thanks only to a $1.5 billion guaranteed loan provided by the federal government.

While Chrysler's bailout by the government bordered on being the business disaster story of the decade, Ford was having its own nightmare when its 1980 losses came in at a staggering $1.5 billion. By 1982, the combined three-year total loss was $3.3 billion, an estimated 40 percent of the company's net worth. If it were not for Ford's profitable European operations the company could have been forced into bankruptcy proceedings. Auto analyst Maryann Keller of Paine Webber Mitchell Hutchins commented, "Caught between GM, with all its money, and Chrysler, with a federal sugar daddy, Ford has to husband its limited resources."

One reporter described 1980, Ford's most disastrous year, by writing, "U.S. car and truck sales slammed into reverse, the company lost a devastating $1.54 billion, and morale and credibility were slipping like the transmission on an overloaded Edsel." For good reason, the members of the press dubbed Ford as "Chrysler II." The talk around Detroit was "First it was Chrysler and next it would be Ford."

David McCammon, vice-president of finance and treasurer, describes Ford's sorrowful state of affairs: "In 1980 and 1981, everything was reversed. The prime rate was higher than our market share, and in 1981, the price of our stock was a lower number than our market share. We never saw anything like that before. The prime rate should be by far the lowest number, and then the market share followed by the stock price, but everything was in the wrong place. If it wasn't so tragic, it would have been humorous.

"I remember eating upstairs in the penthouse executive dining room with some other vice-presidents. We made a pact that each day somebody in the group would bring in a piece of good news before lunch to cheer us up, and only then would we break bread. But business was so awful that had we stuck to the pact, we would have starved. It became a short-lived ritual."

By the end of the 1970s, Ford had still another problem: The company's image was badly tarnished by poor publicity resulting from a series of lawsuits over what were referred to by the media as "exploding Pintos."

Consumer advocate Ralph Nader and *Mother Jones,* a San Francisco magazine, launched an attack on the top-selling subcompact, calling it unsafe because its gas tank was placed too far back and, therefore, might explode on impact when hit from behind at a high speed. In 1978, a record $128.5 million was awarded to a young man seriously injured in a fire resulting from a rear-end collision in a Pinto. While the actual amount paid was reduced to $7.0 million, the $128.5 million figure put the story on the national networks and front pages across the country.

Another Pinto rear-end collision in 1978 resulted in the deaths by fire of three teenage girls near Elkhart, Indiana. This dreadful accident received even more attention due to a recently passed Indiana law that declared criminal charges could be brought against a manufacturer found guilty of making an unsafe product. As one of the nation's largest and best-known corporations, Ford was a prime candidate for a prosecutor to test the law. In early 1980, the case was tried in Winamac, Indiana, a tiny town of 2,300. The trial caught the attention and imagination of the national media. With the full drama of a "Perry Mason" episode, the prosecutor displayed a cut-in-half Pinto to the jury to demonstrate that the car was poorly constructed in comparison with other cars. He argued that Ford was, therefore, negligent in manufacturing a faulty product. The defending attorney responded by doing the same to four similar cars of other manufacturers. Because the four cut-up cars were unable to fit inside the courtroom, the location of the trial was temporarily moved to a lower floor of the courthouse. The jury determined that the Pinto was not unsafely constructed. Instead, the accident resulted when the Pinto's driver stopped on a highway after she noticed that the gas cap had not been put back on at a filling station. Instead, the cap was placed on the roof of the car and the woman saw it fall off and roll on the road. When she stopped the car to retrieve it, a van crashed into the rear end of the Pinto with a force of more than 50 MPH, resulting in three fatalities.

Although Ford was acquitted, the popular Pinto's sales were cut nearly in half by the poor publicity and the car never again won the favor of the American consumer. While *Mother Jones* claimed that there were as many as 500 deaths, the federal government found only 27 deaths by early 1978, eight years after the bestselling car had been on the road. Federal data on auto accidents revealed the Pinto performed as safely as other American and foreign small cars. The damage, however, was done; the alleged design defects had raised too much doubt in the minds of the public, and the good name of Ford was deeply tarnished.

Philip Caldwell, who replaced Henry Ford II in 1980 and remained as

CEO until 1985, explains, "It takes a long time for people to forget a lousy experience; reputation is a very perishable product." The quality of all Ford automobiles was in question. It wasn't long before FORD was being used for such sayings as "Found On Road Dead" and "Fix Or Repair Daily."

Some company executives became personally annoyed with the poor quality of Ford automobiles. Philip Benton returned from England after a three-year stint as vice-president of Truck Operations for Ford of Europe Incorporated, and he became acutely aware of the problem when ordering the new car that top managers receive each year. "When I came back to serve as vice-president and general manager of Ford Division in 1979," Benton remembers, "I had a hard time making my selection of a car. There weren't any I had a desire to drive. That's when it really hit me how badly things had deteriorated during the brief time I was overseas. Just a few years before, it was always a case of 'which one shall I get?' Suddenly, I realized how much trouble we were in."

Lee Miskowski recalls attending a 1981 Las Vegas dealers' convention to introduce the following year's models. At the time, he was the Ford Division's general manager and the company's only new products were the Granada station wagon and the Escort four-door model, which had previously been limited to two- and three-door models. "It was the fourth year in a row that we had nothing really substantial in our product line to offer," he notes. "So we made a lot of fanfare and played some great music. Our theme that year was, 'Look out world, here comes Ford.' We put on a good show, but that's all. There was a lot of hype but little to sell."

Doug McClure, former executive director of marketing, served as advertising manager during the hard times. "Back then, I didn't want my friends and neighbors to buy one of our cars because I didn't want to hear their complaints."

And Don Petersen, who was Ford's president at the time, says, "I used to shy away from going to cocktail parties in the early 1980s because when I did, people would come up to me and say, 'Why don't you do this?' and 'Why don't you do that?' Every comment was negative and oriented to our weaknesses and inabilities."

Joe Kordick, who took an early retirement in 1989 after rising through the ranks to serve as vice-president of parts and service, comments, "When I joined the company in 1954, my parents, who were immigrants, were so proud of me that you would have thought I had descended from heaven when I got the job. Twenty-five years later, we had frittered all of that [pride] away."

During the 1970s, internal strife was also brewing at Ford. In his autobiography, Ford's former president Lee Iacocca states, "I often ask myself why I didn't quit at the end of 1975. Why did I accept the fate Henry was dishing out?" The conflict between the company's top two officers became the source of considerable tension in the Ford executive suites of its Dearborn world headquarters building, and it had had an adverse effect on the morale of other executives. At the very least, the feud was distracting to and draining on Ford and Iacocca.

Caldwell attributes some of the Ford-Iacocca conflict to an ego clash that caused confusion at a time when harmony was essential. "As a result, the business planning process broke down and the company was left without a blueprint for the future. We had become an overly centralized bureaucracy. The organization did less and less on its own. There were too many decisions being made at the top. It became '*I* will decide everything.' Note that while not mentioning any names, the *I* to which reference is made was not Henry Ford, but someone else with the initial *I*."

When Iacocca was fired and then went to Chrysler in 1978, the Ford camp was left temporarily divided. A dynamic leader, Iacocca with his magnetic personality had attracted several loyal supporters who gave their allegiance to him rather than the company. A handful of Ford executives followed Iacocca to Chrysler. The publicity surrounding the firing had a negative impact on Ford, and millions of Americans sided with Iacocca, thinking he was unjustly treated. To many, it was a case of the giant corporation picking on the little guy. Later, Iacocca made convincing appearances in television commercials as Chrysler's spokesperson. When the nation's number three automaker began to operate again in the black, Iacocca became an American folk hero, receiving the credit for saving the company from bankruptcy and giving the government millions in profits by paying off a $1.3 billion government loan early. His popularity was attested to by his book's number one bestselling status.

By the beginning of the 1980s, the country was in the throes of a recession, one that dealt such a severe blow to the automobile industry that Detroiters refer to it as "the depression." At its peak, the unemployment rate in Michigan soared to nearly 16 percent compared to the national average of 9 percent. In Detroit, the number of laid-off workers hovered around 20 percent, and in some communities it was as high as 25 percent. Only in the Great Depression of the 1930s had the Motor City experienced a comparable swelling of the ranks of the unemployed. All in all, 269,000 hourly autoworkers and more than 50,000 salaried employees lost their jobs. The U.S. auto industry closed 38 plants across the country. The U.S. car market fell from 10.5 million units in 1979 to 8.9 million in 1980; it slid to 8.5 million in 1981 and dropped again to 8 million in 1982. While the American piece of the pie continued to get smaller year after year, the sales of foreign cars grew to nearly 30 percent of this shrunken market.

To avoid a strong U.S. protectionist reaction, in the spring of 1981 the Japanese automakers reluctantly self-imposed an annual ceiling of 1.68 million cars exported to America. Soon, in response to possible import quotas, Japanese auto manufacturing plants were built on American soil. Honda was the first to do so when it opened its automobile plant in Marysville, Ohio, in late 1982—at the same location where three years previously it had begun assemblying motorcycles. Those units made in America by the Japanese "transplants" are not included in the count of cars exported to this country.

With the foreign car sales picking up the slack, Ford's U.S. cars sales volume dropped from 2,632,190 units in 1978 to 2,044,462 in 1979; 1,397,431 in 1980; 1,385,174 in 1981; and 1,270,519 in 1982. The Company's 1978 market share of 24.4 percent had dropped to 16.9 percent by 1982. After a long drought with little in the way of good news during the company's four-year fall, Ford's 1982 annual report had the following positive remark to offer its stockholders: "Although unit sales were 1% below 1981 because of the decline in total industry sales, we are encouraged by Ford's 1982 improvement in the U.S. car market share to 16.9%." As a result of Ford's 1981 market share dipping to 16.6 percent, a three-tenths of 1 percent gain was hailed an improvement.

What the 1982 annual report did not show, however, was that during the last quarter of the year, Ford had only a 16.7 percent market share. Even worse, during one ten-day period, it slipped to an embarrassing low of 14 percent. In the meantime, Chrysler captured about 10 percent of the U.S. market share during this period, which stirred up talk at its headquarters about taking over the number two spot.

With a three-year loss of $3.3 billion during the 1980–1982 period, Ford's shareholder's equity dropped from $10.6 billion to $6 billion. For the first time since Ford became publicly owned, dividends were suspended. The company's debt-to-equity ratio rose from 19 percent to an all-time high of 79 percent, and, subsequently, the company's AAA credit rating declined to a BBB rating. "Even worse, our commercial paper rating went from A1P1 to A2P2," says William Odom, chairman of the company's credit and insurance subsidiaries.

Daniel Coulson, who served as manager of the profit forecast and financial statements department from 1977 to 1980, comments on Ford's hard times during this period: "Our cash planning process provides an estimate of anticipated financial planning based on market trends, which we overlay with a moderate economic cycle. Then we observe it and build several worst-case scenarios, which include the possibility of a disaster, its effects, and how we can sustain such a calamity. Well, it would suffice to say our disaster scenarios didn't approach what actually happened. It's an understatement to say that we were caught off guard. In reaction to the shock of the drastic drop in our market share following the second oil crisis, we cut production schedules and simultaneously did some immediate cost cutting to stop the bleeding. But the market drop was so severe it wasn't possible for us to adjust fast enough."

By late 1979, Ford executives were aware that their problems were more severe than just dealing with a second oil crisis. It became apparent there were underlying conditions that surfaced as a result of the energy shortage. "We had been focusing too much on the competition across town," Caldwell states. "While we were looking at what was going on in our own backyard, we didn't pay close attention to the Japanese. It wasn't enough to reduce our overhead while we weathered out the depression. In addition to our costs being too high, our quality was too low."

Donald Jesmore, general manager of Body and Assembly Operations, thinks that although the government regulations were a constant bone of contention to Ford, they were more a distraction than the source of the real problem. "The depression in the early 1980s was the stimulus that caused us to do a lot of introspection," he claims. "For years, the Japanese threat was taken lightly and viewed more as academic and on the theoretical side. Sure, we knew the competition existed, but because it inched up on us so gradually, always with slow but steady year-to-year increases, its presence was never regarded as a serious threat. Then out of the blue, our 1979 sales dramatically nosedived and we reacted by taking off shifts and ordering massive layoffs. When it became abundantly clear that the Japanese cars were better quality, the media attacked the American assembly line worker for his or her shoddy workmanship. It was grossly unfair, however, for the worker to take the brunt of the blame."

As sales tumbled, the assembly-line worker was the first to get hurt. At first, his 1979 paycheck was only reduced when the company had no need to work him overtime. When conditions worsened, plants working two shifts were cut back to one shift. Initially, workers with little seniority were the ones to lose their jobs. Then plants began shutting down for weeks at a time, and even those with seniority took cuts in their paychecks. As the depression deepened, many plants were permanently closed, which put everyone in the unemployment lines. The average number of Ford's U.S. employees in 1978 was 256,614. By 1982, only 155,901 remained on the company's payroll. Ford's worldwide number of employees also went down during this period, dropping from 506,531 to 379,229.

Today, Robert Adams is general manager of Ford's Transmission and Chassis Division, but in 1978, he was transferred to the Cleveland Engine Plant as its new plant manager. At the time it was Ford's biggest engine complex, with one facility that made big engines and a second that made small five-liter engines. When Adams first arrived, the complex was operating at full capacity, working three eight-hour shifts, seven days a week, which meant paying overtime to many of the 15,000 workers. Ford was Cleveland's largest employer, and with the popularity of big cars, many workers were being added to the payroll. "Everyone was working under a lot of stress in an effort to make as many engines as possible; as a result, quality sometimes suffered," Adams relates.

"When the oil embargo hit, the demand for our bigger engines dropped immediately, so we were forced to cut back to two shifts and eliminate all overtime. Next, we closed the big-engine plant altogether and operated the small-engine plant with two shifts. Then as Ford's sales continued to slide, it went from two assembly lines to one, at which point the total employment of the Cleveland Engine Plant shrunk to about 2,500 workers. Needless to say, the massive reductions in the work force had a devastating effect on morale. The stressful conditions operating at full capacity when I took over as plant manager were *nothing* compared to a different kind of stress we endured when we had to cut back.

The layoffs at the Cleveland Engine Plant were mirrored in other Ford plants across the country. One such plant that was permanently closed was the company's 180-acre complex in Mahwah, New Jersey, the largest single assembly plant in North America. When its doors shut in April 1980, a total of 3,732 workers were let go, a catastrophic blow to the community's economy. "This is a total, all-out disaster," wailed union local president Joseph O'Hara.

During these hard times, Jack Hall headed personnel for North American Automotive Operations (NAAO). In this capacity, he dealt with the tens of thousands of Ford people who lost their jobs once such decisions were made. "It was the worst time imaginable. It was absolutely devastating," Hall says sighing. "In addition to the hourly workers, we were downsizing organizations throughout the company which meant restructuring and consolidating jobs across the board. Entire layers of management were wiped out. I was receiving telephone calls in the middle of the night from foremen, engineers, and managers seeking advice and even pleading with me to do what I could to help them. Many of these callers had never worked anywhere else and they didn't know where to turn. Needless to say, GM and Chrysler were also making substantial cuts in their payroll, so they weren't hiring. The job market had completely dried up in Detroit. My heart went out to these people. It was very painful, and for a while, it didn't look like there was much hope. There was some concern that Ford might cease to be a manufacturer in North America. Perhaps we'd make cars overseas and only sell them here."

Perhaps hardest hit were the 10,000 plus Ford and Lincoln-Mercury dealers spread out across the country. Each of these entrepreneurs had more than his or her job in jeopardy—most often savings that were accumulated over a lifetime were on the line. Many of the Ford dealers began their careers as salesmen who, for the most part, were attracted to the business by their love of cars. The top sales producers were those who were hungry and hardworking. If they were smart, they were promoted to sale managers. The most ambitious sales managers sought the pot of gold at the end of the rainbow—a dealership of their own. To them, this was the epitome of the American dream. Because it required large sums of money, they found backers, who ranged from the dealer who employed them to the Ford Motor Company, itself. Still others received large bank loans. Regardless of the source of funds, owning a dealership is a highly leveraged and risky undertaking. This was particularly clear to Ford dealers when the bottom fell out during the great automobile depression.

Typically, the owner of a dealership has millions tied up in real estate and equipment, and in addition, a substantial inventory of cars. Monthly budgets for high overhead such as advertising, salaries, and utilities also have to be paid—regardless of how cars are selling. And in the tough times, the expense that's the big killer is the interest payments on the financed inventory. The year 1979 marked the beginning of a nightmare come true.

Ross Roberts, now vice-president and general manager for the Lincoln-Mercury Division, says, "To describe business then as dismal is putting it too good. It was absolutely terrible! We were building cars the way we wanted to build them rather than the way our customers wanted. It wasn't just Ford; all the domestic automakers did the same thing because we had a monopoly. We were doing that for more than 70 years, and when the market collapsed, we kept putting the same cars in the showrooms with the hopes that our dealers would move them out. For a while, the dealers had an eternal hope that the business would turn around, but it didn't."

During the depression, Roberts was appointed district sales manager for the Ford Divisions' Louisville district in the summer of 1979 and then was named to the same position for Lincoln-Mercury Division's Los Angeles district in the summer of 1981. "My first question to my predecessor in Louisville when I arrived there on day one was, 'How many units do we have on the fence?' In other words, I was asking him for the number of cars owned by the company that hadn't been sold to dealers."

" 'We've only got one,' I was told.

" 'That's amazing. How can you just have one?'

" 'We know what we're doing down here. We've got it under control,' he replied optimistically.

"Well, within three months we had over 2,000 units on the fence! That's how fast the business went downhill. Now, for a small district like Louisville to have 2,000 unassigned cars and trucks, we were in deep trouble. And this district was typical of what was happening in the Midwest in such places as Chicago, Cleveland, and Detroit. The manufacturing base of this country was going down the tubes.

"We had dealers who had been with us for 5, 10, even 40 years, who were going under. Some of them went broke so fast, they didn't know what was happening, and those who did, couldn't do a thing about it. That's how fast we got hit."

Two years later, when Roberts was transferred to Los Angeles, he went out of the proverbial frying pan into the fire. While Ford dealers were bleeding profusely in all parts of the country, there was no place where the blood ran so thick as it did on the West Coast. "In LA, about 25 percent of our dealers were closed, and an equal number were up for sale," Roberts recalls. "The banks were even deserting us. One major bank, for example, wrote to all of our dealers in the area and bluntly told them that it didn't want to do business with them anymore. The bank said it didn't think Ford was a good investment and the dealers should find a new source of finance. Imagine the panic that went through the district when our dealers were informed the bank was cutting off their credit for cars and their retail paper."

In 1980, Lincoln-Mercury's largest dealership in the LA district went bankrupt. "The dealer got in trouble as a result of repossessions," Roberts explains. "Customers got fed up with their poor gas mileage and were tired of having to make so many stops and then wait in long lines at the service stations. So they'd drive their cars up in front of the dealership and hand the keys over. They might have only made five or six payments, but it didn't matter. They just walked away, not caring about what it did to their credit.

"There was one dealership that went out of business," Roberts continues, "that I tried to sell for over a year. Interestingly, I contacted one Buick dealer who refused to give me the courtesy of even looking at it. The company was willing to let him have it at a price far below the value of its inventory. He could have written his own ticket for the place, maybe have even picked it up at 50 percent below book value. We would have worked out any kind of deal to sell it. This dealer was typical of so many—they wanted no part of Ford or Lincoln-Mercury. Most California car dealers were convinced we weren't going to make it. A few years later, the same Buick dealer tried to buy that Lincoln-Mercury dealership at least three or four times. In fact, he even offered to pay a million over blue sky [the value of the net assets] to get it."

"Our monthly sales dropped from 7,000 to 3,000 in 60 days when the second oil crisis hit us," remembers Thomas Wagner, vice-president and general manager of Ford Division, referring to the time when he was the sales manager for the Los Angeles district office. Wagner assumed this position in January 1979, just before the bottom fell out. "When I arrived in LA, there was a ton of Japanese cars sitting on boats in the Long Beach Harbor, with no place to unload them. So, I was right there on the scene of the cutting edge of all the changes that overtook the American automobile industry. Literally overnight, the domestic business went sour."

Wagner explains that there is always a turnover in the automobile business, which occurs in the bottom half of the Ford dealer organization. "The top half is fairly stable," he points out. "For the most part, it was the small, mom-and-pop shops that found it too difficult to compete. But back in the early 1980s, we even lost a few of our big dealers. More than 1,000 dealers in the United States went under between 1978 and 1982. Our number of dealers worldwide dropped from 13,500 to 10,500 during the same period."

Now a Ford vice-president in charge of sales operations in North America, Robert Rewey was named general manager of Lincoln-Mercury Division in September 1980. "While the Japanese automakers knew how to build quality cars, at the time, they were not proficient in marketing and selling their products in this country," Rewey explains. "So they took the easy route and raided the Big Three for experienced people. It was amazing how well their intelligence system worked. I remember one young person from California, who, upon graduating from our college training program in Detroit was sent home to LA and the same day he walked into the office, he received a call from a Japanese firm offering him more money to work for it. I won't mention names, but one Japanese automaker hired nearly 70 of our field people who then became the main source of their sales organization.

About the same time, the Lincoln-Mercury Division suffered another blow when its advertising agency, Kenyon & Eckhardt, abruptedly resigned and took on Chrysler as a client. With rare exceptions, advertising agencies represent only one national firm in the same industry because they are privy to so much confidential and strategic information. So, in the midst of all of its problems, Lincoln-Mercury was thrust into the tedious and hectic chore of going on a shopping spree to find a new ad agency. All the while, its advertising program remained in a state of limbo. Eventually, after an exhaustive search, the division hired Young & Rubicam, which, to this day, represents Lincoln-Mercury.

Ford executives brought back home from Europe where business was profitable were shocked to find out how bad conditions really were. They received calls from Europeans who expressed their concern, often inquiring about whether Ford's North American Automotive Operations would survive, and if it did not, what was to become of the overseas operations. Others, both inside and outside the company, questioned whether Ford would come out whole or if it would emerge from the depression only a mere shell of the powerful company it once was.

Ford was a company that had deep roots that traced back to the turn of the century and had played a leading role in American industry. It was worth saving.

THE OLD FORD MOTOR COMPANY

Ford's rich, often turbulent history is a fascinating story, sometimes reading more like a television–miniseries script than the journal of an industrial phenomenon. Its roots go back to the turn of the century, and although there are some major corporations that can be traced back further, no other company has played as significant a role in American history. Certainly few other members of the same family have ever remained in the limelight for as many years as Henry Ford and his grandson Henry Ford II.

Ford is synonymous with automobiles. Ask who invented the car and most Americans will reply, "Henry Ford, of course." For a time, the Japanese word for automobile was *fordo*. The automobile, however, was conceived in Europe, and as with the airplane, no single individual can take credit for its invention. The automobile age began in the mid–1880s, and an estimated 3,500 makes of motor cars have since been produced around the world, although, at present, less than 100 automakers remain in business. The first automobiles to be manufactured were built around 1885 by Gottlieb Daimler and Carl Benz. In America, the debut was in September 1893, when Charles and Frank Duryea publicly demonstrated their version of a gasoline-powered vehicle in Springfield, Massachusetts, six years before the Ford name was first associated with automobiles.

Born on July 30, 1863, on a farm near Dearborn, Michigan, Henry Ford, as a young boy, showed an early interest in mechanics. By the age of twelve, he had spent most of his spare time working in a small machine shop, and three years later he had constructed his first steam engine. Ford served as machinist's apprentice in Detroit with James F. Flower and Bros., and later became a chief engineer for the Edison Illuminating Company. In his spare time he tinkered with internal-combustion engines and once built a small one-cylinder gasoline model on a wooden kitchen table in his Detroit home. His engine was mounted on a frame fitted with four bicycle wheels and was the first Ford automobile to hit the street. The year was 1896.

Three years later, in 1899, after resigning from Edison, Ford formed the Detroit Automobile Company with a group of businessmen. He obtained a one-sixth interest and was named chief engineer. Two years later, the firm went into bankruptcy. In the year 1900, at least 38 American companies had begun producing automobiles. In 1901, there were 47 more, and by 1903, another 57 firms entered the field. One of the 57 new entries was Ford Motor Company, founded on June 16, 1903. It had been captialized with $150,000; only $28,000 was in cash, paid by a group of 12 investors. Included were a coal dealer and his bookkeeper, a banker, two brothers who owned a machine shop, a carpenter, two lawyers, a clerk, the owner of a notions store, the owner of an air rifle company, and, of course, the forty-year-old Henry Ford. A doctor expressed an interest in investing in the new company but was rejected because the superstitious Ford felt 13 investors was courting bad luck. Ford had a 25.5 percent interest in the newly formed corporation.

Ten workmen were hired at $1.50 per day and immediately began producing a two-cylinder eight-horsepower (HP) car that could run at a top speed of 30 MPH. (The first model received the letter *A*, and as new models were designed, they were assigned sequential letters of the alphabet.) The first 1903 Model A was completed in early July and advertised as "the most perfect machine on the market and so simple that a boy of fifteen could run it." Selling it, however, was not so simple. The company was on the verge of running out of cash when, on July 15, Dr. Ernst Pfennig, a Chicago dentist, placed the first order for a Ford product. Prior to the dentist's payment of $850, the Ford Motor Company's bank balance had dwindled to $223.65.

From a converted wagon factory on Detroit's Mack Street, 1,700 Model A's chugged past the company's gate during the first 15 months of business. Some models were experimental and never reached the market. The Model B was a luxurious four-cylinder touring car priced at $2,000. The Model C was released in 1904 and sold for $800. These two expensive models had a large per-unit profit, but few were ever purchased. When one of his employees remarked to him that automobiles would someday be the most common means of transportation, Ford replied, "Only if a manufacturer can make cars at a price so more people can afford to buy them." He added how it bothered him that the company bearing his name was producing a product unaffordable to the majority of Americans.

Alexander Malcomson, a coal dealer and Ford's first financial backer, suggested that a publicity stunt was necessary to drum up business for the higher-priced models. So in the middle of the winter of 1904, Henry Ford was chosen to drive against the clock over a one-mile straightaway course on the frozen surface of Lake St. Clair. It was a daring ride, and, driving a Ford racing car known as the 999, he clocked in with a time of 39.4 seconds, establishing a world record. Having risked his life for the company, he was determined to gain control of it.

The Model K, an expensive $2,500 six-cylinder luxury car, was released in 1906 but, in spite of its attractive styling, its reception was only modest. This heightened Ford's resolution to sell a lower-priced car "designed for everyday wear and tear and affordable by the average person." Heated discussions occurred when Malcomson opposed Ford's "absurd notion," and caused a bitter conflict about which market the company should pursue. Should it produce more small cars, or fewer of a luxury model? Malcomson argued for fancy cars with price tags in the $2,200 to $4,700 range, pointing out that more than half the cars sold fell into this catagory. A stubborn Ford insisted, "The way to make automobiles is to make one automobile like another automobile, to make them all alike, to make them come through the factory just alike, just as one pin is like another pin when it comes from a pin factory."

In July 1906, concluding that it was impossible to convince Ford to do things his way, Malcomson sold his shares to him for a tidy sum of $175,000 (Malcomson's bookkeeper, James Couzens, who scraped together $2,500 to be one of the original investors, sold his interest to the company in 1919 for $29 million). The transaction with Malcomson gave Ford a 58.5 percent ownership in the company. That same year, he replaced John Gray, a Detroit banker, as president.

Another hurdle was a legal problem that resulted when George B. Selden, an attorney, claimed to own a patent on "road locomotives" powered by internal-combustion engines. The Rochester lawyer applied for the patent back in 1879, and, amazingly, it was granted to him in 1895. Rather than risking an infringement suit, the major companies, including Cadillac, Olds, and Packard, formed the Association of Licensed Automobile Manufacturers (ALAM) and actually paid Selden a royalty of 1.25 percent of the retail price on every car they sold in America.

Among the companies to join ALAM was a new conglomerate that was being put together by a successful carriage maker, William C. Durant. Durant's firm was buying up such automakers as Cadillac, Buick, and Oldsmobile, and using the John D. Rockefeller approach, paying for his acquisitions by offering stock in his parent company in lieu of actual cash. Unlike Ford, Durant was not a car man, but a shrewd entrepreneur who knew how to build big businesses. After debating what to call his new enterprise, Durant named it General Motors rather than International Motors. He even made an offer to purchase the Ford Motor Company for $8 million on the condition that Henry Ford would stay out of the automobile industry. Ford agreed to sell, but insisted on cash. However, Durant was unable to convince his bankers to loan him the money and the deal fell through.

In the meantime, Ford refused to submit to what he believed was an attempt to monopolize the industry, and for nine years engaged in a legal battle with ALAM and Selden. His legal expenses exceeded $1 million. Ford also had to contend with newspaper advertisements placed by ALAM that contained explicit warnings stating any person making, selling, or using unlicensed automobiles would be prosecuted. Many potential dealers and customers heeded the threats, and in 1909, the courts upheld the Selden patent. Ford appealed, believing that if the upper courts did not rescind the earlier ruling, his company would be forced out of business. To combat the infringement charges, he, too, ran full-page advertisements voicing his strong opposition to the Selden patent. By bucking the establishment, Ford became a folk hero across the country. Later, following highly complicated court proceedings, his company emerged as the victor of a battle that freed it and the rest of the industry from Selden's monopolistic grip.

During the Selden suit, Ford continued to produce new models, and, following a series of improvements, reached the 19th letter of the alphabet with a variety of cars. Some had two-cylinder engines, others had four, and one had six. Some had a chain drive while others had a shaft drive. Two models had the engine under the seat. In 1908, Ford introduced the Model T. Priced at $950, it was an affordable and an overnight success. "No car under $2,000 offers more," boasted its advertisements. By this time, a suspicious American public had become accustomed to false claims in the automobile industry, but the Ford Model T was all it was claimed to be. Its first year sales reached 10,660, establishing a new industry record. Henry Ford attributed his success to what he believed was splendid timing. "I invented nothing new," he said in 1909. "I simply assembled into a car the discoveries of other men. . . . Had I worked 50 or 10 or even 5 years before, I would have failed."

Henry Ford was in his glory. The Model T was the car he had always dreamed of building. It was uncomplicated, durable, affordable—and without frills. It was a car that a farmer could afford, and Ford viewed himself as an agrarian populist. Although he personally despised farming, it was his heritage, and he considered farmers "his kind of people." In fact, for a while his ambition was to provide a detachable engine, one that a farmer could take off a car and use for performing other chores such as sawing wood, pumping water, and operating farm machinery. His goal was to produce the Model T in large quantities and, in turn, bring down the price so the average man could own one.

To fulfill his dream, Ford hired Frederick Winslow Taylor, a scientific industrial management expert who had previously introduced time-and-motion studies to the steel industry. That same year, in 1908, Ford offered a huge $20,000 bonus to Walter Flanders, an industrial efficiency expert, if he could install a system to provide the Ford factory with the capacity to produce 10,000 automobiles per year. Flanders earned the bonus with two days to spare. In doing so, he convinced Ford to move into larger quarters in Highland Park, Michigan, where, in 1910, the company's first assembly plant opened. It was a new concept in auto-making replacing the garage-shop facility with a process referred to as the *line*. Ford became obsessed with implementing new production methods, no matter how slight, to increase efficiency on the line. No increment that enhanced the speed of production was neglected, nor was any means to reduce costs as long as it did not greatly compromise quality. "Every time I reduce the charge for our car by one dollar, I get a thousand new buyers," Ford once exclaimed.

The acceptance of the automobile as a mode of transportation started slowly but increased rapidly. For example, in 1902, the year before Ford entered the business, one car existed in the Unites States for every 1.5 million people. Within two years, there was one car for every 65,000 Americans. By 1909, the numbers changed to one car for every 800 people. The need for mobility was never in question. Henry Ford was right; it was simply a matter of money. If automobiles were affordable, people would buy them. The Model T, first introduced on October 1, 1908, was a rugged, simple car and was priced low enough that it was not considered a rich man's toy. It was to become the most famous automobile ever manufactured. Nicknamed the "Tin Lizzie" and the "Flivver," its popularity was such that it became commonplace in American literature—songs were even written about it. Perhaps no other product ever captured the nation's imagination like the Model T.

The Model T was brilliantly simple; still, it promised efficiency and utility at an exceptional value. Unlike other vehicles, it was not a threat to farmers and they accepted it; yet it appealed to sophisticated buyers as well.

The first year's production of the Model T set an industry record. Its U.S. market share was 9.4 percent. By 1911, the Model T sales reached 54,000. The Model T, which had initially sold for $950, eventually was priced at $360 due to a series of cost-efficient, mass production innovations. By 1914, Ford Motor Company became the world's top-producing automobile company. Ford's U.S. market share reached an incredible 48 percent. Its work force of only 13,000 assembled 267,720 cars while the 299 other American auto companies with 66,350 workers assembled 286,700 cars. Americans were buying Fords as fast as they came off the assembly line.

Although Henry Ford is rightfully heralded as the father of mass production in America, he was not the inventor of the assembly line. Forms of an assembly line date back to the pyramids. But in the automobile industry, Henry Ford and the assembly line were one and the same.

At first, it took 12.5 hours to produce a single Model T. Yet in 1908 Ford announced his ambition to produce one car every minute. That meant he would have to increase his production by 750—an ambitious goal by any standard. During Ford's first attempts to assemble an entire car via a "moving line," its frame was placed on skids with workers pulling it by rope from one end to the other of the 250-foot-long building. A small team, consisting of a handful of workers, followed behind Charles Sorensen, Ford's top production manager, gathering and assembling parts stacked in large piles at various stations. This led to what is believed to be the world's first *moving* assembly line, which began in 1913 when groups of workers were assigned stations at the Highland Park plant. Rather than moving with the mobile car down the line, they waited for its arrival. In its original crude form, it is probable no one present recognized that what they had witnessed would forever alter the course of civilization. That same year, an elevated, motorized conveyor belt was introduced. Soon, every piece of the car (and its assembly) were traveling down the line, some by a moving platform, others on hooks and overhead chains.

Obsessed with the stopwatch, Ford carefully analyzed methods to eliminate every human step possible. "Let the conveyor do the walking," he insisted. Ford once calculated that if ten steps could be saved by each of his workers, he could conserve 50 miles of wasted motion on a daily basis.

Sorensen, who played a major role in the assembly-line operations, spent several years working as a pattern maker for other automobile companies prior to joining Ford in 1905. A tall, powerful Dane, whose family emigrated to America when he was four years old, Sorensen worked relentlessly, putting in 14-hour days, including most weekends. He expected the same effort from his workers during their 60-hour workweek at two dollars a day. Ford nicknamed him "Cast-Iron Charlie" and the name quickly spread throughout the plant. With Sorensen in charge of production, Ford spent less time in the plant, but on occasion the boss would make the rounds. Undoubtedly, Sorensen's stringent and demanding management style eroded the morale of the work force. On one tour through the plant while accompanied by Edsel, his nineteen-year-old son, Ford sensed a resentment toward him by the workers. Edsel confirmed that he, too, had experienced the same feeling.

Ford had a strong need to be loved and was hurt by the thought that his 13,000 workers no longer adored him. In search of a quick remedy, he summoned Sorensen, James Couzens, his principal business partner, and a handful of bookkeepers; a quick review of the company's financial statements was soon completed. Ford became embarrassed when he saw the company's incredibly high turnover of employees. He was well aware of the high cost of the constant training of new workers. Futhermore, turnover was inefficient and it reduced quality.

"What if we increase a worker's daily pay from $2 to $2.50?" he questioned. "What would that do to our profits?"

The accountants made projections revealing that profits would still be exorbitant.

"What happens if we pay $3?" he inquired. After reviewing the numbers, he ordered, "Up it to $3.25 and let's see what we get."

The more his consultants protested, the more the obstinate man raised the wages. Finally he stopped at $5. On January 4, 1914, a public announcement was made that Ford Motor Company planned to increase wages to more than twice the going rate of the current nine-hour day, while decreasing the work load to an eight-hour shift. The business community was furious. *The Wall Street Journal* wrote that $5 a day was not only unsound but unethical. Another publication stated that it would ruin America's lower class and bring unhappiness to the masses. Businessmen across the country said that Henry Ford was crazy, and worse, he was dangerous. Some went as far as to express that his action could wreck the U.S. economy. Cartoons appeared in newspapers across the country with workers dressed in fur coats reclining in chauffeur-driven limousines. One caption read, "Pull over to the pay window, James, and get my wages. I quite overlooked to do so last week."

While Ford did indeed have the workers' best interest in mind, he also wanted what was best for his company. He wanted to attract the most highly skilled workers. After all, it made little sense to have expensive machines operated by inept and uninspired workers. He also planned to reduce turnover of employees. His accountants estimated that it cost $100 to train each worker, and in 1913, 963 workers were hired for each 100 who permanently remained on the payroll.

Once the word was out, the public reaction was reminiscent of the great Gold Rush. At least 10,000 workers from across the nation headed to Detroit to apply for work at the Ford Motor Company. They camped outside the plant's gates for days to be hired on as a Ford man. Special policemen were hired to keep the crowd under control. Henry Ford had stated he wanted his pick of the best—and with thousands of workers eager to work for him, he certainly got his choice.

The $5 day was one of Ford's smartest decisions. In addition to attracting better-qualified workers, as an extra bonus it generated so much favorable publicity that the company was able to reduce its advertising and sales soared. Ford also believed that a well-paid American work force would have the ability to purchase more Model Ts. In retrospect, the $5 day did go a long way toward converting a segment of the working class into the middle class.

Ford's mass production–assembly lines were saving so much money that the company could have paid $10 and still have generated huge profits. During the Christmas holidays in 1913, two lines were installed at waist level, and by doing so, production time per car was reduced from 12 hours and 30 minutes to 1 hour and 33 minutes. Henry Ford was so far ahead of his competition that his only challenge was to compete against himself.

As more cars rolled off the assembly line, Ford kept reducing the prices. Profits per car in 1913 dropped to $93 as compared to $200 two years earlier. However, sales jumped from 78,440 cars to 248,307, with net profits rising dramatically. In 1908, less than 10 percent of the new cars on the American roads were Fords. By 1914, nearly half of them carried the company's crest. After-tax profits hit $30 million in 1914 and $60 million in 1916.

As one Model T after another rolled off the assembly line, Henry Ford was on his way to becoming one of the world's richest men. And in this role, he was constantly in the limelight. The September 7, 1916, issue of *The Nation* stated:

> Men now hardly past middle life were brought up with the idea that the Astor fortune represented the boundless possibilities of profit in real estate investments, the Vanderbilt fortune the result of the control of transportational opportunities.... Now two or three decades later they were thrown into the shade by the names of Carnegie and Rockefeller. But even the Carnegie and Rockefeller fortunes appear to have been piled up by a slow and lumbering process when one sees the great golden stream flowing into the coffers of a man who not long ago was a simple mechanic, who has no recourse to combination or manipulation or oppression or extortion, who has simply offered his wares to a public eager to buy them and distanced his competitors by no other art than that of turning out his product by more perfect or more economical methods than they have been able to devise or execute.

Henry Ford was indeed a legend in his own time, and to many he was a saint. For instance, he showed deep compassion for the handicapped. More than a half century before the rest of the country indicated an awareness of the needs of the disabled, he instructed his employment office to be especially lenient when hiring disabled workers; only people with contagious diseases were automatically rejected. By 1919, the company employed more than 9,000 handicapped workers in a work force that totaled nearly 45,000. Included were the blind, deaf, and amputees. Each received the full rate of pay. Also on the payroll were an estimated 500 ex-convicts, many of whom received early parole when guaranteed a job at a Ford plant.

Yet, there was another side to the man, a dark side. Ford did not hesitate to express his opinion on many issues, and when the influential industrialist spoke, millions of Americans would listen. While he possessed genius in the automotive field, when it came to unrelated topics, he was frequently misinformed and unsophisticated and—worse—he was malicious. Ford bitterly opposed America's entry into World War I and stated that he would give away all of his possessions if it would put an end to the war and America's stockpiling of arms. He even went further. In 1915 *New York Times* interview, Ford declared, "The word, 'murderer' should be embroidered in red letters across the breast of every soldier." This statement was made at a time when the country's patriotic pitch was at a record high—and, needless to say, his unpopular sentiment did not win friends or influence many people.

And on whom did he blame the war? "The Jewish bankers caused the war," he declared. Henry Ford was an unabashed anti-Semite, although, in fact, he had never actually met a Jew. In an editorial in the *Dearborn Independent*, a Ford-owned weekly newspaper, he made such outlandish statements as: "Rising rents stemmed from the Jewish landlord" and "The present Jewish government of Russia was transported almost as a unit from the lower East Side of New York," and, to him, this proved that "the Bolshevik revolution was a carefully groomed investment on the part of international Jewish finance." Another editorial offered to pay $1,000 to anyone able to furnish him with an example of a Jewish farmer. (This was part of his belief that Jews avoided "honest" manual labor and instead pursued careers in "criminal" banking activities.) He gave strict orders that no Jews were to be employed by the company.

His anti-Semitism resulted in lawsuits and threats of lawsuits. Hollywood magnate William Fox was so appalled by Ford that he threatened to fight fire with fire. Fox stated that if Ford did not stop flooding the newstands with anti-Jewish propaganda, he would flood theater screens across the country with scenes of broken-down Fords.

As one of the world's most celebrated figures, the outspoken former farmer always attracted reporters who gathered around him and eagerly devoured every outlandish quote that came from his lips. Some statements were bigoted. Others were sheer nonsense. Nonetheless, Henry Ford said them and this made them newsworthy. A nonsmoker, he said, "Study the history of almost any criminal, and you will find an inveterate cigarette smoker." A nutrition buff, he claimed, "Most people dig their graves with their teeth." A chauvinist, he excluded women from the company's profit sharing, declaring, "We expect the young ladies to get married. I consider women only a temporary factor in industry. Their real job in life is to get married, have a home, and raise a family. I pay our women well so they can dress attractively and get married." On the subject of history, he once said, "I don't know anything about history and I wouldn't give a nickel for all the history in the world. The only history that is worthwhile is the history we make day by day." Ford also believed it was not necessary for people to wear glasses, but instead, they should exercise their eyes. And having once observed that men who worked in oil fields were seldom bald, every day of his life he greased his head with a light grade of kerosene as a substitute for a hair cream. Amazingly, in spite of his laughable beliefs, two attempts were made to draft him as a candidate for president of the United States.

While Ford actually contemplated seeking residence in the White House, he was too busy making automobiles and money to ever get around to doing it. His driving obsession was to produce more and more automobiles. The Highland Park plant had become the world's largest factory complex, yet by 1915, with annual production at a quarter of a million cars, Ford wanted to build an even larger facility—one that would have the capacity to process all the raw materials that went into the final product. His vision was to build the ultimate factory, a self-sufficient industrial complex where all of the raw materials such as iron, coal, wood, and rubber would come in at one end and automobiles would be driven out on the other end. This desire prompted him, in 1915, to personally buy 1,200 acres of marshland located on the Rouge River in Dearborn. His goal was to build the largest industrial complex in the world. Construction on "the Rouge" began in 1917. Upon completion and during its heyday in the 1920s, the massive plant was a mile and a half long and three-quarters of a mile wide. Generating its own power, the Rouge used enough electricity every day to light the homes in a city of more than 1,000,000 people. Its coal supply could heat 330,000 homes. With a complete railroad system of more than 85 miles of track and 20 diesel locomotives, it was the largest industrial railroad in the nation. The Rouge had 229 coke ovens, three blast furnaces, rolling mills, one of the country's largest production foundries, an engine plant, a stamping plant, a tool-and-die plant, a frame plant, a glass plant, a radiator plant, and an assembly plant. It also included a steel mill, making Ford the only automobile company to ever own one. All in all, there were 93 buildings, and at its peak, more than 100,000 workers were employed at the Rouge.

Everything that went into the Rouge, from its blast furnaces to its electrical systems, was the best of its kind. The best efficiency experts were hired to make it so. Large barges loaded with raw iron ore pulled into its docks on the river, and by the following day, that same ore was part of a cast-iron engine. It was just-in-time delivery in the purest sense.

The demand for the Model T was so overwhelming that only production limitations stood in Ford's way. To increase the number of cars manufactured, Ford kept pouring profits back into the company. In his mind, this was the best use of money. He despised bankers and financial people, referring to them as parasites who lived off the labor of others. He also considered the paying of dividends to stockholders as wasteful because, as "idle investors," they never made contributions to the company.

This belief was not shared by the stockholders. During the same year of the ground breaking at the Rouge, Ford was sued by John and Horace Dodge, two brothers who operated a machine shop. In the early days of Ford Motor Company, the Dodge brothers had accumulated stock in exchange for parts they manufactured. Now they were suing because they believed Henry had withheld stock dividends to which they were entitled. In a heated trial that received national attention, the court ordered the company to pay $19 million in dividends. Although $11 million was paid to Ford himself, he resented distributing money to stockholders. To him, it was "money gone idle" instead of back into plants and machines.

The Dodge suit prompted Henry to seek complete control of the company, and after paying out a total of $105 million to outside stockholders, the Fords owned 100 percent. The $41,500 invested by the original group of investors netted them the largest return on risk capital ever recorded in the United States. With the buyout, Henry owned 59 percent and the 41 percent of the acquired minority stock went to his son, Edsel. During the 16 years that minority stockholders had owned a piece of the Ford Motor Company, they received dividends totaling $39 million. Each Dodge brother pocketed a tidy sum of $12.5 million, enough for them to start up their own company. Had Alex Malcomson, the investor who sold out to Ford back in 1906, waited another 13 years, instead of getting $175,000 for his stock, the buyout formula would have netted him $64 million. With the Fords owning 100 percent of the company, Henry was in a unique position of power that no other American industrialist ever enjoyed. Even the famed John D. Rockefeller at the peak of his business career only owned 27 percent of the Standard Oil Company.

A few years after the Fords acquired 100 percent of the outstanding stock, a financial syndicate offered them $1 billion for the entire company. While the offer was promptly rejected, it accentuated the bargain Ford received when he bought out the minority stockholders for $105 million.

As America's first billionaire, Ford was once questioned about how he compared his wealth and privilege to that of the pharaohs. Ford responded by suggesting that a better story would be the comparison of a Ford worker (who at this time was paid $7 a day) "with a fellow on the pyramids who worked for ten cents a day."

In January 1919, Edsel was named president of the Ford Motor Company, receiving an annual salary of $150,000. Although Henry, now age fifty-five, announced that the reins were being turned over to his only son, he let it be known that, title or no title, it was still his company, and he was the one who would make all major decisions. It was unfortunate that Edsel was not permitted to assume command; he was a talented executive and well respected throughout the industry. Edsel was also highly regarded by company employees. Called "Mr. Edsel" in the factory, he was a gentle and modest man who possessed an unusual mixture of nobility and the common touch. He adored his father and constantly sought his acceptance. Edsel realized his father's greatness, while he understood his faults. As John Dodge once told his former business associate and later rival, "Henry, I don't envy a damn thing about you except that boy of yours."

By 1920, Henry Ford's goal of producing cars at the rate of one per minute had become a reality (five years later, the company was producing cars at the rate of one every ten seconds). Yet 1921 marked the first time that the nation experienced the cyclical nature of the automobile industry. In the midst of a postwar slump, the American consumer realized that he or she could do without a car during tough times. As auto sales dropped, Ford reduced prices. The price tag of a fully equipped Model T, for example, dropped from $995 to $795. If they accomplished nothing else, Ford's large price cuts were brutal to the competition, contributing to the demise of many small automakers. Ford's cost reductions caused General Motors to suffer such severe difficulties that its founder, William Durant, was forced to sell his interest to the Du Pont family.

In 1922, Lincoln Motor Company was forced into receivership. Lincoln had been formed in 1917 by Henry Martyn Leland, the former president of Cadillac, who resigned earlier that year because Durant, a pacifist, refused to make World War I aircraft engines. Twenty years earlier, Leland had been brought into the Detroit Automobile Company by stockholders to straighten out difficulties, causing Ford to resign in a fit of anger. Leland reorganized the company as Cadillac Automobile Company and manufactured luxury cars until 1909 when it was acquired by Durant for $4.5 million. Lincoln made Liberty V-12 aircraft engines, and following the war, in 1920, Leland chose to launch a quality car. His timing was terrible. The U.S. economy was hit by a recession, and the new stodgy-looking Lincoln was priced at $6,600. There were also serious postwar material shortages, a supplier's strike, and a federal tax claim.

On February 4, 1922, Ford bought Lincoln Motor Company at a receiver's sale for $8 million. Although Leland wanted to remain president, on June 10, 1922, both he and his son, a company vice-president, were fired. Not only did Ford make his entry into the luxury car market then dominated by Cadillac and Packard, but, in the process, he settled an old score.

Once the nation's economy got back on its feet, Ford's sales skyrocketed, and by 1923 its founder celebrated his sixtieth birthday with annual sales of 2,120,898 cars—57 percent of all the cars sold in America. An estimated half of the car sales in the entire world were Fords. By 1927 more than 15 million Model Ts had rolled off the assembly line, making it by far the most popular automobile ever; a record that has never been approached.

While Ford's greatest strength was his production expertise, it later worked against him. He paid less attention to technological changes in the product and instead became obsessive in his pursuit of technological changes in the manufacturing process. As a consequence, Ford lost touch with the market. The Model T was a good value and it was dependable. And although it lacked glamour, for years its dependability was a selling point. However, the tastes of America were changing, and an automobile was no longer simply a mode of transportation. Just as a home provided more than shelter and clothes were chosen not just to cover one's body, an automobile made a statement about its owner. And while it was the men who bought cars, women had an important say in the decision. By now, the competition was offering a variety of styles and an assortment of colors, but Henry Ford was basking in the past success of the Model T and refused to alter his plan. Edsel and other company managers did their best to persuade him to change with the times, but he retorted: "Sell 'em any color they want as long as it's black." He refused to recognize that people would buy a car for any reason other than dependable transportation. He would publicly boast, "A Ford will take you anywhere except into society."

By 1925, although Ford hit the 2 million annual sales mark for the third consecutive year, GM's Chevrolet car division was beginning to increase its market share. So much so, in fact, that in 1925, Ford's market share dropped from 57 percent to 45 percent, and the following year it dipped to 34 percent. GM offered several innovations to spur sales. For example, it provided installment financing—a significant selling point to low-income buyers; Ford did not believe in extending credit. Furthermore, GM had a wide range of products and made annual model changes. Alfred Sloan, who became GM's president in 1923, preached, "A car for every purpose, and a car for every pocket." Each year the company would bring out slight improvements in both performance and style. While the Model T was still the best value, GM's marketing skills far surpassed Ford's. Sloan was the industry's first advocate of what was later to be known as planned obsolescence. He preached that a new model should create dissatisfaction with a year-old model.

One employee of Ford who advocated change was William Knudsen. Knudsen was the driving force in building Model T assembly lines, and in a two-year period set up 14 plants across the country. Nicknamed "Big Bill," the 6-foot, 230-pound Dane was hardworking and highly capable, but he did not fit the mold that Henry wanted for his executives—he smoked, drank, and swore—automatically putting him in poor favor with the boss. Knudsen was a tough taskmaster, but he was fair and was well liked by the workers. The rugged, independent Knudsen was one of the few employees in the company who spoke his mind freely to the boss. Ford misinterpreted independence of this nature as disregard for authority. Even worse, he viewed it as disloyalty. With Edsel, Knudsen tried to convince the old man that the Model T must be improved. For instance, one new feature the two men recommended that did not meet with Henry's approval was the convenience of two doors instead of one. Although Ford acknowledged Knudsen as "the best production man in the United States," he made it clear to one and all that he made the decisions and there would be no changes.

Knudsen simply reached a point where he could not tolerate working for Ford and maintain his self-respect. Inevitably, there was no choice but to leave. One day in 1921, he walked away from his $50,000-a-year job, and shortly thereafter was hired by GM. So Knudsen was out and Charles Sorensen, who never disputed the boss's orders, was in. With a free rein at GM, the highly experienced Knudsen performed magnificently, and Ford's superiority in manufacturing was no longer a given. Other Ford executives also left to join GM. Alfred Sloan surrounded himself with top managers and not only did GM emulate and then improve on Ford's production expertise, but it excelled in the management and marketing end of the business as well.

In 1926, the sales of the Model T dropped to 1.67 million, and Chevrolet sales rose from 280,000 to 400,000, and even though Ford cut its prices twice, sales kept plummeting. On May 26, 1927, the 15 millionth Model T rolled off the assembly line and it was the last one ever built. In a ceremonial 14-mile trip, with his father in the passenger seat, Edsel drove it from the Rouge to the Dearborn Engineering Laboratory where the first had been produced. It was the end of an era in American history.

That same day, all Ford plants were shut down, including the Rouge, the world's biggest factory, to retool for a new Model A. The closings laid off more than 60,000 workers in Detroit alone. There were 10,000 Ford dealers across the country who were forced to endure the months that followed with only the sales of leftover inventories and spare parts to help pay their overheads. With Ford's absence, U.S. car sales were down nearly 1 million from the previous year, which some blamed for causing a mild recession. Many simply delayed making a decision until the new Model A was unveiled. There were armies of loyal Americans who still believed in the man who had put them in the seat of their first automobile.

The sixty-four-year-old Henry Ford worked with the same passion and dedication he had in his youth. His enthusiasm spilled over to his designers and engineers, and they, too, put in long hours building the new Model A. Edsel was in charge of styling, which included the body, interior, and instrumentation, and for the first time in years, Henry stayed out of his way. A monumental effort was put into the new Model A, and upon its completion, it consisted of nearly 6,000 new parts. Its changes were mind-boggling—major improvements were made throughout. With only a four-cylinder engine, it accelerated faster than most six- and eight-cylinder cars. The new Model A left the Model T in the dust. It had comfort, speed, and power. What had been previously unavailable was now included as standard equipment—niceties such as hydraulic shock absorbers, a gas gauge, a standard gearshift, rubber-cushioned seats, and a speedometer. Priced at $495, it was about $100 cheaper than the equivalent Chevrolet. What's more, unlike the Model T, it could no longer be called utilitarian. It oozed with contemporary styling.

If Ford had learned anything about marketing from GM, it was how to masterfully launch a new model. In late November, days before the unveiling, full-page ads appeared in the nation's newspapers announcing the new and improved Ford. Millions of Americans eagerly awaited its arrival. Their anticipation was heightened by the sight of the first cars being hauled into dealership showrooms—fully concealed in oversize canvas bags. Perhaps the only event in 1927 to receive more news coverage was Charles Lindbergh's solo transatlantic flight.

When the Model A was finally revealed on December 2, millions of people poured into Ford showrooms. By 3:00 A.M. on the day of the unveiling, hordes of curious car buffs had gathered at New York's leading dealership located on Broadway. When the massive crowd exceeded

100,000 by midday and became too difficult to handle, the manager arranged to occupy Madison Square Garden as a temporary showroom. That same day, in New York City alone, 50,000 orders were taken, each with a cash deposit. Across the nation, an estimated 10 million saw the Model A during the first 36 hours in the showrooms, and within a week, the number reached 25 million, a staggering 21 percent of the entire U.S. population. Yet, so few cars had been produced that in some dealerships in smaller communities the Model A did not actually arrive until several weeks later. In many cases, a single car was put on exhibit for a few hours, only to be driven to the next town, again for a brief stay. By Christmas, an estimated 500,000 advanced orders had been received— still, few customers had been given the opportunity to test ride the new vehicle. Ford plants worked overtime to produce orders that would take months to fill.

The launching of the Model A appeared to be a huge success, and gave Henry Ford good reason to believe that once again his company would dominate the automobile industry. But the competition was also making new innovations. In 1928, Chevrolet came out with a new six-cylinder model, slightly higher priced than the Model A, but a good value. Ford also had to contend with Walter Chrysler, the former president of Buick, Willys, and Maxwell, who started up his own company in 1925. His early successes included his De Soto and Plymouth lines, which rapidly advanced to the number three spot behind Ford and General Motors. Chrysler's fast rise as an automaker allowed him to acquire the Dodge Company in 1927. So while the Model A was a fine automobile, its success was short lived. In 1929, Ford's sales were 1,851,000 for a 34 percent market share compared to Chevrolet's 20 percent. This was the last year that Ford held the number one spot; it was relinquished in 1930 and has been held by GM ever since.

On Black Tuesday, October 24, 1929, the stock market crashed, rocking the nation, and, in particular, the automobile industry. Within a year, 5,000 banks went under and 6 million workers lost their jobs. The Depression hit Detroit hard. In 1929, approximately 5,294,000 cars and trucks were sold in the United States; by 1933, only 1,848,000 were produced. The unemployment rate exceeded 50 percent in Michigan. Yet, working on the theory that higher earnings would enable workers to buy more cars, Henry Ford reduced the prices of his cars, and, at the same time, guaranteed a $7 a day wage. He theorized that the bankers and financial men who played with money were the people who caused the Depression and it would be men like him, who created wealth, who would solve the nation's economic woes. But this strategy did not work in the Great Depression. Eventually, Ford had to reduce daily wages to $4 while its work force dropped from 101,000 to 56,000. There were few jobs to be found, but one sure way to find employment at the Rouge was to put down enough cash to purchase a new car—or to come up with a rich relative who could buy one. Unfortunately, unemployed men in desperate need of a job did not possess large savings nor did their families.

With millions of Americans subjected to the misery caused by the Depression, Henry Ford, the billionaire, soon lost his status as a folk hero. For a while he came to work with patches sewn on the elbows of his suit jackets to project the image that the tough times had caused even him to make sacrifices. But the masses who stood in soup lines were not taken in by his masquerade. His popularity dwindled even further when he blamed the Depression on the excesses of the Jazz Age. Once he declared that it was "a wholesome thing in general" and commented that it could be "the best times we ever had." On another occasion, he said, "If there is unemployment in America, it is because the unemployed do not want to work." His lack of compassion for those who were victims of the Depression was shocking, particularly when he stated that the only problem with the Depression was that it might be over too soon and people would not have learned enough from it.

During the troubled thirties, Alfred Sloan continued to build General Motors into what would someday serve as a prototype of the modern corporation. He pioneered a decentralized form of management, establishing industry divisions that served as integral units, each headed by its own executive structure, but all under a single corporate umbrella. Unlike Ford, in addition to its manufacturing effort, GM emphasized other areas of business such as marketing, financing, and long-range planning. Sloan introduced to GM the organizational chart in the shape of a pyramid, whereby opportunities for advancement were available to those people at the bottom. Henry Ford opposed a structured organization and wanted no part of an organization that defined authority and contained lines of succession. Edsel tried to convince his father that a formal structure was essential to a company of Ford's size. Henry refuted him and any advice that advocated professional management. The old man would frequently say that if he wanted a job done right, he would always pick the man who didn't know anything about it. Furthermore, he had a strong dislike of accountants and bookkeepers. He put them in the same category as he did most other white-collar people: They were parasites who made no contribution to the company. His intolerance was so great that on occasional walks through the bookkeeping department, he would suddenly fire workers by the rows of desks, insisting, "They are not productive, and don't do any real work. Get them out of here today." As a result, one of the world's largest industrial companies had an accounting system that functioned with the same degree of sophistication as a mom-and-pop operation. The system was so archaic that, on occasion, bookkeepers actually estimated how many millions of dollars of accounts payable were due by measuring stacks of invoices by the foot. Had Ford been a publicly owned corporation and thereby accountable to the public, such gross mismanagement would not have been legal.

In retrospect, it is a wonder that the Ford Motor Company survived the 1930s at all. Ford's lack of professional management is perhaps best epitomized by one highly influential company figure, Harry Bennett, a man whose climb to the top of the corporate ladder is a remarkable story. Bennett's career stands out because it reads like an old B movie script— one that the critics pan for being "too Hollywood." They'd insist a screen-writer, who knew nothing about business, must have invented the Bennett character for he could not exist in the real world. But, in fact, Harry Bennett did exist, and, for a while, he had immense influence in the company.

The recruitment of Bennett began in the streets of downtown New York in 1916 on a day when Arthur Brisbane, an editor and columnist of the Hearst newspapers, was on a brisk walk to visit his good friend Henry Ford who kept an office in the financial district. Brisbane was attracted by a crowd of people that had gathered to witness a sailor being brutally beaten up by a large, powerful man. Suddenly, a short, stocky sailor stepped in to rescue his buddy. Although considerably smaller, the second sailor proceeded to pulverize the bully. He did such a thorough job that, had it not been for two policemen separating them, the bully would have surely suffered severe injuries. As the police were about to arrest the sailor, Brisbane stepped in and identified himself; the sailor was released to his custody.

This sailor, an ex-fighter recently discharged from the navy, was Harry Bennett. As the two walked down the streets of New York, Brisbane said that he was on his way to meet with Henry Ford and invited Bennett to meet the famous industrialist. At the meeting, Ford listened in awe as Brisbane gave a blow-by-blow account of the fight. "I can use a man like you," an excited Henry Ford said. At the time, the Rouge plant was under construction, and Bennett was hired as a company policeman. His pugilistic talent would be used to help control the tens of thousands of often-rowdy construction workers.

For years, Henry had been paranoid about kidnappers and wanted to guarantee his only child and grandchildren were well protected. In 1917, following the birth of Henry Ford II, Bennett became the personal body-guard of the Edsel Ford family. While no attempt was ever made on the lives of Edsel and his four children—Henry II, Benson, Josephine, and William Clay—Harry Bennett claimed full credit for their safety. By the 1930s, Bennett was running an organization within the company known as the Ford service department. Its main function was to enforce disci-pline. For example, because Henry forbade smoking on the premises, one day Bennett, with a pistol he kept in his desk, shot a lighted cigar out of the mouth of a union official. The boss was delighted. There were also times when Bennett punched employees in the mouth for insubordina-tion. Others received severe beatings by "Bennett's Boys," a collection of ex-cons, retired boxers and wrestlers, cops thrown off the force for mis-conduct, and scores of other undesirables, who, like their department head, were not opposed to employing scare tactics. The service depart-ment did its job well. It also had a devastating effect on morale.

The old man admired Bennett and saw in him a toughness that he wished his own son had. Edsel, however, was never exposed to the school of hard knocks that his father and Bennett had endured. To his father, Edsel's gentleness was a weakness. As the father and son relationship deteriorated, Bennett was treated more like a relative than an employee, and in Henry's mind, he could do no wrong. He was fond of saying, "Harry gets things done." In Henry's mind, that's what counted.

Bennett liked to practice his marksmanship from behind his desk. Each day, he would sit in his office with an air pistol and shoot steel pellets at a target on the wall. While some visitors were impressed that he could shoot of the tips of sharpened pencils that were standing in a container on his desk, they always felt intimidated, and that is exactly how Bennett wanted people to feel in his presence. Once, in 1932, when a Communist-inspired mob of 5,000 marched in protest at the Rouge, Bennett's troops resisted violently and drove them off the premises. Dur-ing the confrontation, four men were killed and scores injured, including Bennett, who was knocked out. It was hand-to-hand combat, the kind Bennett liked. The body of one dead man was found sprawled over the unconscious Bennett.

Bennett was well compensated for his services. In addition to his generous salary, he was able to take advantage of the utter chaos that existed within the accounting department. He engineered ways to sift money from the company till and amassed enough wealth to own several homes and live a lifestyle far more lavish than his salary could support. Yet nobody in the company dared to challenge Bennett. Those few who did not fear him still knew that the elderly Ford would always side with Bennett. The old man was totally taken in by his henchman.

In addition to his service department activities, Bennett served as personnel director. In this capacity, he could control who worked for the company, and he never let anyone forget it. The mystique of Harry Bennett was enhanced by his basement office in the old Ford administration building. Behind clouded glass in a public corridor, the department had but a single room from which Bennett operated. The man was an awesome enemy, not somebody whom anyone would want to displease.

The apprehension and terror Bennett instilled created a horrendous work environment, certainly not one conducive to attracting and keeping key executives. Hence, good men left by the droves. Those who remained did so with the hope that the old man would someday retire or die and finally Edsel would be in command. Unhappily, however, it was Edsel who was suffering from failed health, not his father. For several years a severe case of ulcers forced him to lie still for long periods on a couch in the executive restroom where he was fed crackers and milk.

The thirties were turbulent times at Ford. The company's U.S. market share dropped to 22 percent in 1936, while GM had 43 percent and, most embarrassingly, Chrysler's jumped up to 25 percent. One of the few upbeat happenings at Ford was its Lincoln division's production of the Zephyr in 1935. The Zephyr was Edsel's baby. He bought the rights for it from the Briggs Manufacturing Company, after seeing its prototype at the 1933 automobile show. Edsel wanted to have a car priced between the Ford and the Lincoln to compete against GM's middle-of-the-line products. The popular Zephyr was the forerunner to the Mercury, which made its debut in 1937. Edsel also introduced the Lincoln Continental in 1939 as Ford's answer to the great European touring cars. "Father made the most popular car in the world. I would like to make the best," Edsel said with pride.

On July 30, 1938, the city of Dearborn had a celebration in honor of its most famous citizen's seventy-fifth birthday. At a ceremony, Henry Ford donated 20 acres of land to be used as a municipal park, on the condition that alcoholic beverages would be banned. A dubious honor was then bestowed on Ford when Detroit's German vice-consul presented him with the Grand Cross of the German Eagle. Ford's accepting the highest honor that a foreigner could receive from Hitler outraged Americans. After Hitler invaded Poland and the European war was under way in September 1939, Ford joined Charles Lindbergh, himself a 1938 recipient of the Grand Cross of the German Eagle, in opposing U.S. aid or arms to Britain and France.

Ford Motor Company did, however, support the war effort. In late 1940, General James H. Doolittle asked the company to build 200 B-24 Liberator bombers. Although the government was considering Consolidated Aircraft as a custom builder to produce one to two planes a day, following a tour of its San Diego plant by Charles Sorensen, Edsel, and two of his sons, Henry II and Benson, the Ford men announced that if given the contract, the company had the capacity to mass produce in excess of 500 Liberators a month. The concept of mass producing airplanes appealed to Henry. The idea of operating the world's first integrated aircraft assembly line excited him. So he approved the project with only minor reluctance, believing that it did not matter anyhow because the war would be over in Europe before the planes were ever used.

Had Ford refused to cooperate, there were some prominent government officials who were pressing for the government to step in and operate the company altogether. Had there been no World War II and the defense contract work Ford received, it is likely that the company would not have survived as an automaker.

Willow Run, a huge plant just outside of Dearborn, was constructed to produce the B-24 Liberators. When it opened in early 1942, it was the world's largest industrial structure under one roof. Albert Kahn, its architect, called the L-shaped plant, "the most enormous room in the history of man." Its around-the-clock shifts turned out bombers at the rate of one per hour. Willow Run became a symbol to the entire nation of what Americans at home could do to help the war effort. And once again, Henry Ford was given hero status for his support.

Ford was America's third largest defense contractor, behind GM and Curtiss-Wright. By the end of World War II, the company had built 8,600 B-24s; 57,000 aircraft engines; 250,000 jeeps; 93,217 military trucks; 26,954 tank engines; 4,291 gliders; 1,718 tanks and tank destroyers; 13,000 amphibians; 12,500 armored cars; and numerous other pieces of war machinery.

During the war years, Henry and Edsel each put in long, tedious hours, while both were failing in health. Henry had recovered from a mild stroke he suffered in 1938, but a subsequent stroke in 1941 took a heavy toll. It permanently impaired his speech. Worse, the stroke caused frequent lapses of memory. Still, as far as Henry Ford was concerned, he was as fit as a fiddle, and it was out of the question that he turn over command to Edsel, Sorensen, or Bennett—the three contenders for the top spot. In the meantime, Edsel's health continued to deteroriate even faster than his father's. By 1940, Edsel's stomach caused him so much agony that only with painkillers and sedatives was he able to work. To make matters worse, in 1942, he suffered a serious bout with undulant fever as a direct result of the milk he drank for his ulcers—milk that was not pasteurized or sterilized and was, in fact, fresh from the cows of Henry's dairy farm. Edsel's condition grew worse, but all the time his father insisted that there was nothing wrong with his son that could not be cured with a change in lifestyle and a proper diet. When it was finally diagnosed that Edsel had stomach cancer, it was too late. The cancer eventually spread to the liver, and on May 26, 1943, at age forty-nine, Edsel died. Henry's only son's death was devastating to the old man. In his own way he had loved his son and undoubtedly felt guilty that he never adequately expressed his feelings.

Upon Edsel's death, Henry resumed the title of president, although, in reality, his son had only served in that capacity as a figurehead. The company had always been run by Henry—Edsel had never made a major decision that did not need the approval of his father. Even though the old man was severely incapacitated and incapable of running the company, the worst-possible scenario would have been having Bennett take command.

The possibility of Bennett as CEO was cause for great concern to many, both insiders and outsiders. In particular, Washington was troubled by the prospect that one of its major defense contractors was being run by a senile and paranoid old man, who, in turn, could be controlled by the sinister and unscrupulous Harry Bennett. Plus, the octogenarian who founded the company made his hatred of President Franklin Roosevelt quite clear. He believed that the president, in cahoots with General Motors, DuPont, U.S. Steel, and General Electric, plotted to take over his company or destroy it altogether. The government's anxiety was based on sound reason.

So when the Ford family made a request to U.S. Secretary of Navy Frank Knox for Ensign Henry Ford II, the oldest grandson of the company's founder, to be honorably released from the military in August 1943, the discharge was quickly approved. Although the twenty-six-old ensign had been in the navy for less than two years, the government was delighted to ship him home to Detroit. Young Henry offered a flicker of hope that perhaps he could have a quick ascent to a key management position in Ford. Recalling a controversy that erupted after his father's deferment in World War I, his initial response was to remain in the navy. He was convinced, however, that his duty and inevitable destiny was in serving the Ford Motor Company and by doing so he would also be more valuable to his country than as a junior naval officer.

At this stage in his life, the young ensign had nothing notable to list on his résumé but his name. He attended Yale, but, having turned in a paper titled "Folkways and Thomas Hardy" that inadvertently included the crib notes receipts, he was forced to quit college during his senior year sans diploma and work in the family business in 1938. Years later, he returned to Yale to address the Yale Political Union, and, waving his written speech to the audience, he grinned and said, "And I didn't write this one either."

After reporting to the Dearborn world headquarters, the young man received no assignment, nor did he have a desk to sit behind. His grandfather had been on vacation, and nobody offered any suggestions about what work he was to do. So, for a while he simply wandered around on his own, observing people at their jobs and asking a lot of questions to find out how things worked. Wherever he went, and to whomever he spoke, the service department's spy system always relayed the word to the boss. Young Henry received the cold shoulder from many employees because they feared that Bennett regarded him as a threat. They were right. Ironically, the young Ford, whom Bennett had protected during his infancy and early childhood, had now become his antagonist.

By early 1944, the company was again losing large sums of money. Another loss was the resignation of Charles Sorensen, one of Ford's prominent figures in the early mass production successes. He simply could no longer stomach being hassled and tormented by Bennett and his cronies. Sorensen's departure opened the door for young Henry's promotion to the office of executive vice-president. It was also now the time for the company to brace itself for a postwar program of civilian production. A complete reorganization program was essential, and it was certain that the eighty-year-old Ford would not be the one to lead in the rebuilding of the company. Edsel was gone, and Bennett didn't have the slightest notion about building, let alone managing a giant industrial empire.

Thus Henry Ford II, "the Deuce," by default, became the one to lead the company and restore its former greatness. To an impartial bystander, he had only one qualification: his name. There were, however, two important individuals who had faith in the young man—his grandmother, Clara Ford, and his mother, Eleanor. Both women were still stricken with grief over the loss of their beloved Edsel. They had resented Henry for his heartless treatment of his only son, and they were enraged over the degradation and humiliation that Bennett had ruthlessly inflicted on him. These two Ford women were powerful allies because they were shareholders of Ford stock. First, it was Clara who pleaded with her husband and then later insisted he must yield the presidency to her grandson. Next, Eleanor met with her father-in-law, and she, too, argued a strong case for her son. She then took it a step further: She threatened to sell her stock to an outsider if he did not abide by her demands.

On September 20, 1945, the old man invited his twenty-eight-year-old grandson to meet with him at Fair Lane, the old family estate. Old Henry expressed his decision to pass the reins to the younger man. To his surprise, instead of a "thank-you-very-much-sir-and-I-promise-not-to-let-you-down-sir," young Henry said, "I'll take it only if I have a completely free hand to make any changes I want to make." Old Henry appeared displeased with his grandson's response, but after a few obscenities and some shouting, he consented to do as his grandson had requested.

The president-elect and CEO left his grandfather's house and immediately drove to the administration building to arrange for a board of directors meeting on the following day. A few hours later, Bennett, who also served on the board, had the gall to telephone him to say, "Henry, I've got some wonderful news for you. I've just talked your grandfather into making you president of the company."

After a unanimous vote, Henry II's first official act was to fire Bennett. It was simple and to the point. "Harry, we've got to part company," and there was nothing else to be said. Bennett was told that he would be paid his salary for a year and a half until his retirement income would start. With that out of the way, he drove to his grandfather's to inform him that Bennett was out. He prepared himself for a difficult meeting. After all, to the old man Bennett could do no wrong.

When young Henry broke the news to his grandfather, he braced himself for a harsh tongue-lashing. There was a silence, and finally, the old man spoke, "Well, now Harry is back where he started from."

His next official act was to rid the company of Bennett's goons. John Bugas, a former FBI agent, who was originally hired by Bennett but had sided with Henry II, volunteered to do the firings for his new boss. Ford refused, commenting that he did not want people to ever accuse him of shirking his responsibility and letting somebody else do the dirty work for him. Within weeks, more than a thousand cronies of Bennett had also received their walking papers. Now it was time for Ford Motor Company to get back into the automobile business. After all, the company had not built a civilian vehicle since early 1942 when its military output started.

Never before or since has any individual in American industry advanced so rapidly up the corporate ladder to the office of chief executive as did Henry II. After a brief two-year apprenticeship, at age twenty-eight, he was thrust into the awesome responsibility of running one of the world's largest industrial complexes. The advancement of a junior officer to the top spot at Ford was tantamount to promoting a second lieutenant to the rank of a five-star general. Here was Henry Ford II, the little rich boy who had lived the most privileged life of the very, very rich and famous, never having to bother with financial worries like the common people. He was raised in a 60-room mansion in Grosse Pointe, and as a little boy, had a scaled-down version of an authentic coal-burning locomotive. By age ten, he was the proud owner of a small imported sports car that enabled him to scoot about on the grounds of his family's 90-acre estate. His world included yachts, summer homes, trips abroad, country clubs, and many, many servants. Young Henry's reputation as a rich playboy was well deserved. It was hardly a background to prepare Henry II for a successful career as the CEO of a giant industrial company.

To complicate young Henry's smooth transition into the top position, Ford Motor Company had been, for years, riddled with a steady egression of its top managers. Some departures were a result of being either abused or fired by an irrational Henry or a truculent Harry Bennett, others had joined the military, and still more simply abandoned what was viewed as a quickly sinking ship. There was nothing left that even resembled a management team. On top of all of these woes, the company was losing money at the rate of $10 million a month. It had, in fact, been 15 years since the company had operated in the black.

Fortunately, Henry II had the good sense to know that he did not know how to nurse the family business back to good health. The unproven and untested president innately understood an important management principle that few managers implement: *Surround yourself with good people.* In 1945, in what has since been called a brilliant move, Ford put in a call to Ernest R. Breech, a former GM top executive who had spent the war years serving as president of Bendix Aviation Corporation, which was partially owned by GM. The word on the street was that in only a matter of time, the forty-nine-old Breech would be tapped as GM's CEO. Breech agreed to see Henry—out of curiosity and courtesy—he had no real interest in accepting a job offer. In particular, he did not want to offend a customer and Ford Motor Company routinely purchased a variety of

Bendix parts. To Breech's surprise, Henry said he would come to GM's headquarters. The meeting was casual and there was no mention of a job offer. The only thing that Ford did accomplish was to get Breech's word to accept an invitation to tour the Rouge and Willow Run plants. Henry II proved himself to be a subtle, effective salesman. After personally witnessing the sorry mess that the company was in and realizing the challenge that existed to restore it to its former greatness, Breech found himself attracted to coming to the aid of this enthusiastic young man who was barely older than his oldest son. In short, Breech joined Ford as executive vice-president. To sweeten the deal, because the company was not publicly owned and stock options were not available, Breech was given a 20 percent interest in Dearborn Tractor, a subsidiary company. With federal income taxes being so high at the time, the stock was an added attraction; so much so, in fact, that ten years later, its value was $6 million.

With Breech came several other talented GM executives. These included Harold Youngren, a brilliant engineer who made important contributions to the Oldsmobile Division, Louis Crusoe, a top finance man; and Delmar Harder, a vice-president of operations who is credited with coining the word "automation." This trio brought expertise in areas where Ford was particularly lacking. Also brought into the fold was Alberg Browning who had managed billions of dollars as a director of the War Department's enormous purchasing department. Henry II, an admirer of Alfred Sloan, took particular delight in recruiting experienced GM managers. Like Sloan, Breech was a student of modern corporate management techniques, and he and his fellow ex-GM executives set up procedures to begin the tedious task of reorganizing Ford. A training program to develop young college graduates was also established. The number of new recruits from the class of 1945 was set at fifty. However, a bright young engineer with degrees from Lehigh University and Princeton College wanted the job so badly and gave such a sales pitch, the company consented to hire him as the fifty-first. His name was Lee Iacocca.

The GM men set up "profit centers" so, for the first time, the company would be able to identify those areas that were making money and those that were not. No longer would the amount of accounts payable be determined by the height of stacked invoices. Even courses in human relations were introduced, a revolutionary concept in the 1940s. And Peter Drucker's classic *The Concept of the Corporation* became mandatory reading—even the CEO himself was instructed to read it. During 1946, Henry II and his new team swung a heavy ax in a radical cost-cutting program. All measures that could be executed to help reduce the huge monthly losses and rid the company of dead wood were considered. Before the year's end, obsolete plants had been closed or sold, and gone were the company's rubber plantation in Brazil and a soybean processing factory that had been used for extracting milk for consumption while shaping its pulp into steering wheels. By now, the eighty-three-old Henry was a recluse, oblivious to the alterations.

The biggest hurdles to overcome were the price freeze measures that the Office of Price Administration (OPA) set for 1946 cars in its attempt to control runaway inflation following the war. With Ernie Breech, Henry II was able to persuade the OPA to permit a $62.50 per car increase. By the end of the year, after having losses running at the rate of $10 million a month, the company actually eked out a $2,000 profit for the year—the first in a long time. Being in the black was cause for celebration, and producing its first automobiles since 1942 was viewed as a healthy sign. It told a car-hungry American public that the Ford Motor Company was still in business.

About the same time that Ernie Breech joined the company, an unusual telegram addressed to Henry Ford II arrived at Ford's world headquarters. It was sent by Charles Bates "Tex" Thornton, a colonel in the U.S. Army Air Force. The wire explained that ten young officers who worked as a team at the Office of Statistical Control in the air force were seeking employment by a single company. The telegram included Robert A. Lovett's name as a reference. Ford was familiar with Lovett, who, as under-secretary of war for air, worked with the company on the Willow Run operations. Lovett gave a strong recommendation for these men, and during a November 1945 meeting, the young CEO met with Thornton. At age thirty-two, Tex Thornton was one of the older team members; their ages ranged from twenty-six to thirty-four. Thornton had a distinguished service record and in his late twenties had been promoted to full colonel. His work in unraveling the chaos of military buildup and employment of men and arms was outstanding. To complete such a Herculean mission, he sought out the brightest young men in the air force, enrolled them in crash courses in economics and management at the Harvard Business School, and then incorporated their brain power into his "think factory" in Washington and at Wright Paterson Air Force Base near Dayton, Ohio. The group is credited with saving hundreds of millions—perhaps billions of dollars—for the military.

When the war ended, Thornton assembled nine of his best men and suggested that they should work together as a unit for some giant industrial firm that was in serious trouble and needed their assistance. When the word was out that the young Henry Ford was seeking talent to rebuild the once-mighty industrial firm that his grandfather founded, Thornton dispatched the telegram.

Thornton's pitch was brief and to the point. He talked about what his team had accomplished during the war and mentioned that certain military management systems could be applied to private enterprise. He pointed out that while none of his team members knew anything about cars, they had known nothing about airplanes but were able to implement revolutionary management concepts that benefited the air force. It had to be a package deal. Ford would either hire all ten men at annual salaries of $12,000 each, or get none of them. It didn't take long for Ford to recognize what a prize he was buying. On a handshake, all ten men were hired and scheduled to start work on February 1, 1946.

Two of the Thornton team would eventually rise to the presidency of Ford. One such man was Robert S. McNamara, a former assistant professor of accounting at the Harvard Business School, who was tapped as Ford's president on November 9, 1960, and who resigned from the company when John F. Kennedy appointed him secretary of defense on January 3, 1961. Arjay Miller was another of the group who became a Ford president, and later served as dean of the Stanford Business School. J. Edward Lundy, who, before the war, taught economics at Princeton, eventually worked his way to the top of the company's financial department. The remaining six were Wilbur R. Andreson, Charles E. Bosworth, Ben D. Mills, George Moore, Francis C. Reith, and James O. Wright. These were extraordinary individuals as is witnessed by their later accomplishments: two became presidents of Ford, six became vice-presidents of Ford, and three became chief executive officers of other companies. Tex Thornton himself founded one of the nation's first conglomerates, Litton Industries, in 1953, which, ten years later, had sales in excess of $1 billion.

Thornton's group initially spent most of its time wandering around, learning and studying the company. For a while, they were nicknamed the "Quiz Kids" after the radio show featuring child prodigies. Only later were they called the "Whiz Kids," a name they liked no better than the first. They collected mountains of data and put together countless reports about the company. Insecure automobile executives felt uncomfortable and inadequate around them, claiming that the Whiz Kids knew only numbers but nothing about cars. It was McNamara who received the most flak; he was described as being overly calculating, lacking warmth, and having no enthusiasm. Some claimed that he had no feel for cars and might as well have been selling ladies' underwear.

The Whiz Kids asked a lot of questions and soon they began demanding answers. They revealed that one plant was still manufacturing propellers for pre–World War II Ford trimotor planes that had not been produced for several years. When it was discovered that the old Henry Ford had put millions of dollars in noninterest-bearing accounts in banks scattered all over Michigan, the Whiz Kids quickly found better uses for the money. It was also discovered that in the 43 years since the company was founded, there had never been an audit. On the recommendation of the Whiz Kids, the firm of Lybrand, Ross Brothers and Montgomery was retained to audit the books for the year ending 1945. The firm (renamed Coopers & Lybrand) is the company's auditor to this day.

With the arrival of Ernie Breech and the Whiz Kids, Ford became the "in" place to work for top students from the nation's universities and business schools. For the first time in two decades, new blood was injected into the company's upper echelon, and with it came a new discipline. Professional management, coupled with the nation's pent-up hunger for cars made Ford once again a highly profitable enterprise. In early 1947, $72 million was invested in retooling costs for a new chassis body and engine—the 1949 model would be only the fourth major Ford product built from scratch.

While the company's founder did get to see a full-size painted clay model of the new car, complete with a grill built around its futuristic bullet-shaped body, he was too old and feeble to appreciate it. And on April 7, 1947, at the age of eighty-four, Henry Ford passed away. President Harry Truman, Winston Churchill, and Joseph Stalin were among the world leaders who gave eulogies, and more than 100,000 people passed through the Henry Ford Museum, where his body rested in state.

The new Fords were introduced on June 8, 1948, at New York's Waldorf-Astoria. A postwar America craved cars, and more than 50,000 people swarmed the hotel's main ballroom. In 1949, approximately 807,000 Fords, 187,000 Mercurys, and 38,000 Lincolns were sold and profits were $177 million, up from the previous year's $94 million.

For the first time in years, there was stability in the top echelons, and executives worked in harmony. By 1950, net profits soared to $265 million. In 1954, the new V-8 engine was introduced and sales jumped to 2.3 million vehicles; in 1955, sales hit the 3 million mark for the first time. Also, for the first time in 20 years, more Fords were sold than Chevrolets. That same year, the Thunderbird was introduced in response to Chevrolet's highly successful 1953 Corvette. The T-bird was a smashing success. Ford was on a roll.

While the experienced Ernie Breech served as executive vice-president, the young CEO gave him a free hand in running the company. Slowly, Henry II developed into a capable and strong leader, and gradually, it was his presence at executive meetings, not Breech's, that was the decisive factor. Younger brothers Benson and William Clay joined the company, and each ascended through the ranks to senior management positions, where like their older sibling, they, too, proved to be effective executives.

To those who were intimate with the three young Fords, it was Henry II who seemed to possess the better attributes of his grandfather and father. He had an immense level of energy like his grandfather as a young man. Other Ford executives marveled at how he could party the night before and show up bright and early at an early breakfast meeting without a trace of a hangover. And somehow he managed to do his homework, always arriving fully prepared, notes and all. And he had a passion for cars—they were in his blood.

Henry II always knew that he would someday rule the Ford empire. Having an acute awareness of his destiny gave him an inner strength; he could have easily succumbed to overindulgence because his need to achieve was not motivated by monetary gain. And although he had a well-deserved reputation for being a rich playboy, when he was called to assume his responsibility in the family business, he did so in the true spirit of a royal succession.

Growing up in an immensely affluent environment isolated him from the poor. For years, Grosse Pointe was a restricted community where blacks and Jews were not permitted to reside. The private clubs to which the Fords belonged had strict rules to keep non-WASPS from becoming members. In such an atmosphere, young Henry had no exposure to minorities, the exception being the family servants. And given the influence of an anti-Semitic, strong-willed grandfather, one could expect Henry II to be prejudiced. Yet, in his later years, when Henry II became a powerful industrial and civic leader, he used his influence to help minorities. Grosse Pointers who knew him since his boyhood expressed surprise at his sensitivity and comprehension of social problems and racial injustice. His leadership role in Detroit civic matters remains unequaled. No other U.S. corporation has provided as much opportunity for minority groups, as witnessed by its employment practices, and minority-owned dealership and supplier programs.

Unlike his grandfather, Henry II was a good friend to the Jewish community and the recipient of many honors from B'nai B'rith. He campaigned to get his close friend, Max Fisher, a wealthy man who owned large oil and real estate interests, and two other prominent Jewish businessmen voted into the Detroit Club, an elite city club that previously blackballed Jews. Fisher, North America's leading fund-raiser for the State of Israel, arranged two trips for Henry II to visit Israel, which included personal meetings with Golda Meir, Moshe Dayan, and Shimon Peres. In 1966, when it was announced that Ford trucks and tractors were to be assembled in Israel by a Jewish entrepreneur, Henry II refused to give in to the threat of an Arab boycott. His decision was made in spite of the much larger market within the Arab nations that contained a population in excess of 100 million. In comparison, Israel's population was less than 5 million. The boycott lasted for 20 years.

Henry II was a compassionate man, yet he was tough like his grandfather. Within the company, anyone with good sense knew not to con the Deuce. He had learned to protect himself because all of his life people had tried to use him.

The 1950s and 1960s were incredibly good years for the Big Three. In 1955, an estimated 80 percent of all of the world's car registrations occurred in North America, and until the 1960s, U.S. auto sales surpassed the combined total of the rest of the world. Between 1947 and 1967, the Big Three averaged a return of 16.7 percent on net worth. GM, by far the leader with more than a 40 percent market share, enjoyed a 20.7 percent average return. In the 1950s, Ford recaptured a distant number two spot relinquished by Chrysler, which continued to lose ground to the top two. GM set the pace with its market segmentation and model change strategies. There was virtually no competition from abroad. In 1952, Japan's largest automaker, Toyota, sold its Toyopet in the Japanese market at a $167 price disadvantage to a made-in-America Ford.

During the golden years of the fifties, the car was king. There were no challengers. The automobile industry equaled nearly 20 percent of the nation's gross national product (GNP). Detroit set the standard for quality, which evidently pleased everyone because cars kept on selling—the gas-guzzlers, the tail fins, and even three-toned cars. A land of plenty, the country evolved into a disposable society. Each year, as new models were introduced, last year's models were traded in for new ones. It was called planned obsolescence, and everyone accepted it as a way of life. The nation had an insatiable appetite for cars and Detroit did its best to feed it.

In January 1956, the public offering of the initial 10,200,000 shares of

Ford common stock by 722 underwriters was made available to the investment community, and it was hailed as "a landmark in the history of public ownership" by the president of the New York Stock Exchange. In a speech to commemorate the occasion, Henry II said, "The one-man band owner-manager is fast being replaced by a new service class of professional managers, dedicated more to the advancement of the company than to the enrichment of a few owners."

Prior to the offering, the company was owned by Mrs. Edsel Ford, her four children—Henry II, Benson, Josephine, and William Clay Ford—and the Ford Foundation. This organization was created by the old man so that on his death, his heirs would not have to sell their shares to raise funds to pay inheritance taxes and consequently lose control of the family business. While the Foundation received the bulk of the stock, its shares had no voting rights; the family kept the majority of voting stock and thereby retained control. Old Henry's intent was to reduce the burden of inheritance taxes, but what resulted was the establishment of one of the nation's most richly endowed charitable foundations.

After his death, the family was left with only 5 percent ownership, with the foundation owning 95 percent. At the time of the offering, the family's share increased to 12.1 percent, and in exchange for more ownership, the family's voting rights were reduced to 40 percent and the foundation received voting shares. The remainder went to the new 300,000 owners who bought first-traded shares at a value of $64.50 each. With the far-flung ownership, the Ford family's 40 percent voting stake is more than enough to make the company impregnable to a hostile takeover. The market value of the family's interest was worth $70 million in 1956. Today its value is in excess of $2 billion.

Ford prospered during the fifties, with the exception of one notable failure: the introduction of the ill-fated 1957 Edsel. The company's strategy was to offer a medium-price car to fill the slot between the Mercury and the Lincoln, a slot dominated by GM. That led to the formation of the Edsel Division, complete with its own assembly line, apart from other Ford plants. The Edsel also had its own network of dealerships. The company designed a new car with controversial styling and innovative equipment, such as push-button transmission controls on the steering wheel, self-adjusting brakes, and safety rim wheels. To launch this new venture cost an estimated quarter of a billion dollars.

The name was a tribute to the man who was the first to advocate style and change within the company. While insiders were familiar with what the name stood for, outsiders were not. Prior to the naming, marketing researchers revealed that the man in the street associated the name with *pretzel* and *weasel,* each projecting a weak image. The Edsel bombed. One problem was the speed with which it went from conception in the spring of 1955 to the market in the summer of 1957, causing quality problems. Then, too, 1958 was a recession year. But most significantly, the Edsel was an eyesore. It has been said that a camel could only be the result of design by committee, and if this is true, then most certainly it was the same committee that designed the Edsel. For years, its ridiculous "horse collar" grill served as the butt of many jokes. It was simply, ugly. What was meant as a tribute to a beloved member of the Ford family became an embarrassment. The Edsel's main contribution is that it has, in business courses on campuses across the country, become a classic example of what can go wrong. The word Edsel has become synonymous with a faux pas of epic proportions. When it was all over, a mere 110,000 Edsels were produced before the division permanently closed its doors.

While the Edsel was Ford's dismal failure of the fifties, the Mustang was its smashing success of the sixties. For starters, it had the good fortune to be introduced in 1964, an upbeat year for Americans. The nation was enjoying relative peace, the economy was healthy, the dollar was strong, and Lyndon B. Johnson was mesmerizing the country with his Great Society. The nation's love affair with John Kennedy was still going strong—he had become even more popular after the assassination—and the accent was firmly on youth. In addition to the young adult buyers, the multicar family was steadily increasing. But research and sales experts revealed that a two-seat passenger car, even a relatively successful one, would only sell a marginal number of cars in the United States. Within this climate, the sporty four-seat Mustang had tremendous appeal.

While business professors have since lectured that the Edsel failed because the company marketed a product for which there was no need, the opposite was true with the Mustang. There was, indeed, a strong demand in the marketplace for such a car. Furthermore, the components of the existing Falcon could be used, including its engines, transmissions, and axles. Instead of having to overcome several hundred million dollars in start-up costs for an all-new car, the cost to develop the Mustang was a drop-in-the-bucket $75 million. And the car was conceived in 1961, giving it a full year's more development time than was allowed the Edsel.

There was also a great deal of talent supporting the Mustang's development. As general manager of the Ford Division, Lee Iacocca was hailed the father of the Mustang. However, Donald Frey, the product manager, is considered by company insiders as the man who originated the concept of an inexpensive sports car that would appeal to the young. Frey also worked on its initial development, as did Don Petersen. But it was Iacocca who took the idea and ran with it. Without his superb salesmanship, particularly to the skeptical finance department as well as his boss, Henry Ford, the project probably would have never been implemented.

The success of the Mustang placed Iacocca squarely in the spotlight of the automobile industry—both the car and the man became legends across the country. In what could well be the publicity coup of the decade, the division's public relations manager, Bob Hefty, was able to jockey simultaneous cover stories in both *Newsweek* and *Time* magazines, each featuring Iacocca as the hottest young man in the car business. No company employee had ever publicly upstaged a Ford, and it has been hinted that this was the start of the infamous rift that later occurred between the two men. If Henry Ford was upset by Iacocca's instant fame, he was also pacified by the immense success that the Mustang enjoyed. During its first year, sales totaled 418,812, far more than the 100,000 units projected by marketing research, setting a first-year sales record. Profits exceeded $1 billion.

Beginning in the 1950s and continuing through the present, the company's international growth spiraled, and today, the sun never sets on the Ford empire. To reduce the risks inherent in the cyclical nature of the automobile industry, Ford has expanded into diversified fields ranging from aerospace to financial services. Today its nonautomotive businesses generate sales in excess of $13 billion, more revenue than the entire company realized as recently as the 1960s.

The 1970s were tumultuous times for the nation. America had not yet recovered from Vietnam, Watergate bred mistrust of our national leadership, drug abuse had emerged as a major problem, double-digit inflation was rampant, and there was an unsettling oil embargo. The ensuing social and economic upheavals deeply affected the country, and by no means was the automobile industry immune. Ford Motor Company was experiencing internal unrest. Lee Iacocca, who had served as president since 1970, was favored to be the successor on Henry Ford's anticipated retirement, at age sixty-five, in 1980. However, a personality conflict had drawn the two men apart for several years—Iacocca, one of the highest profiled executives in corporate America, had become too big for his britches, and there could be only one star at Ford Motor Company, Henry Ford, the Deuce. The beginning of the end occurred when Philip

Caldwell was named vice-chairman in 1977, and in this position, also became a strong candidate for the number one position. Shortly thereafter, at a press conference, with Ford sitting between Iacocca and Caldwell, a reporter asked, "The three of you serve as members of the office of Chief Executive, so who would be in charge, Mr. Ford, when you are out of the country?"

At first, Henry II remained silent, choosing to ignore the question. But when the reporter pressed him for an answer, Ford replied that the responsibility would rest on his vice-chairman . . . Philip Caldwell. Iacocca was visibly incensed, and consequently appealed futilely to other board members for their support. Thereafter, the estrangement between Ford and Iacocca grew increasingly more intense, causing considerable strife and dissension on the top floor of Ford's world headquarters, the Glass House. It culminated on July 13, 1978, when Henry Ford fired Iacocca. The firing received front-page coverage across the country.

The same day that the board of directors made the firing official, Iacocca met with Henry Ford. William Clay Ford, his brother and company vice-chairman, sat in on the strained encounter. The conversation was short and to the point. When a frustrated and tearful Iacocca inquired what he had done wrong, Henry answered, "I just don't like you." Iacocca argued he had done a good job and that the company had earned $1.7 billion after taxes in the previous year. "You'll never do it again," was Iacocca's parting prediction.

Ford Motor Company's net income dipped slightly to $1.6 billion in 1978, and the following year, it dropped to $1.2 billion. These were still respectable years, though, and no cause for alarm.

However, when the 1980 *losses* came in at $1.5 billion, Iacocca's prophecy caused tremors throughout Ford headquarters. Such losses would continue for three consecutive years and total more than $3 billion before the company would again operate in the black.

FORD THUNDERS

During his thirty-five-year reign, Henry Ford II became a public figure, projecting an image that fittingly has been described as "bigger than life." He was as much a statesman as a businessman, and certainly a household name throughout America and Europe. When he toured plants, eager assembly-line workers sought his autograph. Whatever he did received headline coverage in business publications and tabloid sheets alike. The Deuce was a powerful industrialist, yet a man with human frailties, which he never denied. Henry II was one of the nation's richest men but with a common touch. Respected by the hundreds of thousands who worked for Ford, and loved by those who personally knew him, Henry Ford II was a tough act to follow.

When Philip Caldwell, chief executive officer, was elected chairman of the board in 1980, it was a significant milestone for the Ford Motor Company. For the first time since its formation in 1903 the company would be headed by somebody with a last name different from its own. For years, the company prided itself in being a family company. Many Ford employees felt as though they knew Ford personally; nearly all of them, including many who had since retired, worked their entire careers under his leadership. Henry Ford II was their supreme commander, and throughout his reign there were no candidates to challenge his command.

The turbulent times that the company was experiencing made the transition all the more difficult. The company's losses were running in the billions, its market share was drastically down, and thousands had already lost their jobs. All one had to do was read the newspapers to see that on March 13, 1980, the day that Henry II officially stepped down, little in the way of relief was in sight. Uncertainty raged throughout the organization.

Caldwell became chief executive officer on October 1, 1979, while his predecessor continued on as chairman of the board. The chairman title was in name only because, contrary to what employees and the public thought, Ford was no longer involved in the business on a daily basis. In February 1980, Henry II walked into Caldwell's office for an informal meeting, and following a few minutes of small talk, he said, "You know, Phil, this really doesn't make any sense. It's not possible to run this company not knowing what's going on around here all the time. And frankly, I don't know what's going on here all the time. What's more, I don't want to know." Henry II decided to stop being chairman and have Caldwell assume the title.

"So Henry actually accelerated his departure by a year or so. And once he departed, he never interfered even though he certainly had the power to do so," Caldwell notes. "He could have stepped in and said, 'Now, that's not what *I* think we should do,' or 'We're not going to do that!' But our team had full rein. Of course, if I wanted to talk to him, he always made himself available. As far as I'm concerned, Henry played his role perfectly."

At the end of the first day as CEO, Caldwell recalls running into Henry II on the elevator. "By the sheerest concidence, we rode down to the parking garage together. He said to me in a soft voice, 'You know, Phil, I'm really sorry to leave you with all these problems.'

" 'Well, all the history that I've read,' I answered, 'says that you had a lot of problems when you took over.'

" 'Yeah, that's true. But we had one thing going for us. The market would take anything we built. The market won't do that any more.'

"I suppose that of all the things he might have said to me," Caldwell continues, "there was nothing that could have given me a greater sense of comfort. Although it was a brief interlude, it made me feel a strong loyalty to him. The chance meeting left me with a feeling of comradery that meant a lot to me."

A previous chance "meeting" happened a few days before the World's Fair opened in 1939 on Long Island, New York. As a nineteen-year-old college student, Caldwell was visiting the fair grounds and was attracted to the commotion at one exhibit building still under construction. "What's going on?" he asked one of the workman.

"Henry Ford is coming to view the Ford exhibit," he was told.

Edging his way through the crowd, young Caldwell was able to catch a glimpse of not only the senior Henry Ford but also his son Edsel and grandson Henry II who were accompanying him. As Caldwell looked in awe, a flashbulb went off, and the following day a picture of the three famous Fords appeared in the *New York Times*. Seeing the photograph in the newspaper article, Caldwell observed the exact location where he had stood and, to his disappointment, his image had been deleted.

"I joined the company in 1953," Caldwell reminisces, "and one Sunday afternoon my family and I were visiting the Henry Ford Museum. Well, lo and behold, there was a life-size, blown-up copy of the original photograph of the three Fords at the 1939 World's Fair, only this time it included me in the background! I have often wondered what the odds were of the three Fords and me as the first nonfamily member appearing in the same photograph . . ."

At one time Lee Iacocca appeared to be the heir apparent, so Ford had a definite choice. The differences between Iacocca and Caldwell were remarkable. Iacocca is a super salesman and a showman who thrives on center stage. The cigar-chomping executive is outspoken and, although an eloquent speaker, he is prone to use locker-room language in private conversations or while addressing a small group of executives or workers. His ego is enormous and so is his temper. He could bring grown men to tears by reading them the riot act. He feels comfortable drinking beer with the boys and is equally at ease sipping champagne with heads of state.

Caldwell is a less emotional man. He is soft-spoken and conservative. Above all, he is always a gentleman, a bit on the old-fashioned side, seeming to be from an era when people were more courteous and respectful. He never has shouted at a subordinate, and for that matter, seldom raises his voice. Caldwell does not use obscenities, and he readily admits that he is ill at ease in the presence of those who do. Caldwell, like all top business leaders, has an ego, yet he is by no means egotistical. Caldwell's family farmed in Ohio, although he personally did few farm chores. A fine student, he graduated high school at age sixteen and Muskingum College by age twenty. Following his graduation, he enrolled in the Harvard Business School and on December 8, 1941, the day after Pearl Harbor, was interviewed on the Harvard campus by a navy recruiter. By the following June he was Ensign Philip Caldwell. The navy taught him a very valuable lesson that he has since applied throughout his business career. "One of my officers never asked anyone what he thought he could do. Instead, he said, 'This is your job,' and then he'd explain in detail what was to be done," Caldwell explains. "I think it's essential to make it clear to people what the objective is, otherwise they go off in different directions. The navy taught me at a very young age that people are an organization's greatest asset when they are properly managed."

Eventually, Caldwell served in the Pacific theater, assigned to a variety of projects that included building bases, airfields, ammunition depots, and harbors in such places as Guam, Saipan, and Okinawa. When the war ended he served as a civilian in naval procurement and, in this capacity, gained valuable legislative experience working with the codification of laws and regulations. "Most importantly," Caldwell says, "I observed how the government works, and I gained firsthand knowledge that has helped me throughout my business career. It was especially valuable when it came to knowing my way around Washington during the 1970s."

The Unified Procurement Act saved America billions of dollars by combining the purchasing of the army, navy, and air force. It also provided excellent experience for Caldwell, who joined Ford in 1953 as head of procurement training. Here he met up with an old Harvard Business School acquaintance, Robert S. McNamara, who at the time was general manager for the Ford Division. "The important lesson I learned from my procurement experience was that in the automobile business, it's not the concern about making a single part that matters but the capability of making millions that counts. Repeatability is the key." Caldwell worked his way up through the ranks with key assignments, such as vice-president and general manager of the Truck Operations, president of Philco Ford, vice-president in charge of Manufacturing of North American Automotive Operations, and chairman of Ford of Europe. Caldwell's experience and fine performance made him a prime choice to head the company. He was not, however, a flamboyant and colorful executive like Iacocca; and the publicity generated by Iacocca's firing overshadowed Henry II's selection of Caldwell as his successor.

Throughout the history of America, times of crisis have resulted in a significant change. When Caldwell took command, Ford was on the brink of bankruptcy and could not continue with the status quo. Change was essential. The eleventh-hour nature of the crisis served as a blessing in disguise. It was a powerful catalyst that created an alarming sense of urgency. Nothing was so sacred that it could not be challenged; everything was subject to change.

"It became very clear to our management team," Allan Gilmour explains, "that we were uncompetitive in every element of our business. We didn't have the cars people wanted to buy. We didn't have good quality and our costs were too high. Furthermore, we had poor relationships with practically everyone—our employees, dealers, suppliers, and the government. While we cried for years about the things we couldn't do, we finally reached a point where we became aware of the necessity to concurrently mend all of our problems. We realized that we couldn't say, 'Well, we'll fix our costs, and then improve our products. Afterward, we'll deal with the government problem and then tackle the employee relations problem, and so on.' There were problems that simply couldn't wait. Certain ones had to be simultaneously tackled."

Caldwell's "cocaptains" were Donald Petersen, president and chief operating officer, and Harold "Red" Poling, executive vice-president in charge of NAAO, the domestic division in which the red ink was the thickest. These were the three key individuals who would guide the giant sinking ship to port. The future of Ford Motor Company, if there was to be a future Ford Motor Company, was contigent on their skillful leadership.

Upon assuming their positions as the company's top officers, Petersen recalls the triumvirate's first conference: "Phil simply said, 'We must assume that we're the ones who have to get this company back on track. So let's get on with it. We must have some stability.'

"He then said that the immediate objective was to formulate a game plan. First, the North American operation was out of control, and he wanted to establish a cycle plan. In the automobile business, it meant we should lay out our existing and future products and determine which ones must be changed in two years, in four years, and so on. It's a highly integrated process that involves reviewing external factors such as the market forces, the competition, and the government. This long-term planning maps out the company's strategy and plays a major role in future decision making."

The difficulty of the task was compounded because, by taking a specific action to solve a short-term problem, the company's ability to compete in the long run might be hindered. For example, a drastic reduction of all costs could impair the quality of future Ford products. So it was necessary to carefully prioritize problems and clarify all implications of each solution.

Caldwell drew on his days in the navy. "Once when I attended a staff meeting headed by Ed Andrews, who is now assistant secretary of the navy," he recalls, "the subjects of logistics and procurement were discussed. He posed a thought-provoking question to several heads of bureaus: 'Gentlemen, if war broke out at four o'clock in the morning, what would you do?' Then, he went around the room, giving everyone an opportunity to voice an opinion, and did it ever generate some food for thought! Later, when Louis Johnson became secretary of defense, Andrews suggested that the same question be addressed by the rest of the services." At a series of meetings with the senior managers throughout the organization, Caldwell asked the same kind of thought-provoking and direct questions.

"In response to my own questions I stated, 'We've had our eye on the grandstand with some highly exposed products like the Mustang. But while the Mustang standing alone sold a lot of cars, in total, Ford sold fewer and cannibalized itself while we became complacent. The records show that for 15 years, we've been losing market share. Why? For starters, our quality is poor. Then, there's the damaging publicity we've received regarding the Pinto fires. However, it's a lame excuse that our face is no dirtier than anyone else's.

" 'In addition to poor quality, our products need major overhauling in the areas of fuel economy, emissions, and safety requirements. These are difficult problems because fuel economy calls for weight reduction while the safety issues require increased weight. As a result, we're faced with constant trade-offs.

" 'In recent years, our European operations have been our biggest source of profits, but before that it was trucks and the finance company,' I'd hammer away. 'However, our car business in North America has been sick for a long time.'

"After my review of the major factors that had caused our business to nosedive, we concentrated on reinstating the business-planning process. Most significantly, our product planning had fallen to three years, when it should have been ten years. Otherwise, the research and development program doesn't run properly. Then, too, the advance engineering suffers, which, in turn, adversely affects productivity in the plants. New technology is also impaired. In short, everything was in an uproar."

Caldwell's immediate task was to communicate the planning process to top managers of the company. "It was up to these individuals to focus on planning ahead and not cope with the daily problems like 'How is such-and-such plant running today?' That's not what our senior people should be doing."

The most glaring problem that the domestic automobile industry faced was a message that was repeated across the country: *Americans just don't build cars like they used to.* Japanese goods now represented quality and reliability, and, ironically, *Made in America* had come to mean inferior workmanship. In 1980, industry surveys indicated that Ford was viewed as the worst offender of the Big Three. It was with this in mind that at the first board meeting that Caldwell was to chair, he scribbled a note on a piece of paper and proceeded to read it aloud: "Quality is the number one objective of the Ford Motor Company." At first there was a silence. Then, each of the board members nodded their heads in agreement. This single small act shaped the course of action that was to follow.

Improving quality is a noble and desirable ambition, but a chairman of the board can't dictate good quality, or simply rely on a clever slogan to achieve it. And the words declaring it as a company's number one objective are certain to get nods of approval in any American company. After all, who's going to argue with the chairman that he or she opposes quality? As Allan Gilmour says, "Quality is right up there with motherhood, baseball, and apple pie. However, saying you want quality is one thing. *Achieving it* is quite another." It is particularly difficult in the automobile industry, in which changes in products require considerable lead time to implement. Ford management recognized that the quality of its products could only be gradually realized, so while this worthy goal was given top priority, other pressing changes could be expedited during the current year. Most glaring was the reduction of costs.

Ford's 1979 U.S. market share was 20.7 percent, down 3.7 percentage points from 1978. Although the company had earned $1.2 billion in 1979, its North American operations had operated in the red. By this time, it was an accepted fact that Ford didn't have the products for the U.S. market, and it was likely that sales volume would continue to decline during 1980. Management clearly understood the problems it faced, and with reduced U.S. car sales, it was evident that NAAO's expenditures would exceed its revenue.

The individual who seemed best suited to implement a major cost-reduction program for the sickly North American operations was Red Poling, a feisty company veteran, who appeared to have the track record to tackle the immense undertaking. His career at Ford was his life's work and had been ever since the summer of 1950 when, as a MBA student at Indiana University, he did an internship at the Rouge steel plant. Prior to this summer job, he had no intention of working in the automobile industry, but, as he puts it, "I got carried away with the enthusiasm about the business, and upon graduating in 1951, I was hired as a cost analyst in the rolling mill at the steel plant." Following several staff and divisional positions, Poling was promoted to assistant controller of the Transmission and Chassis Division. Later, he was named controller of the division and, in 1968, became controller of the product development group. In 1972, he was named vice-president of finance of Ford of Europe. In Europe, Poling was able to gain valuable overseas experience, a common denominator shared by most senior managers.

"Back in 1972, Ford of Europe was a relatively small contributor to the total profitability of the company," Poling explains, "so career-wise, the promotion didn't appear to be a significant advancement. I went because Ed Lundy personally requested me to go, and it turned out to be the best thing in the world for both my career and my family (although initially, my thirteen-year-old cheerleader daughter opposed it). Although Ford of Europe had record earnings of $300 million in 1973, that November we were hit by the Arab oil boycott and it absolutely wrecked the overseas economy. We were having such a wonderful year, and then I got word that December was going to be a disaster."

This prompted Poling to request a comparison of the August figures, a shutdown month in Europe and thereby the worst period of the year. Upon reviewing the report, it was obvious to Poling that December would be even worse than August. Furthermore, he projected a first-quarter loss of $25 million. "With that, I met with Ford of Europe's chairman, Bill Bourke and recommended that we cut our costs by $50 million for the next three months," Poling continues. "Acting on this advice, we structured a program and turned a projected loss into gross profits of $25 million. Despite a very poor European economy in 1979, we worked extremely hard to keep from getting in the red and actually eked out a $2 million profit for the year. With the energy crisis behind us and an improved economy, we went on to some fantastic years in Europe."

Poling's role did not go unnoticed. In 1975, he was named president of Ford of Europe, and two years later its chairman. With Poling at its helm, the subsidiary realized annual before-tax profits in excess of $1 billion for 1977, 1978, and 1979. It was these 1979 earnings that kept Ford Motor Company in the black that year.

Under Poling's leadership, Ford of Europe enjoyed several triumphant years, and in 1980, a repeat performance was just the ticket to cure NAAO. So on the evening of March 12, Poling received a telephone call informing him that he would be named executive vice-president of North America Automotive Operations at the following day's board of directors meeting.

"It occurred to me that I couldn't have taken the job at a worse time," Poling tells, "but then, as things turned out, they did get worse."

The following day, Poling called Ford's controller to request an up-to-date forecast. It increased the projected losses by $300 million. "This was the environment that I walked into when I came back to Dearborn," he sighs. "Within three weeks, I had my first scheduling meeting, which determined what production will be for the rest of the year. I concluded that, based on the economic conditions, the production schedule was too aggressive for the industry so I ordered 500,000 units to be taken out of production. I also set an objective to take $1.5 billion of costs out."

In an industry that increases and decreases a production schedule in units measured in increments of 15,000 and 20,000 units, Poling's cut of 500,000 sent tremors that were felt in every Ford plant across the continent.

Shortly thereafter, Poling met with the company's two top officers, Caldwell and Petersen, who had been named president at the March 13 board meeting. "There was surprise, and, of course, concern," Poling explains, "but they fully understood what the impact of this decision would be; so nobody second-guessed my decision. I felt I had their support." Caldwell, Petersen, and Poling concluded that it was essential to get back to the basics of the business to regain control. It was informally agreed to divvy up the responsibilities, with Caldwell, as CEO, providing meaningful direction, a vital ingredient that had long been absent. Poling would concentrate on instilling control and discipline, which was also noticeably missing. And Peterson would initially reacquaint himself with Ford's existing products as well as those cars that were on the drawing board. He, therefore, spent a great deal of time conferring with designers and engineers.

Each had his work cut out for him. Caldwell was faced with the seemingly insurmountable task of instituting crucial change in a giant-size multinational organization riddled with a burdensome bureaucracy. Poling had the unpopular job of closing down plants and laying off workers. Yet, in a way, Petersen's assignment was even more difficult. It takes a long time in the automobile industry to realize significant change in product and public perception, and this was Petersen's responsibility.

During the weeks to follow, Ford's sales continued to decline, and at the next scheduling meeting in May, Poling ordered another 500,000 units to be pulled from production. "The customers just weren't buying our cars," Poling explains. "Had we produced those million cars, our dealers would have come to us for floor plan financing, and the interest charges would have been disastrous to both them and us. Then we would have had to offer incentives to buy those cars. I personally don't think we could have moved them out. At some point, people would have started questioning why we were pricing them so low in the marketplace. Had that happened, we would have put our entire future in jeopardy. Although the market continued to walk away from us in 1981 and the following two years, we reduced our losses and improved our break-even point."

As a consequence, 60,000 hourly and salaried Ford employees lost their jobs, thereby reducing the U.S. Ford payroll from $6.2 billion to $5.2 billion. Poling met his objective of cutting costs by $1.5 billion in 1980 with another $500 million reduction in overhead by closing five plants during the year. Called "Mr. Hatchet Man" by union leaders, he took a lot of the heat for the mass layoffs. "Nobody likes to put people out of work," he says. "The union didn't like it, and I didn't like it. Making those tough decisions caused me a lot of sleepless nights. Everyone likes to build. I don't like tearing things down; but the alternative was even worse. Our 1980 worldwide losses were $1.5 billion, and we would have lost even more money had we not cut our costs, which, in the long run, would have meant even more jobs lost."

Throughout the year, Poling made a concentrated effort to communicate with United Automobile Workers (UAW) officials as well as plant managers. To do so, he went to the plants, an unusual practice at the time. Big Three executive vice-presidents simply did not meet with union leadership in the plant. "The message I gave plant managers and union leaders was the same," he relates. "I said, 'The perception of the American public is that we can't produce vehicles in the United States that have the quality of the Japanese products, and unless we change that perception and reality, there is no future for any of us.' I told the union people, 'Your members, our employees, know better than anybody else what it takes to improve quality and efficiency. We need your help.' The union leaders' reaction usually was, 'Is this another one of those damned programs or are you really serious?' I assured them I was serious.

"In my meetings with union representatives, the real question was deciding which plants would have to close. 'Was it realistic? Was it equitable?' I assured them that we'd assess each plant's quality, history, and cost competitiveness. While the UAW didn't want to close any plant, the company had to prove to them that we would back our words with action. This could only be accomplished by demonstrating that our decisions of which plants to close, would, indeed, be based on the quality of the products they made."

Using quality as the criterion for closing a plant was a major departure from how the automobile industry had always operated. Cost reductions had always been the determining factor—quality never even made the list. Plant shutdowns or plant closings were long viewed to be a quick fix during a recessionary period. So the UAW leadership had good reason to question Ford's sincerity. Poling confirmed that he meant what he said when he announced the closing of the assembly plant in Mahwah, New Jersey, in mid–1980. Although a financial analysis revealed that it would be more cost-effective to close the 50-year-old Norfolk, Virginia, assembly plant, the company decided to close the Mahwah plant instead. The Mahwah plant was a much newer and larger facility and had a better location, but it had the poorest quality record. The word of how the decision had been made spread throughout the organization. It did wonders to validate management's commitment to quality.

"The New Jersey plant was a vast property employing about 6,000 workers," explains Wayne Doran, chairman of Ford Motor Land Development Corporation. "Considering the huge real estate investment it represented, a more cost-effective decision would have been to close the Norfolk plant. But the company's objective was to evaluate quality, and consequently, we never allowed the value of real estate to be a factor. Plant closings were strictly governed by the manufacturing issues of quality and productivity."

Politics also was a nonissue. Shortly before the Mahwah plant was closed, Phil Caldwell was meeting with the Michigan delegation at the Capitol Building in Washington. Bill Bradley, then a freshman senator from New Jersey, was informed that the Ford CEO was in town and came barging into the meeting, determined to talk to Caldwell. "I wasn't about to excuse myself," Caldwell says, "so I said I'd come to his office as soon as I finished.

" 'You say you're going to close the Ford plant in Mahwah,' Bradley said. 'You can't do this!'

" 'Senator, I can, and let me explain why,' I said. Then I told him about the depression our industry was in and how the demand was off. 'We're up to our neck in alligators, Senator.'

" 'You didn't come to see me about it,' Bradley exclaimed.

" 'I am sorry, and I should have told you about it ahead of time. I apologize for that. But frankly, Senator, it never occurred to me, and it doesn't now, that I have to get your permission to do what we have to do.' "

In what David Scott, vice-president of external affairs, views as a symbolic act affirming that Ford had no sacred cows, he tells about the scrapping of the G M-34, a sports car that had generated a lot of internal excitement. "We had a soon-to-be-introduced $30,000 deluxe two seater on the back burner," Scott remembers, "that was billed as a revolutionary model. It was designed and built in France and Italy to be distributed in the United States. Due to considerable changes made by various manufacturing and marketing people, the car went over its budget. 'Each car line and each truck line must stand on its own in terms of profitability,' Poling declared. He insisted that unless the G M-34 could represent a profit center, it wouldn't be manufactured.

" 'Launch it anyway,' the marketing people said. 'It will attract showroom traffic and help sell more Thunderbirds and Continentials.'

"Poling held firm. 'Absolutely not,' he announced. 'Every Ford product is a business and must be a profitable project or it will not be made.' Although throughout its development Poling was one of the G M-34's staunchest supporters, he still vetoed it. By doing this, he sent a strong message to everyone that this was the beginning of a new discipline for NAAO."

Poling recalls the incident, "Initially, I was really enthusiastic about that program. I thought its styling and interior package were outstanding. The G M-34 was approved to the first status report, but then it deteriorated so badly that there was absolutely no way we could continue the program.

"Sure, the dealers wanted it," he continues. "But I don't believe in losing money on anything. Period. It's wrong. Where do you stop? If you want to talk about the future of this company, we have to earn a profit."

Ford's U.S. car sales were down 50 percent from 2.6 million in 1978 to 1.3 million in 1980, and its 1981 models scheduled for an autumn introduction offered no encouragement that good times were imminent. Even looking ahead to Ford's 1982 lineup showed no promise of increased acceptance by the American car buyer. The huge reduction of expenditures was not enough by itself to make up the lost sales volume. Massive cutbacks were certainly vital for survival but were not a long-term solution for gaining increased market share. Ford had to make better automobiles. This meant Poling had to maintain a delicate balance—he had to cut excessive fat without damaging healthy muscle. His cost cutting must be performed with a scalpel, not a meat cleaver. In addition to the strict austerity program to save billions of dollars, large sums of money had to be invested in making new products with improved quality.

Quantum leaps in quality and innovation, however, do not happen simply by throwing large buckets of money onto the problem. Besides,

Ford's pockets were not so deep that the company could survive if its market share continued to slide.

By the spring of 1981, the company was feeling a cash squeeze. There was only about $1 billion in the coffers with which to run the entire company, a mere pittance for a business of such magnitude. Furthermore, it was becoming increasingly more difficult and expensive to borrow funds. As a result of its many problems, Ford no longer maintained the credit rating it once enjoyed. Both *Moody's* and *Standard & Poor's*, two major bond-rating services, lowered their opinions of Ford's financial health. Its AAA long-term debt rating dropped to BBB, and, even worse, its commercial paper rating (credit for short-term money) declined from A1P1 to A2P2. "Our debt-to-equity ratio went up to an unprecedented level in the range of 75 percent in 1982," David McCammon, vice-president of finance and treasurer, points out. "To put that number in perspective, today's debt-to-equity ratio is 14 percent."

"In addition to having major financial difficulties," Petersen explains, "our free fall in market share made it glaringly clear to us that we had to be as aggressive about improving our products as we were about improving our efficiency. There was no alternative; with the fuel economy laws, we had an absolute requirement to resize our cars in the United States. It was mandatory that we continue spending on the development of new products. We realized that we had to do it right the first time. We wouldn't get a second shot."

To achieve this far-reaching goal, Petersen realized that an attitude change at all levels of the organization was vital. This would be a monumental task, and would necessitate reshaping one of the most autocratic and politicized corporate cultures in the United States. Throughout its history, Ford had been a company headed by individuals driven by big egos. There were the two Henry Fords at the top, there was Lee Iacocca, and scores of others who managed their own fiefdoms in different pockets of the organization. These were men who believed that pushing people rather than pulling people up was the best technique to motivate subordinates. When Petersen became president in 1980, he knew a new style of management was essential. "What we are doing now obviously isn't working," he declared. "We've got to find a better way."

He did, and toward the end of the 1980s, Don Petersen was named Chief Executive Officer of the Year by numerous publications and national organizations because of the remarkable management style that had emerged at Ford. Petersen plays down his leadership role and, instead, insists on giving credit to Caldwell, Poling, and scores of other key Ford managers. "It was a team effort," he says.

Petersen's roots can be traced back to a humble beginning. He was born on a farm in Pipestone, Minnesota, in 1926. Petersen served in the Marines during World War II and afterward received a mechanical engineering degree in 1946 from the University of Washington, graduating magna cum laude. He received his MBA from Stanford in 1949, and, following a job interview on the campus, he boarded a cross-country bus to Dearborn. When the bus accidentially overdrove a bus stop, a determined Petersen carried his suitcase under his arm, jumped a fence, and made his follow-up interview in the nick of time. "I was dusty, but they liked me," he says with a grin.

He received a paycheck of $300 a month and throughout the 1950s, the young engineer's career centered on car product planning. He worked on the legendary Thunderbird, and, later in the 1960s, in a management capacity he played a key role in the development of such cars as the Mustang, LTD, Maverick, and Mark II. In 1969, he was elected vice-president of car planning and research, a position requiring him to orchestrate the company's future cars by coordinating design, engineering, and finance. From 1971 to 1975, Petersen served as vice-president and general manager of Truck Operations. He became an executive vice-president of Ford Diversified Products Operations in 1975, and in 1977 he was promoted to executive vice-president of Ford International Automotive Operations. Since becoming the company's president and chief operating officer on March 13, 1980, industry publications have consistently referred to Petersen as a *car guy*, a high compliment in Detroit automotive circles. Not since Henry Ford I has the company had a top manager with an extensive technical background in product development.

When Caldwell determined that quality was Ford's highest priority, Petersen recognized that the achievement of this goal would take a commitment by tens of thousands of men and women working at all levels of the company. This, he understood, would require an unprecedented drive to push responsibility into the ranks of workers. A team effort was essential—the job at hand was too big for only a handful of players to manage. In this respect, Petersen was an ideal candidate to rally the troops, for he is not only referred to as a car guy but a *people* guy as well.

It is no easy matter, however, to gain the support and cooperation of such large numbers of people, particularly those employed in an organization consisting of warring fiefdoms, an adversarial union, and a corporate culture with a 75-year history of autocratic management. Many didn't believe it was possible for Ford to change. There had been too many past instances of talk about improving quality and efficiency, but little ever changed. It would take concrete action to make believers out of nonbelievers. In the words of Ralph Waldo Emerson, "What you are thunders, for I cannot hear what you say."

Petersen began meeting day and night with managers, starting each talk with a sermon on teamwork and quality. The closing of the Mahwah plant also relayed a powerful message to every plant manager and worker. It became quite clear that, if and when other plant closings were ordered, those with the poorest quality really *would* be the first to go. UAW leaders began to stress to their members that efficiency and quality were their best job security.

Again and again, Poling demonstrated that he meant what he said about quality having priority over cost savings. At a monthly scheduling meeting, Poling ordered all plants to be shut down for a two-week period while the workers were on vacation. In the past it had been a standard practice to hire part-time workers during vacation periods. Poling pointed out that these part-timers would not be able to produce products of the same quality as the full-time workers. In spite of the protests that the lost production would cost the company an estimated $100 million in profits, Poling replied, "There is only one thing we're after and that is quality. Shut the plants and take the loss."

Throughout Ford's long history, if there was a most hallowed tradition it was to never delay a Job One date. (Job One is the first unit off the assembly line.) For years, Ford, like the other domestic carmakers, planned its business activities around the date that a new model was scheduled to be released. If an automaker fails to meet this goal, a vacuum is created: The inventory of the previous year's models has been sold, yet there is no inventory of new models to sell. However, in mid-June 1980, Donald Jesmore, who headed manufacturing and engineering, informed Poling that he was not satisfied with the quality of the Escort. "It's just not ready for production."

"Well, if it's not, it's not," Poling replied. "Tell me when it is going to be ready and that's when we'll introduce it."

This was a particularly bold action to take at a time when the company was losing huge sums of money, and the Escort was one of the few models that Ford was sure would sell.

"The delay of Job One sent shock waves through the operating side of the company," Jesmore recalls. "The engineering community and the manufacturing community knew that *nothing* ever delayed Job One. But now there was this exception. *Quality.* It's easy to quote clever slogans such as 'Quality is our first priority,' but what Poling did when he delayed Job One was, in my opinion, the first tangible act that anyone had really seen on the part of senior management that the company was committed to quality above all else."

In the early 1980s, it was feared that Ford could not remain competitive in the long run unless large sums of money were invested in upgrading its manufacturing facilities. Prior to Poling's arrival at NAAO, there was an unwillingness to commit the funds to plant modernization, and as a result, Ford was behind GM and Chrysler, let alone the Japanese automakers. So, even at a time when the red ink was flowing at its thickest, Poling asked for a long-term commitment to spend $20 billion. Caldwell consented, and between the years 1980 and 1982, when the company lost $3.3 billion, it also spent about $13 billion in plant improvements. And this came at a time when Caldwell demanded "to leave no stone unturned in any part of the business. And to challenge everything we are doing. Challenge it to make sure it is absolutely necessary, and challenge ourselves to find if there is a better way to do what is necessary."

Caldwell, Petersen, and Poling also began to spend a major portion of their time visiting Ford facilities across the country, speaking and listening to plant managers, foremen, and workers, repeatedly communicating the same message that quality and efficiency require a team effort. At the same time, an employee involvement program was implemented. It invited every employee to furnish ideas that could improve every facet of the company. High-ranking executives at every level were seen making the rounds in their shirt sleeves, stopping to talk to workers, asking for their suggestions. "We didn't simply ask for opinions," Petersen explains. "We responded by implementing hundreds of ideas that came pouring in. It was wonderful because time and time again, workers would say to one of us variations on, 'I just want you to know that I have been with Ford for 25 years and never before have I been asked what I thought about my job, and how my job might be done better. For the first time in my life, I now actually look forward to coming to work.' And it was just because we asked him what he thought. Soon we could feel a snowballing effect and it served as a tremendous reinforcement that our hard work was paying off."

That Ford was truly serious about quality was further demonstrated when the company stopped penalizing supervisors who did not make their quotas because they prioritized quality. It was reinforced when products, which a worker on the floor said were not right, were not shipped from the plant. When it was announced that a single worker had the authority to stop the assembly line if he or she detected anything that would jeopardize the quality of the product, there was little doubt about Ford's top priority.

A visit to a plant was a difficult day's work. As Poling explains, "I'd meet with the managers and review the quality data, and not only would I critique the plant's quality, but how it stacked up against the best in class of all the competition. Then I reviewed the plant's cost performance. But looking at the books was not enough. Afterward, I'd walk through the plant to observe firsthand how it was operating. When you've been in this business as long as I've been in it, you can tell how efficient a plant is by the attitude of the workers. For instance, I can look around and see how clean it is. Sure, every plant will clean itself up when they know I'm coming, but I can spot areas that have been especially cleaned up for my inspection, and I can tell the areas that are not done on an ongoing basis. They can't cover it up. I also look around for parts that are rejects—this tells me something too. And I can spot people who are standing around talking, doing nothing. Sure, everyone takes a break, but I know when there are too many people milling around.

"I remember walking through one plant—I probably shook 3,800 hands that day," Poling adds. "There was a geniune enthusiasm. People were excited about sharing new ideas with me, and they wanted to talk about something special they had previously done. Perhaps a worker redesigned a part for his machine, improving the quality of the product or the efficiency with which he produces the part. It's a great feeling to see the excitement in somebody because he's proud of his work."

While top executives sought suggestions internally from Ford's work force, they also went outside to find solutions. One early study, for example, indicated that the Japanese imports required considerably fewer repairs than domestic cars. This report helped explain why so many Americans who bought Japanese cars were not coming back to buy American cars. It also served as an eye-opener to hard-nosed Ford executives who were unwilling to accept the fact that the Japanese were capable of making better products than they were. This prompted the company to dispatch managers to plants around the world to observe Ford's most cost-efficient competitors. As a consequence, it is rare today to come across a high-ranking manager who has not made at least one visit to Japan.

Today's general manager of the Transmission and Chassis Division, Robert Adams, recalls his early days as plant manager at the Cleveland Engine Plant: "The Japanese car sales took off in 1979, and pretty soon we were reading articles about how good their products were compared to ours. Well, I've been in this business a long time, and I was under the impression that we were doing a good job in this country. Then, in 1982 on my first visit to Japan, I toured a few engine plants and witnessed their work effort and efficiency. I found out that they were doing things we didn't think were possible.

"I studied their engine manufacturing process for two weeks," Adams continues, "gathered a lot of facts, and prepared a presentation to deliver to my people at the Cleveland plant. Now, I knew there were a lot of bad feelings toward the Japanese among my workers. They felt threatened and thought the Japanese would take their jobs. I took advantage of that. I had American flags put up throughout the plant and also displayed posters showing comparisons between Japanese worker productivity and ours. Other posters illustrated how the Japanese quality levels were superior. Then I delivered my state of the plant message to a group of about 150 people, including managers, supervisors, and salaried people. Later I conducted a series of meetings so everybody in the plant would get my message. Each time I wore a Japanese kimono and slippers. Sure, it was symbolic and they laughed. But I got through to them. I told them what the competition was doing and convinced them that they could do it too. For instance, our cylinder block machine line had 32 people on each shift. I pointed out that the Japanese were producing the same production figures with 8 to 10 workers per shift. Their first reaction was denial, but then my message started to sink in, and with a change in attitudes we were able to make some changes."

A 1980 NBC documentary "If Japan Can, Why Can't We?" reinforced Petersen's concern for quality. The program revealed the remarkable work done by W. Edwards Deming, an American business consultant who is considered the godfather of Japan's quality revolution. It showed how, after World War II, Deming (invited to Japan by Ichiro Ishikawa, president of both the great Kaidenran and the Japanese Union of Engineers, JUSE) worked with about 50 heads of Japanese firms, including Toyota, consulting with them on statistical process control and its impact on quality improvement. Deming told the Japanese industrialists who attended his quality-control conferences in 1950 that "within five years, Japanese quality would be known the world over and that other nation's manufacturers would be screaming for protection. I didn't export U.S.

practices to the Japanese. What they learned from me was not American practice. America still has not learned it." Deming's five-year prediction was off by a year. It took the Japanese only four years. The documentary on Deming prompted Petersen to personally meet with Deming.

Ironically, revered in Japan since the 1950s, Deming was ignored in his homeland. Now, however, he is receiving long-overdue recognition in the United States. A crusty old man in his late eighties, Deming's policy when considering a new client is to meet only with the chief executive officer and/or chief operating officer. He insists that the commitment to quality must start at the top of a company. Deming accepted Petersen's invitation to meet with him in Dearborn. At their first meeting, Deming emphasized that Ford did not have a problem with its work force; the problem stemmed from the company's management and systems. During this and subsequent meetings, Petersen and Deming exchanged ideas about corporate culture, employee involvement, and participative management. These discussions played a significant role in the development of the Ford Code of Quality Excellence, which evolved several years later.

Petersen recalls a recent conversation with Deming: "He was the key speaker at a Society of Automotive Engineers' meeting, and I was on the stage as a panel guest. Deming addressed a question to me that caught the attention of the entire audience. 'Considering what Ford has accomplished,' he asked, 'how far along do you think the company has progressed?'

" 'Perhaps 15 percent,' I replied. 'Maybe that much . . .'

"Afterward, he came up to me and said, 'I'm tickled to hear that you think you're only at the 15 percent mark. Truthfully, I was fearful that you might think you had it made.' "

Edward Baker, director of Ford's Quality Strategy and Operations Support, relates Deming has consulted Ford on a consistent basis throughout the 1980s, spending from two days to a week each month in Detroit. Baker describes Deming's work as an educational process that "we continue to study and implement. When you look back to where we were in 1980 and where we are today, we've come a long way. But when you look at where we could be, there's tremendous opportunity ahead for us."

Although a member of Mensa, an organization for people with very high IQs, Petersen has never been accused of being an egghead. He loves fast cars, shares an exotic rock collection with his wife, and comfortably engages in small talk. Yet when it comes to business, his approach to problem solving is executed with the thoroughness of a laboratory scientist. In addition to seeking consultation from Deming, Petersen studied several successful American corporations. He dispatched teams of Ford people to a variety of companies to observe such things as corporate culture, application of teamwork, and commitment to continuous improvement. Petersen was particularly impressed with the team approach at Hewlett-Packard Company. Petersen concluded that the team approach used by the Ford Truck Division was the reason it was able to outperform the Car Division. Hourly workers in the automobile plants were organized to work as teams and more decision making was shifted from the top to those people who did the actual work.

Petersen's quest for knowledge and his love of cars led him to enroll in the Bob Bondurant School of High-Performance Driving at the Sears Point International Race Track in Sonoma, California, in 1982. Petersen was prompted to develop his driving skills so he could personally feel how safely Ford cars handled at high speeds, before being introduced in the market. The Bondurant school instructed him on how to consistently drive a 60-mile lap, which is necessary to have comparable speeds for testing cars with different suspensions. Petersen thought highly enough of the school that squads of company executives have since enrolled. Once again, top management demonstrated that it would go to extremes making sure the product was right.

At a 1982 dinner meeting at the Renaissance Center in Detroit, Petersen addressed a group of 35 members of Ford's dealer council. Those present were elected representatives of Ford dealers across the country. During a question-and-answer period following an after-dinner speech, one dealer made reference to a remark that Petersen had made about dropping the Fairmont from the product line and replacing it with the Tempo, soon to be introduced.

"I think I speak on behalf of the other gentlemen here tonight, Mr. Petersen," the dealer said, "when I say that Ford should keep the Fairmont because we need a low-price car under $6,000 to compete with the Chevy II."

There was a loud round of applause by the group, demonstrating their approval.

The normally calm president slammed his fist on the podium: "I am sick and tired of hearing people say that we should retain a car that will not be competitive in the future. The new Ford Motor Company *will* have integrity and we *will* sell state-of-the-art, quality cars. We will not sacrifice long-term image for short-term profit."

There was a hush throughout the room and nobody challenged Petersen's statement. Pat O'Daniel, president of D. Patrick Ford in Evansville, Indiana, recalls the incident: "Don Petersen is normally soft-spoken, and it was so out of character for him to raise his voice. But, boy was he ever effective! One dealer came up to me after the meeting and said, 'That was the finest speech I've ever heard a Ford executive give. It's about time somebody showed some emotion around here.' I agreed. Petersen's outburst demonstrated his conviction, and he made a believer out of me that the company was committed to quality. Up until this time, I thought it was lip service."

Slowly but surely, Ford was getting its act together. Costs were coming down, efficiencies were being realized, and a feeling of teamwork prevailed. Internally, the company was improving, but there were still external problems that would not go away. The Japanese continued to flood the market with quality cars, and each year they got better. Interest rates remained high and the dollar-to-yen relationship continued to be out of whack. "Our product development people and manufacturing people did incredible work on the 1982 Escort," Petersen says, "and through these efforts, they were able to pass a $400 savings on to the customer. That's quite an accomplishment, which we felt would enhance the Escort in competing against the Japanese cars. But then there was a change in currency that more than wiped out all that had been accomplished. Needless to say, it was very discouraging."

"We meticulously monitored quality to measure how we were progressing," Caldwell notes, "and during the first two years after we started our quality program, we couldn't see any improvement whatsoever. Naturally this was disconcerting, and time and time again, we'd review the entire scenario and ask ourselves, 'What are we doing? What is missing? Is there something we should be doing that we're not doing? Does anybody think that we're doing the wrong thing?' Well, nobody thought we were doing anything wrong, and there was nothing else we thought would work better so we held to our course."

"Quality isn't simply one thing but a composite of many things. So while we were making advances in this area and that area, we kept coming up with new designs and new parts, so the total composite wasn't showing us any particular gain," Caldwell continues. "It's remindful of the Bay of Fundy in New Brunswick, Canada, off the Atlantic coast. That's where the highest tides in the world occur every 12 hours or so. Well, the Bay of Fundy water builds up slowly in the beginning, rising ever so little, and then suddenly, a wall of water rushes in. Likewise, we were unable to detect much progress from our efforts to improve quality, but then, all of a sudden, it was there and everyone knew it."

Caldwell adds, "There's a longer gestation period for a car or a truck than a radio. We Americans are an impatient people. We have instant picture, instant sound, instant cooking in microwave ovens. But it's not possible to have instant production of new cars. It takes time."

In the meantime, Ford was substantially reducing its costs, and its people knew that, sooner or later, the automobile depression was bound to end. As Dan Coulson, accounting director, explains, "We were gradually getting our cost structure under control and our quality was improving. We knew that if we could just hold out, when the economy rebounded, we'd be in much better shape than when it started. We knew that was when we'd be profitable again."

On the top floor of the Glass House, there was a consensus among Ford's executives, who had worked both hard and smart, that, in time, their efforts would pay off. There was also a pent-up demand for new cars. In the April 13, 1981 edition of *Newsweek*, Poling was quoted as saying, "We've got 50 million units in operation out there that are less fuel efficient than the cars the auto industry is turning out today. I think we'll see a gradual improvement this year. We'll build on that in '82 and then I think you're going to see a couple of very, very strong years in the automotive business in the United States."

Ford's 1982 U.S. car sales dropped to 1.4 million, down from the previous year's total of 1.5 million, and the nation's automobile depression continued with total industry car sales declining from 8.5 million to 7.9 million. But although Poling's prediction was correct, it was his forecast of *when* conditions would improve that was off. In 1983 Ford and the U.S. automobile industry would again rejoice.

When the company turned the corner during the first quarter of 1983, and its U.S. operations earned a profit for the first time in 16 quarters, it was a time for celebration. At an informal ceremony, Red Poling, the man who had earned the well-deserved reputation of the "bean counter," presented two big bottles of black ink to Petersen and Caldwell. Then there were more bottles—of champagne. Like the Bay of Fundy, there was a buildup of black ink. Ford enjoyed four profitable quarters during 1983, with annual earnings totaling $1.9 billion.

4

THE PEOPLE DIFFERENCE

A permanent shutdown of a large automobile plant has a devastating effect on the lives of thousands. To a worker, it inflicts anguish, humiliation, and financial hardship. An entire family is victimized. The side effects often include increased rates of alcoholism, wife and child abuse, and suicide.

Ford plants were often the largest employers in their communities. Closing these plants was catastrophic to many areas. A huge number of workers flooded the local job markets making it impossible to provide work for all of the unemployed. Those who did get hired were apt to settle for a smaller salary. The local economy is destroyed as the reduction in spending ruins many small shopkeepers and service-related businesses. The ensuing massive exile of workers, who are forced to relocate, causes the value of local real estate to plummet. Sellers are forced to take losses on their homes, wiping out any equity they may have accumulated over the years.

An economic depression can be measured in hard numbers, consisting of such figures as the number of unemployed, reduced payrolls, decreased spending, and depreciated real estate values. Not so easily measured is the mental depression inflicted on the thousands of unemployed workers and their families.

A total of nine Ford plants were closed during the 1980–1982 automobile depression. It was indeed devastating to the people who worked and lived in those communities. To many, it was the most agonizing time of their lives. One unemployed worker could have been speaking for thousands when he said, "For months there were rumors the plant was closing 'next week.' And when next week came, then it was 'next week.' With all the talking, you'd think I'd be prepared when it finally happened. But when it was officially announced it was shutting down, I was in a state of shock. I had such an empty feeling when I went home that night. I felt so ashamed. It was as if I was letting down my wife and two kids. In the beginning, I thought it would just take some adjusting, but as time went on, the empty feeling turned into despair. The worst part was the guilt I was having because I had failed as a husband and father. It got so bad, I had a hard time looking them in the eyes when I talked to them."

At other Ford plants, however, conditions were not quite so severe. Although cutbacks occurred, Ford kept many factories open at reduced capacity and continued to manufacture cars and trucks. Still, it was a traumatic experience even for those who remained on the payroll. They witnessed fellow workers being laid off, never knowing if they might be next. It was a source of constant anxiety. Almost daily, rumors spread across the plant floor that more workers would be laid off or that a permanent shutdown might occur.

"Everyone's effort can make a difference," visiting executives from Dearborn told them. The message was constantly repeated in newspaper articles and television broadcasts: "Ford must regain its competitive edge. If not, the company will fall victim to the hard times." Looming over their heads was the constant reminder that Ford might be forced to manufacture cars abroad and only *distribute* cars in America. To the workers who witnessed wholesale layoffs of their coworkers, these warnings could not be taken lightly.

Then an interesting phenomenon occurred. Those workers who remained on the payroll refused to be passive victims. They became determined to play a role in their futures. The realization that the fate of their coworkers could be theirs served as a strong motivator on the plant floor.

Adversity makes strange bedfellows. Ford management and UAW leaders were drawn together to fight the common enemy, the Japanese automakers. Both sides emphasized teamwork—as a team, the company and the union would triumph. It was by no means a revolutionary message. The production of automobiles and trucks always required teamwork. Since the first days of mass production, it always required thousands of people working together to assemble thousands of parts to make a Ford vehicle. Teamwork was really nothing new; it has always been a vital ingredient. But now the team had a new competitor.

For the first time ever, the domestic automakers were faced with competition from foreign shores. With the arrival of the Japanese automakers, it was not simply a matter of waiting out a weak economy. The Japanese competition was threatening because their products were very good, and they were unyielding in their drive to gain market share in the United States. With the coming of the second energy crisis, their cars exactly filled the needs of the American consumer. The Big Three were caught completely off guard; their products were no match for the Japanese invasion. Practically overnight, the U.S. automobile industry was thrown into a new arena that demanded vastly improved quality and productivity.

No longer would the company be operated with the smugness exhibited by previous Ford managers. The new regime was aware that solutions must be sought from sources outside its domain. It was decided that the best place to observe new management practices was behind enemy lines, in Japan. In the beginning, a handful of Ford managers journeyed to Japan, and then there were dozens, and they were followed by hundreds of others who went to observe workers and managers in the automobile plants of Toyota, Nissan, Honda, and Mazda. To their surprise, they discovered that the superiority of the Japanese automakers was not achieved by higher levels of automation and advanced technology. *It was not machines but people that made the difference in quality and productivity*. It also became obvious that the Japanese workers were not superior to American workers. The difference was how the Japanese workers were managed.

"For a while, we had a devil of a time trying to determine what the reason was for the difference in quality between our products and theirs," says James Bakken, former vice-president of corporate quality. "Was it Japan's homogeneous society? Was it their technology? Hell, they got their technology from us, and little by little, they improved on it. Believe it or not, there were even studies made to find out if their diet had anything to do with it!

"We put together statistical evidence," Bakken continues, "and it revealed how, in the early 1970s, the American and Japanese automakers had about the same quality. Later when we plotted the entire decade's history, we observed that the Japanese quality showed continuous improvement. Always, no matter how slight, there was year-to-year improvement—it was 2 percent, 1 percent, 5 percent, but never backward, always forward. We then analyzed how Americans were taught to manage a business, and observed the emphasis was always on stability and control. We were instructed to set a budget and meet it—never deviate from the operating procedure. There were five generic inputs: people, equipment, materials, methods, and environment. Once these factors were blended together, a state of stability was attained, and as long as the procedure wasn't altered, the results were predictable. The Japanese, on the other hand, say, no, no. This is just the base from which to begin. Now, it must be continuously improved. We must create change, and it must be meaningful change. We learned from the Japanese that the job of management is to provide leadership to make possible meaningful change. Now because we acknowledge the value in striving to change—every process and system must be continuously improved."

Accepting the concept of constant meaningful change was a radical departure from the Ford's past. Particularly radical was Ford's desire to emulate the harmony that was found to exist between Japanese managers and workers. For years a pervasive "us" and "them" syndrome had existed in Ford. In fact, it had been nurtured. A well-defined line between management and labor prevailed. The segregation between white- and blue-collar workers was clearly intentional. Workers considered managers uncaring and callous. And to the managers, workers were people who lacked motivation and took no pride in their work, who could contribute with their backs only, never with their brains. Little if any responsibility was delegated to workers. The workers understood what was expected of them, and rarely did they do anything additional.

The company's attitude toward workers dated back to the days when Henry Ford I set up the first mass production–assembly lines, employing mostly European immigrants who had difficulty reading English and others who only spoke in their native tongue. The company operated on the premise that a small group of individuals did the thinking while the vast majority of employees could only do what they were told to do. For years the business operated this way, and for the most part, it seemed to work. And Ford was no different from most other American manufacturers. Across the country, in the nation's businesses workers were treated as brainless, interchangable parts.

Not only did Ford believe workers could not make correct choices at work, but he presumed the same was true during their off-the-job hours. In 1915, a company-published booklet titled *Helpful Hints and Advice to Employes* [sic] was distributed to every employee. A subtitle read, "To help them grasp the opportunities which are presented to them by the Ford profit-sharing plan." The following has been excerpted from the booklet.

The Company desires all of its employees and their families to be well housed, live in good wholesome neighborhoods, and be free as possible from danger of disease caused by dark, foul, filthy tenements, and unwholesome localities.

The Company does not undertake to select neighborhoods or plan homes for its employees, but it does expect that they, to be profit-sharers, will choose wholesome and decent neighborhoods and buildings, and keep their homes and surroundings clean, sanitary, and healthful.

This requirement is made that the employees and their families may live healthily and cleanly, and be a credit to the Company, as well as to themselves and the community in which they live.

Every male employee over 22 years of age, who leads a clean, sober and industrious life, and who can prove that he has thrifty habits, is eligible to share in the profits.

Cases have been brought to the Company's attention indicating that some young men, in order to qualify as profit-sharers, have hastily married without giving serious thought to such an important step in their lives. Seldom does such a marriage prove a happy one. If they would give more thought to the uncertainty of business affairs and the certainty of the obligations and responsibilities assumed in the marriage vows, there would be less work for the divorce courts.

A staff of investigators has been chosen whose duties are to explain the profit-sharing plan, and collect information and data from every one of the employees. This information is to be used in deciding who is entitled to benefit from the profit-sharing.

The judgment formed by the investigators, based upon information and figures obtained from the employee, goes a long way in determining whether the employee is worthy to receive or continue to receive profits from the Company, but are by no means final.

Employees should live in clean, well conducted homes, in rooms that are well lighted and ventilated. Avoid the congested and slum parts of the city. . . .

Employees should use plenty of soap and water in the home, and upon their children, bathing frequently. Nothing makes for right living and health so much as cleanliness. Notice that the most advanced people are the cleanest.

Other advice given in the booklet included information on the worker's children, education, thrift, how to use profits wisely, good banking practices, worthy investments, legal hints, and avoiding debts. Interior and exterior photographs of filthy and clean homes were illustrated to enable Ford employees to recognize the differences.

While Henry Ford's intention might have been benevolent, it is certain that his attitude did nothing to enhance the self-esteem of company employees. And for years, while working conditions and employee's rights made slight improvements, up through the 1970s the worker's job was still to do exactly what his supervisor ordered. "Workers had no brains," says Steve Yokich, UAW vice-president, "just legs, arms, and hands. When you worked on an assembly line, you weren't paid to think. No matter what. Even if there were bad pieces and poor production, you didn't dare to do anything differently, because if you did, your reward was that you'd get docked. That's the way it was, and Ford was making lots of money, so they were happy with the way things were. The company was selling everything it made, even when it was junk. Profit was the driving force. The company thought quantity, not quality."

"The whole idea was to take the job and decompose it," explains Ed Baumgartner, program director of Truck Operations. "By making the work very simple, anyone could be hired to do it. That's the way it was done when Henry Ford I was in charge. Following World War II, the company was run by men who were trained in the military in an environment where orders were given and no questions were asked. When we began to feel the heat from the Japanese, we started to pay attention to how they worked with people. We had no choice but to take a good hard look at them because it was obvious that they were doing something right that we weren't. What we discovered was that, to be competitive with them, we'd have to make the best use of everybody's brainpower. This meant that we'd have to create an atmosphere where people take an interest in their work and feel good about themselves."

As Petersen explains, "Our nuts-and-bolts restructuring moves by themselves weren't enough. We had to figure out how to capture our workers' hearts and minds."

So, during the company's restructuring, Caldwell, Petersen, and Poling examined every aspect of the business, including how people were treated. At Toyota, the giant of the Japanese auto industry, for example, 1.4 million employee suggestions—30.5 per worker—were submitted in 1981. Ninety-four percent were accepted. Soichiro Honda, the former auto mechanic who founded the company bearing his name, says, "An industry prospers only when everybody involved in it thinks about how it can be improved." The successes of such automakers as Toyota and Honda captured the attention of Ford. Petersen and Poling concluded that the best way to maximize human resources was to get the company's workers involved by implementing the employment involvement (EI) process.

EI was not a new concept, nor is it one that originated in Japan. The Japanese borrowed the concept from America when they began setting up "quality circles" taught to them by W. Edwards Deming and another American quality management pioneer J. M. Juran in the 1950s. (Ironically, Deming and Juran went to Japan at the suggestion of General Douglas MacArthur to help the Japanese improve the quality of their manufactured goods so they would reach an acceptable standard for competing in world markets.) In brief, a quality circle is a problem-solving team, consisting of a small group of workers who participate in "off-line" discussions on a voluntary basis to devise ways to improve working conditions, quality, safety, productivity, and so on. In order to be effective, Deming states QC circles "must have management's participation so that the suggestions of the workers can be carried out."

As a result of the success that the Japanese were having with quality circles in the early 1960s, several companies in America introduced them to their work forces; by the end of the decade, they were being set up in hundreds of U.S. companies. The quality circles benefited both the employer and the employee, and from their successes, employee participation programs began to evolve. While the concept is practiced by many major U.S. corporations including the Big Three members, no two programs are identical. Ford emphasizes that EI is not a program but a process.

From a worker's point of view, EI gives the worker more responsibility and recognition for the ideas that he contributes. "People like being involved," Petersen matter-of-factly states. "And they like being asked, 'What do you think?' It's just remarkable what that question does to people." The company also benefits from EI because productivity is increased and better quality goods are produced. Furthermore, in a positive working environment, the worker furnishes the company with his ideas, which, in turn, foster an overall improvement.

The acceptance of the EI process at Ford was contingent on gaining the support of the UAW. While in principle EI is a win-win situation, getting initial approval was by no means easy. Some UAW leaders declared EI as a tool used by the company to undermine the union's influence on the worker and protested that it was "contrary to the collective bargaining process." Some said it reminded them too much of the Japanese, and feared it would lead to "doing jumping jacks and singing songs before each shift." They claimed that if the emphasis was put on "the team," the individual would lose his autonomy. Other workers objected, seeing it as another way for management to get something for nothing. Phil Caldwell notes the suspicion and comments, "The mind-set of the worker was, 'I don't know what the game is, but I do know that you're going to get me in the end because you've always done it before.' "

Nor was EI received with open arms by plant supervisors. Foremen said it stripped them of their authority. The idea that a worker should be permitted to express his opinion or, for that matter, voice a complaint would make it impossible for management to maintain control on the shop floor. The fact is that both sides opposed EI because they had little trust in each other. But while EI seemed threatening, nobody was seriously worried that it would become a reality, because it was so contradictory to the existing culture.

Perhaps EI eventually received the blessings of both management and labor simply because its time had come. In the late 1970s, weak car sales caused union membership to dwindle, making UAW leaders aware that the time had come when labor and management must cooperate, lest both suffer. 1979 was the year of the historic pact when both Ford and the UAW endorsed the concept of EI. To make it official, Ford and the UAW signed a letter of understanding (referred to as a "side letter" because it was not written in the contract) in which they agreed to provide joint management and union leadership to employee involvement in an effort "to make work a satisfying experience, improve the overall work environment, enhance creativity, contribute to improvements in the workplace, and help achieve quality, efficiency, and reduce absenteeism."

Both sides agreed that if EI were to work, they must communicate to all workers throughout the organization that it was supported by both management and labor. To get the word out that the company was behind EI, Caldwell, Petersen, and Poling, who by this time had been making regular visits to plants, would talk it up at every opportunity. Union leaders were also making the rounds to inform labor of their support. Meanwhile, although widespread reductions in expenditures were occurring, cutting the EI budget was never a consideration. Ford's cash commitment clearly demonstrated that it was not simply a management rage that would run its course.

Even with the blessings of management and labor, there was much suspicion in the plants, and early attempts to implement EI were no easy matter. After all, when the generals may agree to a cease-fire, the animosity among the troops does not necessarily vanish. "Selling the concept was the easy part compared to the implementation," remembers Ernest Savoie, director of the employment development office at Ford. "And naturally, implementation is the most important part. After we presented the process to 60 plant managers, 4 actually volunteered to try it. Some were hostile and others had a wait-and-see attitude."

"When a culture has been set for more than three-quarters of a century, and then a new path is charted," explains Paul Banas, manager of employee development, strategy, and planning, and who served on the first national EI steering committee, "it's understandable for people to be skeptical. It should be remembered that when we first started EI, most of the people thought they were only paid to come in and do physical labor, even though they might have wanted to make a greater contribution. It wasn't realistic for us to lay something on them and say, 'Here's what we were yesterday, and here's what we are today,' and expect them to respond, 'That's wonderful,' give us a salute, and immediately begin to behave differently. It's only natural for people to judge us on our actions, not our words.

"On the same token," Banas continues, "when we presented the process to our plant supervisors and told them what the workers would now be doing, their reaction was, 'Hey, that's what we do everyday.' To a bunch of engineers, for instance, EI wasn't any great revolution. Depending on where somebody came from, the response differed."

At first, Ford set up pilot programs consisting of about 200 volunteers in each of the four plants. They focused on forming problem-solving groups, new product launch teams, and *ad hoc* quality involvement teams. They were invited to contribute their ideas, their analyses, and their solutions to job-related problems. " '*You* pick the problems that you want to work on,' we told them," Savoie stresses. " 'Here's an opportunity for you to improve your job, your work, and whatever's bugging you. You can choose whatever you want to work on that you feel is going to contribute to a better work life for you. Anything that you feel will make your work easier and better, and add to quality and more efficiency of the process.' "

In time, little successes led to noticeable changes. Hourly employees assumed tasks formerly performed only by supervisors. They became involved in work scheduling, and they were allowed to stop an assembly line when something, such as a compromise in quality, went wrong. After several months, both company management and labor leaders were convinced that EI could improve product quality and efficiency as well as the workers' standard of living.

Banas recalls an early meeting with a group of hourly employees and managers at the Engine Division: "We were discussing EI and somebody raised the point about the relationship between the suggestion program and employee involvement. An hourly worker jumped right in and said, 'I think it is very important that we keep the suggestion program separate from the employee involvement process.' He noted that the suggestion program had always been perceived as a management program, 'but the employee involvement process is for the employee.' He stressed that in an environment conducive to open communication, a suggestion program wouldn't be necessary because ideas would flow freely with it."

Banas explains that the process is set up to provide an opportunity for employees to contribute, and again emphasizes, "It is strictly voluntary, for anybody who wants to come forward and be involved. Whenever a manager asks me, 'How do you motivate employees to participate?' I say, You don't, and I don't want anyone to even talk about motivation. Our employees don't need us to inspire them. They're already motivated. We just have to remove the barriers and they'll participate on their own."

To ensure that EI would not be perceived as a tool to exploit the worker to the benefit of the company, no attempts were made to measure the workers' performances to evaluate how it might be profitable for Ford. No scorekeeping was done to determine if the bottom line showed it was paying off. This policy sharply contradicts Ford's historic emphasis on quantifying results. "We wanted to stress the quality of the process, not the outcome," Banas asserts. "By doing it this way, a message was sent out telling everyone that this was not business as usual."

Julius Sabo, industrial relations manager at the Walton Hills Stamping Plant near Cleveland, explains, "We don't keep score because EI is more than only accomplishing a task. It's changing an attitude, or what you'd call revising a mind-set."

In time, the news spread via the grapevine and in-house organs that EI really could work at Ford. To boost the process, the company held conferences and training programs for EI coordinators at local plants offering courses on topics ranging from instructional skills to creative problem solving. In addition, as the EI process gained momentum, another process called participative management (PM) was set up. If EI was to succeed on a large scale, it was essential to instruct managers and supervisors on how to support it. With this in mind, Ford managers were trained so they would know how to respond to workers who became involved. Petersen explains, "The company is like a pyramid: You have large numbers of people at the bottom and relatively few at the top. Like other corporations, Ford has always been managed from the top down. But to implement EI, it's essential to have people in management capable of responding to the flood of good suggestions that pour in from the work force. To accomplish this, we recognized that EI needed a companion—that's why we set up PM to develop managers' listening skills and so they would know how to *let* people participate. It was also important for managers to understand that EI didn't mean they'd have to abrogate their responsibility. It just means giving anyone with a valid basis for having an opinion a chance to be heard."

In the beginning, the employee involvement process was resisted more by salaried supervisors than by hourly workers. Hugh Merchant, who served as a troubleshooter and trainer in the development of EI and PM across the country, says, "The supervisors had always ruled the workers, telling them, 'I make the decision' and 'The buck stops here.' Well, with EI, that was all thrown out the window, so the supervisors thought, 'Why would they [Ford] need me if they're going to ask these people to participate and make decisions?' In retrospect, we went into it too quickly, we didn't take the time to prepare them properly. We should have spent more time saying, 'Let's talk about how this could benefit you.' Once we got the process going, the salaried and middle managers saw that EI *did* benefit them, and eventually the word got around that it was a good thing."

At each plant that participated in EI, one salaried and one hourly person were elected to be employee involvement coordinators. Trainers such as Merchant went from plant to plant to teach them how to conduct EI classes so the work force could then participate. "We wanted the people in the plant to be the ones doing the training—not some people from Division—so some ownership was there," Merchant explains. "After about 16 hours of classes, the coordinators were able to do it on their own."

One prime example of how EI has succeeded is illustrated by an 1981 incident at Ford's stamping plant in Chicago. For years, after car doors were manufactured, the workers crated them in wood or metal boxes to be shipped to an assembly plant. When the crates arrived at the other plant, the workers ripped them open, took out the doors, and returned the crates to the Chicago plant to be reused. There was no concern at the assembly plant about the condition of the crates that were sent back, and they came back in such poor condition that extensive repairs were necessary. Not only was it annoying to the Chicago workers to fix the damaged crates (called dunnage), it was a time-consuming and expensive process. This led workers in a problem-solving group who identified the problem to tackle it on their own initiative. After taking photographs and video-tapes of dunnage, they sent their findings to their fellow workers at the assembly plant. Next, they invited the assembly-line workers to visit the Chicago plant to see for themselves that considerable expenses were incurred to repair the crates. Finally, the Chicago workers produced a manual and an educational program to instruct the assembly-plant work-ers on how to unload doors properly to preserve the crates. About six months later, the cost of the dunnage was reduced from $400,000 to $80,000. "Before EI," comments Savoie, "they would have never done anything like this. No, not ever in a million years!"

Another EI success story took place at Ford's assembly plant in Louis-ville, Kentucky, in 1982 just prior to when the Ranger was added to the company's compact truck line. Before a single Ranger went down the assembly line, in-depth discussions were held with all hourly employees. Employees were asked to look through the process sheets and make recommendations on changes they thought should be made prior to Job One. More than 800 suggestions poured in and the majority of ideas were implemented. Not only did the company receive ideas providing vast improvements in quality and work efficiency, as an extra bonus, workers' morale skyrocketed.

Once EI was under way at Ford's Kansas City plant, more than 650 design and manufacturing changes for the Tempo and Topaz were sug-gested. More than three-quarters of the suggestions were implemented. One came from a worker who was in charge of all nuts, bolts, and fasteners for the entire plant. He observed that the prototype had two bolts holding the front-door handle that differed from the two on the back-door handle. It didn't make sense to him since both door handles and bolt sizes were identical. The worker questioned the engineer, who, in turn, promised to look into it. It turned out that the difference resulted from the front and back doors having been designed by separate design-ers who had never communicated with each other about the matter. Thanks to the worker's suggestion, identical nuts, bolts, and fasteners are used for both doors—resulting in substantial cost savings, easier installa-tion, and the tracking of fewer parts.

How well was the process received? A 1982 survey of 748 UAW-Ford EI participants revealed 82 percent job satisfaction as compared with 58 percent before the process. Even more significant is the finding that 82 percent of these workers indicated that they now had a chance to accomplish something worthwhile in contrast to 27 percent beforehand. The survey also served as a vote of confidence for the UAW. It showed that 90 percent of the EI participants and 80 percent of the nonparticipants were in favor of the union's involvement in the process.

Paul Banas recalls a visit to Taiwan, when he met with a Chinese plant manager. "We were discussing employee involvement," Banas says, "and he said to me, 'We have done a tremendous job utilizing the physical and mental capacity of our workers.' He then paused and added, 'But the real breakthrough will come when we have captured their hearts.' I thought to myself, 'Boy, this guy really understands people.' "

Everything about a corporation is subject to change. Names of companies change. Products change. Real estate locations change. People change. But the most difficult and slowest change to make is one that involves a change in a corporation's culture. This is particularly true in a mature and established company such as Ford. The acceptance of EI at Ford demonstrated the willingness and determination by both management and labor to accept a change in corporate culture. Ford has clearly come a long way since its 1915 publication, *Helpful Hints and Advice to Employes*.

"It's no easy matter to make a transition from being an autocratic company to one that permits its people to have latitude and promotes teamwork," explains Phil Benton. "When I first started working for Ford, I worked in an environment in which my managers came from the old school. They browbeat their subordinates and rarely asked for opinions. They dictated their orders because that's the way they were treated when they first came into the business. It was engrained in the culture. I recall one vice-president who told me a story about how his boss treated him so rudely. 'That man shouted at me to the point where I was actually crying in his office,' he told me. I was touched by the story, but 15 minutes later, a subordinate walked into the office, and this vice-president jumped all over him in exactly the same manner. So you see, there's a corporate culture that's passed down from one generation of managers to the next, which is extremely difficult to change. As people are promoted, their behavior tends to mimic the managers who supervised them."

As the EI process began taking roots, it became obvious that Ford's work force represented an enormous untapped resource for ideas and energy. Don Ephlin, retired UAW vice-president, states, "When the operator who spends eight hours a day working on a machine began to relay its flaws to the engineer who designed it, the engineer learned all sorts of ways to improve the machinery. Besides, doesn't it make sense that the guy who operates a machine all day has some invaluable knowledge to share with the guy who designed it? Not listening to what he has to say is such an incredible waste." Plus, it was apparent that a dedicated and contented worker was more productive and conscientious about quality. "People find inherent satisfaction in doing a job well. They will strive for excellence, if they are allowed to," adds Petersen.

EI provided enough proof to make Ford management realize that they were on the right track. A significant step in the right direction had been taken, and the next question was, "How do we keep the momentum going and get the entire organization to pull together?"

Remarkably, although Ford Motor Company had been making automobiles for nearly eight decades, a corporate culture had never been articulated. Petersen and Poling were aware that a common theme was needed, one that could unite the efforts of all Ford people. During many meetings with Petersen and Poling, Deming reemphasized this need. He strongly advocated that a company must have certain guiding principles that it lives by and passes on from one generation to the next. Without such principles, he felt a company's drive for continuous improvement was seriously jeopardized.

Deming kept addressing the same question: Does your company have a consistency of purpose? It was a legitimate question, yet at the time when Ford was losing huge sums of money, the Socratic nature of his consulting did not seem relevant. It would have been easy enough to shrug it off and reply, "Yeah, we have a consistency of purpose. We've been making cars for 80 some years." Instead, Petersen and Poling listened carefully and then did some soul-searching. *Did* they have a consistency of purpose? And, if so, was it being communicated throughout the organization? This led them to recognize the need for all Ford employees throughout its worldwide operations to share a common focus and universal goal. This, they felt, was vital, providing direction for the future.

Following a series of informal sessions with top and middle managers, it was agreed that Petersen and Poling would meet regularly with a group of selected people to pursue the development of a central statement representative of common aspirations. The objective was to create a proclamation that clearly stated what Ford Motor Company stood for.

At times, the discussions during these sessions sounded more like a college class in philosophy than a business meeting. Yet, slowly, a statement began to evolve. At Poling's suggestion, it was agreed that it should be worded in a simple fashion so, even though it would not be memorized, its basic message could be recited without difficulty. Through these efforts, by the end of 1983, Ford introduced the company "Mission, Values, and Guiding Principles" (MVGP). It reads as follows:

Mission. Ford Motor Company is a worldwide leader in automotive and automotive-related products and services as well as in newer industries such as aerospace, communications, and financial services. Our mission is to improve continually our products and services to meet our customers' needs, allowing us to prosper as a business and to provide a reasonable return for our stockholders, the owners of our business.

Values. How we accomplish our mission is as important as the mission itself. Fundamental to success for the Company are these three basic values:

People. Our people are the source of our strength. They provide our corporate intelligence and determine our reputation and vitality. Involvement and teamwork are our core human values.

Products. Our products are the end result of our efforts, and they should be the best in serving customers worldwide. As our products are viewed, so are we viewed.

Profits. Profits are the ultimate measure of how efficiently we provide customers with the best products for their needs. Profits are required to survive and grow.

Quality Comes First. To achieve customer satisfaction, the quality of our products and services must be our number one priority.

Customers Are the Focus of Everything We Do. We must strive for excellence in everything we do: in our products, in their safety and value—and in our services, our human relations, our competitiveness, and our profitability.

Employee Involvement Is Our Way of Life. We are a team. We must treat each other with trust and respect.

Dealers and Suppliers Are Our Partners. The Company must maintain mutually beneficial relationships with dealers, suppliers, and our other business associates.

Integrity Is Never Compromised. The conduct of our Company worldwide must be pursued in a manner that is socially responsible and commands respect for its integrity and for its positive contributions to society. Our doors are open to men and women alike without discrimination and without regard to ethnic origin or personal beliefs.

Although on the surface, Ford's MVGP seems uncomplicated, much thought was put into it. Note, for example, as Petersen comments, "There was a great deal of talk about sequence of "the three P's"—*people, products,* and *profits.* It was decided that *people* should absolutely come first. Once the values were defined, the guiding principles fell into place.

The board of directors approved MVGP as an official company statement. Laminated pocket-size MVGP cards have since been printed up and today a majority of Ford managers carry one in their breast pocket, including both Petersen and Poling. One explanation for the popularity of MVGP is that it has received such strong support from the top of the company. Has it made a difference? Definitely. At meetings throughout the organization, commonly heard questions are "What are we trying to accomplish?" and "Is it consistent with the mission, values, and guiding principles?"

The words *dealers and suppliers are our partners* are in bold print in Ford's guiding principles. About 54 percent of the parts in a Ford vehicle are made by outside suppliers. While *supplier* is interchangeable with *vendor* throughout American industry, at Ford, each of these independent companies is called a supplier. "Personally, I think of vendors as people who sell peanuts at the ballpark," says Clinton Lauer, vice-president of purchasing and supply. No big deal perhaps; however, it is a small gesture of respect.

When Henry Ford entered the automobile industry, the company actually made no product whatsoever; instead his firm *assembled* cars. Ford was no different than the competition in this respect. At the turn of the century, there were only a few dozen manufacturers of parts, such as Dodge Brothers, which made axles and power trains. In most incidences, there was only one supplier of a particular part or parts for all automobile assemblers.

When innovations occurred, an automobile assembler would typically ask an existing supplier to make a new part, or, if necessary, would go outside the industry for a new product. For instance, executives from Cadillac approached Charles Kettering in Dayton, a National Cash Register engineer, because he had invented a small motor that electrified cash registers. They asked him if he could adapt it to start cars electrically. Young Kettering accepted the challenge and invented the electric starter to replace the hand crank. Kettering then founded Dayton Engineering

Laboratories Company (later named Delco), which made electric starters. When it came out in 1912, Cadillac sales jumped from 10,000 to 14,000. In 1916, Delco was acquired by General Motors.

It was also common for a small car dealer to go into the parts business. Detroit was the center of the automobile world, and most often, a supplier was a local acquaintance or somebody from the vicinity that somebody else recommended.

Eventually, Ford, as well as General Motors, Chrysler, and other automakers, began making many of its own parts. Sometimes, it was out of dissatisfaction with an existing supplier. Or perhaps, it stemmed from fear of becoming dependent on a supplier. In other cases, the automobile assembler could make it for less money, or make it better, or both. Ego also played a role—it might have been more ego than good business judgment that inspired Henry Ford to make his own steel and glass at the Rouge and to grow his own rubber in Brazil. As the automobile industry matured, the assemblers gradually became producers. Today, Ford makes 50 percent of the content of the cars it produces, General Motors 70 percent, and Chrysler 20 percent.

As the major Detroit automakers became three of the biggest and most powerful corporations in America, thousands of suppliers became dependent on their enormous orders. In many cases, a supplier's only customer would be one of the Big Three, or the auto company represented such a large piece of the supplier's total production that the termination of the business relationship would most likely put the supplier out of business. While doing business with a large automaker can be quite profitable, there is an obvious risk.

The selection of suppliers was often based strictly on the cost of product, with concern for quality an afterthought. Suppliers were requested to bid against one another—with the lowest bidder nearly always getting the order. There were also many instances where the good-ol'-boy network was the determining factor—the drinking or golf buddy received the order regardless of his bid. Still other times, buying decisions were based on payoffs ranging from paid vacations to lavish presents that included under-the-table cash.

One supplier tells about the graft that was commonplace in the 1930s during the Harry Bennett days: "It seemed like everyone at Ford had his own racket. It wasn't just the purchasing agents I dealt with, but workers in the plant as well. The Rouge was known as one of the biggest job-selling places in the world. In the 1930s when it was difficult to find employment, Bennett's thugs would sell jobs to workers. A guy would have to pay ten bucks to receive a slip of paper that would entitle him to get a job in the plant. Without the slip, they wouldn't hire him!"

Philip Gardner, CEO of Findlay Industries, a large manufacturer of seating and interior trim parts for Ford, Chrysler, and General Motors today, recalls the old days: "In the late 1940s and early 1950s I worked for a company that sold automotive interior carpeting, and I remember how one purchasing agent requested us to carpet his house so 'he could test it.' There were other incidents when we took purchasers on Florida vacations and even gave them money to bet on the races. That's the way it was, and we had to play their game to get the business. There were so many who always had their palms out in those days."

Henry Anzuini is the president of Metal Forge Inc., a Columbus, Ohio, firm that was originally the Columbus Bolt and Forge, with roots dating back to the horse and buggy era. "We've been around for a long time," Anzuini says, "and we were part of the good-ol'-boy network. Whenever there was a problem with quality, we'd send one of our guys to Detroit and he'd put his arm around the plant manager, talk it over with him, and then they'd go out and have a few beers and that was it! It doesn't work that way today. Believe me, it's a much nicer industry to work in now."

William Brock, president of Arrow Molded Plastics, describes how "In the past, Ford bought almost strictly on price. Each year, we'd get a one-year contract, which would put us in a very vulnerable position. Today, we have three- to five-year contracts, which allow us to do our planning, especially with the capital equipment we require. [These contracts] also enable us to plan our work force and other expenditures. It's a far better situation today, and we feel a lot more secure."

Today the good-ol'-boy network has gone by the wayside, nor is a supplier's price the number-one selling point in determining which company receives a contract. In the late 1970s, NAAO did business with an estimated 4,500 suppliers but this number has since been reduced to about 2,000. "In 1980, we told our people," explains Lauer, "that we had too many suppliers, and we were going to reduce the numbers. We set no objectives, but instead, we conducted quality meetings with our purchasers and told them, 'Judge your suppliers on quality. Decide on how many suppliers you presently have and how many you think you need. Then show us a plan on how to get there, and do your planning based on quality. Define what your commodities are. List the suppliers you have producing parts for that commodity grouping. Next, we want you to rate them according to those who are potential long-term suppliers and those you consider short-term suppliers. Be sure to get the concurrence of your engineers, designers, assembly people, and everyone who is involved in your commodity group. After you do this, let all of your suppliers know where they stand and inform them that Ford intends to work with some as potential long-term ones while others will be classified as short-term ones and thereby receive only one-year contracts. And since we are reducing the number of suppliers, the long-term suppliers will be given larger contracts.'

"One important reason for doing this was so we could tell a supplier how this company was rated. For instance, we'd say, 'Your rating scores are 75, 85, 80, and 55. You've got to improve on this area.' We could also say, 'You're a long-term supplier, and we'll consider you as very good as long as you maintain your strengths in these areas. When we source something in the future, your affordable cost is one consideration; however, we will evaluate such things as your product's quality, your technology, delivery, and so on.' "

In 1983, Ford devised a system that established formal quality ratings for every supplier. Called the Q1 program (for quality first), it tied in with the company's battle cry that "Quality is Job One." Ford recognized that unless this theme was carried over to the suppliers, it could not build quality automobiles. "When we first started the Q1 program, it came as quite a shock to many of our suppliers," says Lauer, "because we had never told them that they weren't good. We had started to give ratings for eight characteristics earlier in 1981, but with the Q1 program, in order to qualify as a supplier, they'd have to have a score of more than 70 (100 is a perfect score). To qualify as a Q1 supplier, it was required (1) to have a rating of 85 or above and (2) to use statistical process control. In a competitive bidding situation, no supplier would even be considered if its rating was ten points or more lower than a Q1 bidder. In the event that three suppliers placed a bid at the same price, the one with the best Q1 rating would receive the work. The Q1 ratings of 85 or better were announced in 1983, and suppliers had until January 1, 1985 to improve their ratings.

"As business was awarded to suppliers based on their quality ratings rather than having submitted the lowest bids, those suppliers who had doubts about whether Ford would stick to its guns found out that the company was dead serious about quality. Now, while a supplier's quality of its product is the most important criterion, we have several other categories that we rate. For instance, we have a delivery rating that is based on meeting required shipping schedules. We also have a rating scale for technology because our supplier base must keep up with us in this area if we are to remain competitive in the future. In the past, we'd design the parts and say to a supplier, 'We know more about cars than you, so here's what we want,' and they'd do what we instructed them to do. Today, we realize that many of our suppliers have more expertise on what they make for us than we have, so they're rated according to how we perceive their technological capabilities. Other ratings are based on such things as the general management of the business as well as the overall management of the work force."

The Q1 program was initially developed to provide an incentive for suppliers to improve their quality. On January 1, 1990, the rating necessary to qualify as a preferred supplier was raised from 85 to 90. Ford raised the standards to motivate suppliers to improve their manufacturing processes. As of this date, no new business was awarded if a rating was under 90.

Phil Gardner of Findlay Industries comments, "Ford has come a long way since the 1930s and 1940s when I first began working in the automobile industry. At that time I worked for Continental Motors, who made clutches for Ford. We'd put four into a box and ship them to the Rouge on a freight car. When they arrived, they'd put a box of clutches on a moving conveyor, and when it crossed the scale, they knew whether there were four clutches in it. That was the extent of their inspection. The only time Continental Motors would hear about a bad part was when a customer had trouble with his car!"

Gardner sees a striking contrast between the Ford of yesteryear and the Ford of the present. "Later, through the 1970s," Gardner explains, "the standard for quality at Ford and the other domestic automakers was based on making it only good enough to be accepted at the plant. We never were driven to make it any better than to just get by. It was only after the Japanese automakers set new standards in America that the Big Three became motivated to make quality products for the customer.

"When Ford became serious about quality in the early 1980s, they made a strong effort to get their suppliers involved. For instance, they'd invite groups of 200 to 300 to attend seminars at the Glass House where we'd hear Dr. Deming speak on his manufacturing theories. There were also several meetings with people from Ford's purchasing department, including top management such as Clint Lauer. They outlined what we'd have to do to be Q1 suppliers and worked closely with us so we could do it within their time frame. I understood that there would be fewer suppliers, but the ones who survived would end up with more business. I also understood that the bidding would be more competitive in the future, so we might not get as high a price, and possibly we'd have five-year contracts where there would be no price increases. But I realized that by being a quality supplier, we'd also be a more efficient company. And it's true, the big thing we're getting out of quality is that we're saving money.

"Here's how it works," Gardner continues, "For example, about 70 percent of our products are purchased from other suppliers. We used to throw away 3 percent of our products, so on a couple hundred million dollars, we'd have waste in the millions. Today we apply the same quality standards to our suppliers' products as Ford does to ours. By cutting the scrapped products down, we have realized tremendous savings. Then too, by reducing the number of rejects we get back from Ford, we have fewer hassles because our people don't have to run back and forth, spending time in the field to fix parts, and so on. There's no doubt about it. We've become a much better company as a result of Ford raising the quality standards for the products we make for them."

Findlay Industries has more than 1,000 suppliers furnishing it with materials, all of them having to improve quality to meet Ford's standards. And those suppliers have their own suppliers who must meet the up-graded standards. The effects of Demings's vision are, indeed, far-reaching.

There is a closeness that exists today between Findlay Industries and Ford, which, in Gardner's words, is "like being part of the same team. Don Petersen talks a great deal about the teamwork within Ford," Gardner explains, "and it permeates throughout their supplier network. I take pride in being part of the Ford team. Since Q1, they evaluate us carefully to make sure we're financially sound. And they scrutinize our work force closely. For instance, we have a training program in which we bring in our people from our 12 plants about once a month. At these sessions, questions are addressed such as 'What can we do to make this part better?' and 'What are your ideas on how your job can be improved?' Ford sends its people here to observe and advise us on our training program as well as many other aspects of our business. Their know-how in all facets of the industry is a tremendous resource."

Dana Corporation, a $5 billion manufacturer of automotive and truck parts, is one of Ford's major suppliers. Southwood J. Morcott, chairman and chief executive officer, takes special pride in Dana's team approach. "In the past, there was an adversarial relationship between the Big Three automakers and suppliers, much like that which existed between them and the union," Morcott says. "Today, we feel like we're part of the same team, and what we do with Ford is to our mutual benefit.

"Knowing Ford is responsive to our beyond-the-call-of-duty efforts," Morcott continues, "gives us an added incentive to invest in technology. What we did with Ford's Aerostar is a good example of how this works. Historically, Dana has supplied front and rear driving axles, frames, and other parts to Ford. In 1986, when the Aerostar was originally introduced, it was a two-wheel-drive vehicle. Our guys said, 'Let's see if we can develop a four-wheel option for the Aerostar.' We gave them the go-ahead, and using our own laboratories, engineering facilities, and test track, we developed a package and took it to Ford. We told them, 'We can produce the four-wheel drive for x number of dollars, and you can offer it as an option.' They said, 'Let's go to work on it!'

"Once we had their endorsement for the four-wheel-drive system, we worked together as a team on its development. What prompted us to act on our own without first getting their approval? After all, this was a speculative undertaking without a commitment on Ford's part. We did it because, number one, we thought they'd snap it up, which they did. Number two, we were confident that if Ford went for it, they would give us a chance to build it rather than making it themselves in their own factory, which, again, they did."

Perhaps the ultimate partner relationship is illustrated at Ford's Kentucky Truck Plant in Louisville. About a mile down the road, Dana's Spicer Universal Joint Division built a regional assembly facility (RAF), a small plant with about 50 employees that makes only drive shafts and universal joints for its single customer, Ford. The plant was built in 1979 as a just-in-time facility to ensure prompt and reliable delivery and is unique in the U.S. automobile industry. Dana took a calculated risk in building the plant, because, at the time, Rockwell Standard was also supplying the same parts to Ford. "We believed that as long as we had a competitive price and could give them 100 percent just-in-time delivery, we'd be hard to beat," Morcott explains. Dana was right in its assessment and, today, is the sole supplier for these parts.

Dana's RAF in Louisville exemplifies the kind of efficiency that is attainable when two corporations work as a team. There is no paperwork exchanged between the two companies. This means no orders, no invoices, and no checks. All transactions are made by computer. For example, if, by four in the afternoon, x number of units are requested by Kentucky Truck, Dana will make them and have the units on their docks by seven in the morning. And thanks to the computer system, each drive shaft and component is numbered sequentially according to Ford's assembly schedule. What's more, neither Ford nor Dana has the added overhead of stocking an inventory. "We don't even send them a bill," Morcott adds. "We just have to know how many trucks went out of their plant, and this tells us the number of parts we made for them. Every time a truck clears the line, a billing mechanism is triggered, and we're paid by a wire transfer from their account into ours. The float is less than 24 hours."

While the Toledo-based Dana Corporation, with 40,000 employees and operations in 25 countries, is a large company, many Ford suppliers are small firms. Although it generally takes a large, well-capitalized company to supply parts to a member of the Big Three, Ford has devoted considerable effort to award contracts to small companies, and, in particular, minority-owned businesses.

Shortly after the 1967 Detroit race riots, Henry Ford announced his dissatisfaction with the fact that, although many minority people were employed by the company, there were few minority suppliers. Ford felt that if more minority people had a stake in the business community, they would serve as leaders and role models in Detroit's minority communities. A purchasing program was established in 1968 to actively pursue business from minority-owned companies. In the beginning, these firms were mainly engaged in service-related fields such as maintenance, security, and waste collection.

During its first ten years, the program made modest headway, but then in 1978, after a series of meetings with Detroit's mayor, Coleman Young, Henry Ford hired Gary White. White was a black city administrator, whose résumé included a background in public relations and advertising. He was named manager of Ford's program, and, under his guidance, a concentrated effort was exerted to develop minority suppliers, assisting them in all areas, from financing to technology. In 1984, the Minority Supplier Development Committee was formed, which consisted of 18 high-ranking Ford executives. This committee set objectives, guidelines, and review procedures to ensure the program would succeed. These vice-presidents were executives who had the power and influence to make things happen. With this commitment, Ford was soon doing business with large numbers of minority-owned suppliers.

It was Red Poling who said, "If we are going to do this program, let's be sure to do it right. Just purchasing from these companies is a disservice to them. They must also be given the tools of the trade needed to be top suppliers. In this respect, we must think of them as suppliers who just happen to be minority owned." Poling emphasized the importance of bringing them in during the early development stages to work with designers, engineers, and manufacturing people. In the past, it was more common for only large suppliers to participate and be privy to the long-term planning of new cars. Like all suppliers, the minority-owned companies are governed by the Q1 rating system. They do receive special treatment, however, in certain areas. For example, Ford often offers financial assistance and works closely with them in an advisory capacity, particularly in the areas of technology and productivity improvement.

After running the program for eight years White resigned from Ford and, with a leveraged buyout, acquired Jones Transfer. An $85 million company, Jones Transfer is the nation's largest minority-owned trucking company. White's replacement, Renaldo Jensen, has a Ph.D. in aerospace mechanical engineering, spent 20 years in the air force, and held several command and staff positions at the Pentagon prior to joining Ford in 1980. According to Jensen, the minority suppliers program has a dual objective: to be "a good corporate citizen and, from a business point of view, to generate goodwill with the nation's minorities."

"In the beginning, much of this program's motivation stemmed from social guilt," Jensen explains. "It was the right thing to do because minorities are part of this nation. But there is an economic advantage for Ford, as well. If you look at this program in the short run, it isn't one of the most profitable ventures; however, in the long run, it shows great promise. In the future, as minority members become more affluent, they will buy more cars. We recognize there's a constituency out there, and we want to bring it aboard. Ford wants to be a part of their success."

In 1988, there were 475 minority-owned suppliers doing $481 million of business with Ford, averaging more than $1 million per company. The same year, Ford was named America's most outstanding company by the National Minority Supplier Development Council, a council consisting of such companies as Ford, General Motors, Chrysler, IBM, General Electric, Proctor & Gamble, and other *Fortune* 500 companies.

Today, there are many Ford minority suppliers' success stories. One of the most interesting is Mexican Industries in Michigan, Inc., a Detroit-based company that makes sewn products such as spare tire covers, sunroof storage bags, and leather wraps for steering wheels. Its owner, Hank Aguirre, is a former baseball player, who pitched for the Chicago Cubs and Detroit Tigers. Upon retiring from sports in 1975, Aguirre sold construction materials until 1979, the year he formed his own business. Using his home as collateral, he was able to secure a Small Business Administration (SBA) loan for $350,000. The company got off to a shaky start and nearly went under during the early 1980s. In 1981, sales were only $351,000 and the struggling firm showed a negative net worth of $290,000. At the time, the payroll had only eight employees; three were Aguirre's children.

After hearing about Ford's commitment to minority suppliers, Aguirre approached the company, and eventually Mexican Industries was selected as one of the minority businesses to participate in the program. "They [Ford advisers] are there to give assistance," Aguirre says, "they're committed, and they're caring. They're constantly observing us. Ford's engineering, finance, and purchasing people visit us on a quarterly basis for a status update. I'm impressed with their sincerity, and, in fact, it was on their advice that we got into the leather wrap business. They suggested it because it's labor intensive, so we must employ a lot of people, which means filling many jobs with minority workers. The work requires our people to hand stitch a leather wrap around the Lincoln Town Car and Bronco steering wheels, somewhat on the same order as a baseball is hand stitched. This year, we'll do about 130,000 pieces for Ford, and in five years, our production figures should reach 450,000 units according to Ford forecasts."

Aguirre's company has come a long way since the early 1980s. Today, its four plants employ 250 workers. Ninety percent are Hispanics, of whom the vast majority are female. Sales figures are now running at around $50 million, and the business is growing quickly. The company does business with each of the Big Three automakers, plus Nissan, Mazda, and several suppliers in the automobile industry such as Davidson Rubber and Prince Corporation. Ford is Mexican Industries' biggest customer. On the drawing board are plans to open additional plants in other Hispanic communities in Arizona, Texas, and California, employing still more minority workers.

Aguirre gives a lot of the credit to Ford for helping him instill statistical process control methods in his four plants. "It's scrap saving," he claims, "and we're really into continuous improvement. There's a we're-all-in-this-together attitude at Ford that really comes through." He proudly adds that "all four of our plants have qualified for Ford's Q1 rating."

The quality of work performed in Aguirre's plants demonstrates that a motivated work force can efficiently produce quality goods. "I take special pride in what we've accomplished with our Hispanic workers. And look what Ford's plant in Mexico has done," Aquirre exclaims. "They're making the Tracer there, and it has the highest ratings for world-class quality, comparable to the finest Japanese vehicles." William Scollard, vice-president of manufacturing at NAAO, agrees. "We built a brand new plant near Mexico City and hired all new people with no manufacturing experience, most of whom were recent high-school graduates. We gave them extensive training, including sending many to Japan and Spain, and today, they do outstanding work. When you hear somebody knocking the quality of work in Mexico, like anywhere else, the blame should be put on the Mexican management, not the Mexican people."

Earl J. ("EJ") Yancy, the founder and owner of Yancy Minerals Inc., based in Woodbridge, Connecticut, is another black entrepreneur who has benefited by Ford's commitment to minority-owned suppliers. Yancy, who formerly taught architecture at Harvard and Yale, left the academic world in 1977 at age thirty-four to market commodities such as coal, metals, petroleum products, and chemicals. He landed a contract with Ford in 1982 with a spot order to supply coal for a one-month period. At the time, Yancy Minerals was an $8 million company. "Ford was satisfied with the initial order, and soon we entered three-month and six-month contracts with them. As our relationship developed, we were able to sell other products to Ford including natural gas. Those early contracts for coal have since been expanded to a long-term seven-year contract, which is presently in its fourth year."

In 1989, to provide a countercyclical balance to its energy business, Yancy Minerals purchased Peak Electronics, a maker of printed circuit boards for the automotive and computer industries. Based on Yancy's track record as an energy supplier, Ford agreed to a multiyear contract to purchase a majority of the circuit boards produced by Peak Electronics.

"Ford takes a step beyond the rhetoric," Yancy explains. "They told us that if we want to be a better firm internally, they will not only help us do that but will show us how. A case in point of what this has meant to us is how they introduced statistical process control to our electronic business. In a nutshell, Ford has said to us, 'Here is what we think are the important variables in developing your business internally and here is what we are going to do to help you get to that point.' To implement SPC, we attended a series of seminars at Ford, and they visited our plant to give us pertinent advice to develop this process control. We receive some critical assessment on how well we are doing or not doing relative to their expectations for our firm."

Yancy explains that to Ford's credit, the company has made minority suppliers fully aware of the enormous potential available to those who take advantage of opportunity and perform well. "Sure, in the beginning, Ford may pay a premium by purchasing from a small business due to economy of scale in comparison to a primary established supplier. But what happens is that a hungry small entrepreneur becomes very aggressive and consequently highly competitive in an effort to perform well to keep the business. And by focusing on learning to do things the so-called Ford way, a small minority-owned business benefits by also becoming better than its competition in areas outside of Ford." Yancy is living proof of such success. Today, his company is a thriving $43 million business.

A program similar to the one for minority suppliers was started in the late 1960s to develop black-owned dealerships when Henry Ford issued a directive that established affirmative action as a high priority. It was about this time that the Mercury Division began to sponsor "The Ed Sullivan Show," one of the first television shows to feature black entertainers. As a consequence, Mercurys sold well among the black population, alerting the company to the potential of catering to this segment of the market. In 1967, Ford signed up its first black dealership in Chicago when Ernie Banks, the great Chicago Cubs slugger, formed a partnership with another black, Bob Nelson. While Ford was not the first, it is the nation's leader in its development of minority-owned dealerships.

Phil Benton, who served as vice-president of North American Sales Operations in the early 1980s, played a major role in setting up a five-year plan to establish 320 black-owned dealerships by the end of the decade. Benton reiterates, "It was a combination of doing the right thing and doing what was good for business."

Rusty Rustuccia, marketing services and training director, states, "We're committed to taking a leadership role in this area and to developing minority-owned dealerships. Why? In addition to the social issue, the black consumer market represents 11.5 percent of the population yet only accounts for 4.8 percent of the new car purchases. The black income level is lower than the general population so they tend to purchase more used cars. But it's improving. Five years ago, the blacks accounted for only 2 percent of the new car sales. The Hispanics represent about 8 percent of our population and by the year 2010 will be the largest minority group in America. There are also the Asian immigrants in this country who are becoming an important economic factor. All in all, today's minorities in the United States account for about 23 percent of the total population."

A separate dealer association exists for the black dealers. "Ninety-five percent are members," Rustuccia points out. "They formed their own association because they believe black dealerships have unique problems." Ford agrees that differences exist and to help strengthen these dealerships, the company provides additional training to address specific black issues. Presently, there are 263 black Ford and Lincoln-Mercury dealers in the United States, short of the 320 dealers that Benton wanted before the 1980s came to a close. But 57 percent of all black-owned auto dealerships in the United States are Ford dealerships.

Helen Love, Ford's manager of Urban Affairs, points out that the minority suppliers and dealers programs are just a portion of the company's involvement in social issues. The company supports causes ranging from the NAACP and the National Urban League to economic development groups such as Operation Push and the U.S. Hispanic Chamber of Commerce. Love explains, "Our employees are part of our community and don't divorce themselves from whom they are when they walk in our doors. We deal with them within these walls, knowing that they are part of the external community. There's an awareness at Ford that our sole responsibility isn't just to sell cars but to service the people in the general community. We're involved in these programs because we care about what happens in America. Personally, I believe that when minorities perceive us as a caring company, it also has a positive influence on their buying choices. It's reminiscent of the people out there who only buy American-made products. By the same token, there are some people who feel a bond with Ford because they feel we are hiring and doing business with minorities."

In order for Ford to compete against the Japanese automakers, it was vital for its supervisors and workers to be kept abreast in the fast-changing world of technology. Presently, Ford's North American Human Resources Development Center in Dearborn offers technical and apprentice training to all company plants in the United States. The center offers a total of 88 programs ranging from an overview course on the principles of robotics to a course on listening. Other courses cover subjects such as employee involvement, managing conflict, and self-assessment. More than 26,000 employees visited the center during 1988, including hourly workers, engineers, and clerical and secretarial people. Plants send employees to the center on company time, and all travel and lodging expenses incurred are paid by the company. "People are very appreciative," explains Hugh Merchant, a director at the center. "It demonstrates that the company cares about them and is willing to invest in their future."

Petersen has been credited for having radically reshaped Ford's previous highly autocratic and politicized corporate culture. Although he has received many accolades for his role in Ford's switch to participative management, he insists, "The credit here goes to my team, not me. There are no stars today at Ford." He stresses, "There have been times in our history when a star system has been very damaging, so, in choosing between the two, teamwork is far and away the better approach, and anything that interferes with teamwork is destructive."

Petersen uses a sports analogy to make his point: "This does not imply there is no room for individual excellence and leadership. Take, for instance, a basketball player like the Pistons' Isiah Thomas or the Lakers' Magic Johnson. The other players recognize them as team leaders. But because Thomas and Johnson are able to blend in with the team rather than being dominant forces, their effectiveness is maximized."

In early 1983, when Ford was working on its MVGP, a task force was established to observe some of America's most-respected corporations. Its purpose was to study the cultures and management styles of such companies as Hewlett-Packard, IBM, Dana, and 3M and to learn how these organizations were able to make significant changes. Thomas Page, former executive vice-president of Diversified Products Operations (DPO), appointed Nancy Badore, a DPO employee involvement and training manager, to head the task force.

"We conducted interviews with CEOs, presidents, middle managers, and plant workers," Badore explains, "to discover what these companies did that was so special. We also met with some of the nation's top thinkers and writers such as Tom Peters, Peter Drucker, and the late Bill Abernathy. After being on the road for four months collecting an enormous amount of information, we decided to tell our findings in a series of talks instead of a report.

"There were too many reports already, and they frequently have a tendency to get filed or lost altogether," Badore continues. "So we said that anyone interested in what we had to say, would have to attend a forum to hear us out. Managers throughout the organization were invited to attend."

The forums served as an ideal way in which the company could disperse information about values and ideals, objectives and long-term goals. With the reception that the forums received from managers who attended, Petersen assigned Page and Badore to head another task force to study the merits of establishing a permanent school or center for Ford. To accomplish this, Page and Badore visited companies that had succeeded in this area. This time, they traveled across the country and in Europe for nearly a year, observing and collecting information. On April 1, 1985, Ford's Executive Development Center was chartered.

The center received an annual budget of $5 million and today is headquartered in the Renaissance Center in downtown Detroit in the same tower that houses other Ford operations. At present, 2,000 managers go through a six-day course, 50 at a time, every two years. While they are permitted to choose their dates, attendance is mandatory. "Until they retire," Badore states, "they'll come here every other year, and this practically guarantees that they *will* have a concern about what's going on in the CEO's office." Badore explains one of the main purposes of the center is to provide a broad perspective of the total picture.

During their one-week stay at the center, the executives discuss many problems that face the company and envision the Ford of the future. Other activities include trips to the design center and observing focus groups of car owners. A major portion of the week is devoted to executive participation, which is accomplished through a series of small workshops that are broken down into problem-solving teams. In what Badore refers to as a "maxmix" technique, seven managers from a cross-section of areas throughout the organization interface with one another and, in the process, hear different points of view. During these workshop sessions, they wrestle over a business plan as a whole. "While they might not have much in common at the beginning of the week," she explains, "after a day or two, they see things in a different light. For instance, a design manager might come in here having no concept about the financial guy's standpoint or how the plant manager in Tulsa looks at things. But after talking matters over with other managers, he has a different attitude. By the middle of the week, the grumbling has disappeared, and everyone is thinking, 'Well, that senior guy wasn't so dumb after all.' "

Because Ford managers from around the world attend the Executive Development Center, each seven-person team is likely to have two to four people present from abroad. This emphasizes the company's international activities; a strong effort is made to have its executives think in terms of a worldwide market. With the diversity of managers in attendance, it is unlikely that anyone will know more than two or three of the other 49 attendees at the one-week session. Badore thinks this is a plus.

Today the new Ford Motor Company is a people company, and evidently the word is out, because when company recruiters visit campuses, college students are lining up to seek jobs. And Petersen says, "When I visit communities across the country, people come to me and say, 'How can I get a job at Ford?' In 1980, that's something nobody was saying. Today, young people want to be part of our team." Just like when the Whiz Kids were around, Ford has become *the place* to work in corporate America.

"There's a different attitude about working at Ford today," explains

Doug McClure, former executive director of marketing. "During the 1970s, our products weren't any good and it had an adverse effect on employees' self-esteem. Today, we can wear our Ford oval with pride. You know, it's like being a member of the New York Yankees. When a player puts his pinstripes on, he feels like he's a winner."

In the late 1970s and early 1980s, many managers left Ford, but by the end of the 1980s, the exodus had stopped, and in the case of Jerry Sloan, it did an about-face. Sloan, who today heads Ford's public affairs staff, left the company in 1983 to become vice-president of public relations at American Motors. At American Motors, he ran the whole show and reported directly to the chairman of the board. In early 1987, Chrysler announced that it would acquire American Motors, and Sloan figured he was destined for Chrysler. Ford, however, called Sloan in late July and offered him an opportunity to become head of public affairs. "It came down to whether I wanted to work for a *hot* personality, Lee Iacocca, or the *hot* company, Ford. I was told about Lee Iacocca's shouting sessions during which he'd rant and rave, puff his big cigar, pound the table, and humiliate executives in front of superiors and subordinates," Sloan says. "I thought life was too short to work in that atmosphere; I thought of Don Petersen and Red Poling heading Ford and decided to turn in my resignation to American Motors effective at the close of the business day of August 5, the date I anticipated the merger would be executed. As it turned out, American Motors stockholders met on the morning of August 5, and at noon that day, the merger took place. All of AMC's employees became Chrysler employees by lunchtime. This meant that I worked for American Motors in the morning, Chrysler in the afternoon until 5:00 P.M., when my resignation took effect, and the following morning beginning at 8:30 A.M. I was employed by Ford. This probably makes me the only person in the history of this industry who was ever employed by three automobile companies in the period of twenty-four hours!"

5

FORD AND THE UAW

A fter the $5, eight-hour workday announcement on January 5, 1914, Ford was *the* place to work in the United States. The next morning, more than 10,000 job seekers lined up in front of the Model T plant.

Unlike other workers, Ford's prided themselves in working for a family business, not an impersonal corporation. It was clearly a great source of status to be associated with Henry Ford, an individual with whom the average man could identify.

Sadly, as time passed by, the man with the common touch lost touch with the common man. By the 1930s, Henry Ford had become the nation's most outspoken opponent of organized labor. He detested any effort that he perceived as undermining his production of cars. To him it was clear that a union would only work against the best interest of *his* company. Even after the passage of the Wagner Labor Relations Act of 1935, which granted workers the right to organize, he bitterly opposed unionism, more so than any other powerful American employer.

It is no wonder, then, that from the start the Ford Motor Company and the United Automobile Workers (UAW) faced off as bitter adversaries.

What made the moving assembly line work was its simplicity. It was designed so that no thinking was required by the workers on the line. Only the managers were paid to think. It was strictly a top-down management style with all decision making coming from the top. In a period when the work force consisted mainly of immigrants who spoke little or no English, and those who did were almost certain to be illiterate, it proved to be an effective way to manufacture automobiles. Until

113

the mid–1920s, Ford was the world's most successful automobile company.

At an April 1936 meeting in South Bend, Indiana, autoworker representatives agreed to become affiliated with the Congress of Industrial Organizations (CIO), marking the beginning of the UAW. For good reason, the leaders of the newly formed union chose to first organize General Motors. GM was the biggest of the nation's automakers, and it was a publicly held company, while privately owned Ford was controlled by the strong-willed and belligerent Henry Ford. The game plan was to unionize GM, after which Chrysler was certain to follow. Only then would the UAW go after Ford. Following a series of peaceful sit-in strikes in January 1937, GM management sat down at the negotiating table with UAW leaders to discuss such issues as increased wages, seniority rights for layoffs and rehirings, plus a host of other problems. Within weeks, a contract was signed. In April, the UAW zeroed in on Chrysler. In only a matter of days, Walter Chrysler consented to essentially the same terms as GM.

In early May, the city of Dearborn granted a license to the UAW to hand out pamphlets at the main gates of the Rouge plant. The local government officials complied without resistance. They had little choice; to do otherwise would be to violate the Wagner Act. On May 26, union demonstrators began gathering at a pedestrian overpass that crossed over Miller Road, connecting a parking lot to Gate 4 of the Rouge manufacturing complex. Underneath was a long line of big black cars which, to many union sympathizers, appeared to be a funeral procession. In retrospect, that was an ironic observation. Each vehicle was packed with large men dressed in dark suits. They could have been dressed for a funeral, except for the baseball bats and clubs underneath their suit jackets. These men were employees of the Ford service department. Each was handpicked by Harry Bennett. One was a well-known local boxer; two were professional wrestlers; and there were several ex-football players. The rest were common thugs who worked for a variety of Detroit mobs.

An army of reporters and photographers showed up to witness the anticipated showdown between the union and "Bennett's boys." UAW leaders on the scene included Walter Reuther, Richard Frankensteen, Richard Merriweather, and Ralph Dunham. Reuther was familiar with the plant. He was a former worker at the Rouge and had been dismissed for previous attempts to organize its work force.

As the UAW members approached the middle of the overpass, Bennett's thugs moved in, trapping the union leaders on both sides. No match for the club-swinging troops, the demonstrators were mercilessly beaten. Frankensteen's coat was pulled over his head, and with his arms trapped in a makeshift straitjacket, he suffered blows with clubs as well as kicks to the head, kidneys, and groin. Reuther received a similiar workover, and in a semiconscious stupor was thrown down a flight of 36 iron steps. Union members witnessed the assault on their leaders and fled when the service men turned on them. Those too slow to escape, including several women, were also assaulted and beaten. One young girl was the victim of an onslaught of kicks to the stomach. A minister, who was clearly present as a spectator, had his back broken. Bennett seemed pleased by the brute force employed by his troops; in his eyes it was an obvious victory of might. In truth, it was his Waterloo. Hundreds of photographers recorded the ugly event, and the sympathy of the American public was with the union, the suppressed underdog.

"The Battle of the Overpass" made headlines across the nation. The public was appalled and embittered by the ruthless brutality documented by the scores of writers who witnessed the bloodshed. In spite of the many eyewitnesses, Henry Ford denied any wrongdoing. Edsel pleaded with his father to make amends with the union, only to be ordered to stay out of the way and let Bennett handle the problem. Bennett handled it by doing what he did best. He intimidated and browbeat the workers.

After the avalanche of publicity, Bennett's attempts to bribe local and federal judges to dismiss charges failed. The testimony presented on the Battle of the Overpass had been affirmed by too many impartial people. The National Labor Relations Board (NLRB) filed charges against Ford but, due to the work of a battery of attorneys, proceedings were delayed in court for several years. In the meantime, Bennett's service men were always available. In a 1940 UAW effort to sign up workers at the Rouge, Bennett's bullies were dispatched to rip UAW buttons from the shirts of workers. But no sooner did one button come off than another replaced it. In April 1941, Bennett fired eight workers who were active in the union. When the word spread throughout the plant, 1,500 workers staged a massive sit-down. Upon hearing the news, Reuther rushed to the plant but by the end of the day the entire Rouge was idle—50,000 workers in all. Even Bennett and his strongmen could not bully that many men.

Six years after the Battle of the Overpass the company was found guilty of a series of violations charged by the NLRB. These convictions were upheld by the Supreme Court. As a result, Ford was no longer eligible to receive government contracts. Of even more significance was the ruling that both the UAW, in conjunction with the CIO, and the American

Federation of Labor (AFL) were given the right to organize the company's work force. Bennett backed the AFL, in part, because it was headed by Homer Martin, a union leader with a dubious reputation. Bennett knew he could control Martin. Henry Ford was in favor of an NLRB election. Still living in the past, he was under the misconception that the workers remained loyal to him because it was he who gave them the $5 a day wage. Ford believed they would reject unionization. But when workers put it to a vote, the UAW received 70 percent of the votes cast, with 27.3 percent going to the AFL. A mere 2.7 percent of the workers voted against unionization. True to character, Bennett blamed Edsel for the defeat.

Henry Ford was devastated by the outcome. He had been certain that the workers would stand by him and referred to the defeat as "perhaps the biggest disappointment of my career."

On June 17, 1941, a contract was prepared. It contained the most generous concessions yet, providing higher wages than those paid by GM and Chrysler. It included a provision requiring the enforcers of the so-called service department to wear uniforms, caps or badges, thereby making them easily identifiable to all workers, which would undoubtedly curtail their spying activities. In addition, the company agreed to deduct all union dues from its workers' paychecks. Known as the "checkoff," this meant that Ford, in effect, agreed to collect money for the UAW. Even GM and Chrysler had not consented to be dues collectors for the union. In exchange, the UAW agreed to drop all claims against the company. To Ford's advantage, it would once again be eligible for government contracts, and with America getting ready to enter World War II, the company could ill afford to lose the huge defense contracts that were certain to be granted to the nation's automobile manufacturers.

When the agreement was first presented, Henry Ford refused to sign it. "Close the plant down if necessary," he ordered. However, that same evening, his wife gave him a convincing reason to consent. She was tired of the rioting and violence and threatened to leave her husband if he continued to resist the union. The following morning, he signed the agreement in full, giving the UAW everything it demanded. "Don't ever discredit the power of a woman," Ford confided to Charlie Sorensen.

By no means was the signing of the contract a guarantee of harmony between Ford and the UAW. For years they had been dedicated enemies. Some of the same bullying measures used by Bennett's thugs to intimidate prounion workers were now exercised by union thugs. Scare tactics were employed against the workers, who, for the most part, were terrified to speak out against the union. Ford managers were also threatened and sometimes beaten. There were instances when hoodlums belonging to local Mafia gangs were hired by Ford to beat up union members one week and the following week were hired by the union to beat up Ford managers!

While the 1941 contract opened the doors for the UAW, Ford did not put out a welcome mat. Instead it created a working environment with clearly defined sides pitting management and labor firmly against one another, the "us-versus-them" syndrome that has long been the norm throughout the history of unions in the United States. Each side viewed the other as the enemy. From the union's point of view, management sought to exploit the worker by paying the lowest possible wages for the most possible work. Conversely, management believed that the union wanted its workers to receive maximum wages for the least amount of work.

Until the late 1970s, in spite of the constant conflict between management and unions, the domestic automakers enjoyed a sellers' market with practically no interference by foreign competition. Any inefficiences caused by a lack of harmony between management and labor were shared by Ford, General Motors, and Chrysler alike. What was a competitive disadvantage to one was equally so to its crosstown competitors. Labor negotiations at the Big Three took place every three years— simultaneously. As the contract expiration date neared at all three, the UAW chose one as the target company at which the pattern agreement was to be reached. Then the UAW would move to the next company and, finally, the third to get the same contract. Most often, the companies would pass on the cost of wage increases to customers by increasing prices on their cars and trucks.

In the early 1950s, import car sales had a U.S. market share of less than 2 percent, and there were virtually no Japanese automobiles sold in America. By 1976, the Japanese share of the U.S. market was 9 percent, and by 1980, it had soared to 21 percent (projections are estimated at 35 percent for the early 1990s). Ford's U.S. car market share was 17.3 percent in 1980, down 3.4 percentage points from the previous year. In an industry where fractions of a percentage point are fought for, these numbers made it apparent to both management and labor that they were now competing in a worldwide market. The Japanese automakers represented the most awesome competitors and a major threat to both Ford and the UAW. Their presence made it obvious to both sides that productivity and quality had to improve.

In addition, the quality of a company's product must keep pace with its competition. In the late 1970s and the early 1980s, while Ford's quality was comparable to those cars made by General Motors and Chrysler, it did not stack up favorably when measured against those of the Japanese automakers. *Made in America* became synonymous with inferior merchandise.

Ford's U.S. market share nosedived from 23.6 percent in 1978 to 17.3 in 1980, and to an annual low of 16.6 percent in 1981. While the company incurred fewer losses in 1982, its market share had not improved appreciably, and during one ten-day period in the final quarter of 1982, it had actually slipped to an embarrassing low of 14 percent. These figures stirred up talk at Chrysler headquarters of replacing Ford in the number two spot.

Ford's North American car and truck sales fell from 4.92 million units in 1978 to 2.42 million in 1980. In 1981, sales continued a downhill trend and, for the year, had dropped to 2.35 million. In 1982, the sales volume sank even lower—down to 2.26 million. The UAW had a vested interest in these totals. Fewer cars and trucks manufactured meant fewer workers needed. As a consequence, by 1982, Ford's U.S. employment figures had been reduced to 155,901, down from a high of 256,614 workers in 1978. Ford's bad times were the union's bad times.

By the late 1970s enough literature had been written about the Japanese style of management and Japanese worker's productivity to line rows of shelves at business-school libraries. Similar stories appeared in newspapers and magazines across the country, and seminars on the subject were conducted nationwide. It was made quite clear to the majority of Americans that the Japanese workers were significantly outproducing their U.S. counterparts. What had worked for so many years in the American automobile industry no longer was working in the 1980s. Problems in U.S. industry were blamed, in part, on the lethargic attitude of the American worker. Some said a lack of pride in workmanship prevailed. But the undercurrent of discontent had more profound roots. The nation had paid a heavy toll for the assassinations of John F. Kennedy and Martin Luther King, Jr., an unpopular, no-win war in Vietnam, and Watergate. Apathy and anger had carried over to the workplace. In the 1980s, Johnny Paycheck's song "Take This Job and Shove It" reflected the mood of millions of discontented workers across the country.

Along with the price of the market value of Ford stock, its credit rating plummeted. Ford was a battered company getting hit hard from all fronts.

But troubles of this nature were historically not the worry of those who worked on the assembly line; these nightmares were for high-ranking executives and members of the investment community. It was Poling's plant closings and the ensuing massive layoffs that plagued the company's hourly and salaried employees. There was no one who felt the slightest degree of job security because there was no way of knowing where the bottom was. Rumors circulated through those plants still open that if conditions continued to worsen, Ford might altogether cease manufacturing operations in North America. Supposedly the company would continue to market its products here, but it would make them abroad in those countries where the costs of labor and goods were less costly.

Douglas Fraser, who served as UAW president from 1977 until his retirement in 1983, explains: "The Big Three had a monopoly for years. Suddenly, we were confronted with intense competition by the Japanese. When the domestic car business tumbled in 1980, it became obvious that the Japanese were beating us, and we must work with the Big Three to build quality products that could be competitive in a worldwide marketplace. To paraphrase Benjamin Franklin, 'Either we hang together, or most assuredly, we will hang separately.' "

It was under these conditions that the employee involvement programs were able to take hold in the early 1980s. For years, the UAW had campaigned for a more active role in the manufacturing decisions. And it was nothing new for union leaders to ask that its members be treated with respect and dignity. Suggestion boxes had been placed in factories for decades and even Japanese-type quality circles were old hat. This time, however, the timing was right to seek involvement because it was strongly endorsed by top management, and most significantly, it was given a high priority. Not only did the company's highest-ranking executives support employee involvement, but so did the leaders of the UAW. It served as a common ground to bring Ford management and the union together to solve mutual problems. When Ford managers and UAW leaders sat down to communicate and work together to solve a mutual problem, they discovered that they had other common interests and objectives as well. It was a beginning.

In the late 1970s, Ford Motor Company was in constant turmoil. Internal strife on the 12th floor of the Glass House eventually lead to the firing of Lee Iacocca during the summer of 1978. Several Ford executives followed Iacocca to Chrysler. A steady flow of Ford managers accepted job offers with nonautomotive firms; these managers had read the handwriting on the wall and were certain that Ford would have great difficulty in the 1980s. Some high-ranking executives deserted with the belief that the company was destined to follow in the footsteps of Chrysler.

While it was hard times for the automobile industry, the headhunters were thriving and demanding large fees for locating replacements. One such vacant spot at Ford was the position of vice-president of labor relations. After a detailed search that began in late 1978, the field was narrowed to two candidates. When one accepted another offer, only Peter J. Pestillo, a forty-one-year-old vice-president of employee relations with the B. F. Goodrich Company remained. Pestillo, a soft-spoken man, had lived in the Midwest for several years but still retained his eastern accent. A native New Englander with a law degree from Georgetown, he did not appear to come from the same mold as his predecessors. In the past, Ford vice-presidents of labor relations were tough men who had worked their way up through the ranks of the automobile industry, compiling years of firsthand experience with the enemy. Even Harry Bennett had worked his way up the ladder.

Once Pestillo was clearly the choice for the labor relations opening, Caldwell placed a call to Goodrich's CEO, John Ong, who was also a long-time friend. After exchanging brief greetings, Caldwell said, "Let me tell you my reason for calling." After a slight pause, he continued, "John, I am going to ask you for your right arm . . ."

With that, Caldwell explained that he intended to make an offer to Pestillo but he did not want to do so without first discussing it with Ong. While Goodrich has since ceased to be in the tire business and today is strictly a chemical company, at the time it was one of Ford's tire suppliers. Of course, with Ford being a major customer, it was difficult for Ong to turn down Caldwell's request.

After a final meeting with Caldwell in January 1980, Pestillo accepted the offer, but not without some reservations. He confessed his lack of hands-on experience in big-time labor negotiations, and he "didn't profess to have solutions to the problems that existed between the two. But it was obvious that things were not working then."

"Right from the start, I liked Peter. He is articulate and has a good sense of humor," Caldwell recalls. "Although he's an attorney, he doesn't take a legalistic approach. And unlike many labor relations executives, Peter is not a hardball-type guy but instead he is low-keyed and a real people person."

Pestillo also gets high praise from Fraser. "He's a fine communicator who can relate to anybody. He can speak the same language as the guys on the assembly line. Pestillo understands their problems and can relate to them. Unlike some of his predecessors, he isn't pompous."

While union leaders generally take a wait-and-see approach to a labor relations executive brought in from the outside, Pestillo's outgoing and sincere personality quickly won him acceptance. He credits the reception to the times. "In early slumps, the union never believed the company when it was in trouble. Instead, Ford managers were accused of crying wolf," he explains. "The shop people would say, 'We went through this back in 1958 and we will do it again.' But this time was different. There were simply too many bad quarters of red ink back to back. Everyone knew things had to change, so they were willing to work with us."

Pestillo quickly took the initiative to establish open channels of communication. Not one to stand on ceremony, he broke tradition; rather than having only scheduled formal meetings with union leaders, frequent, informal sessions became routine. His philosophy was that "it is better to resolve differences and problems as they occur rather than to deal with them at a grievance or during negotiations." Pestillo also made it a point to visit with union leaders on their turf, not just at Ford headquarters. UAW vice-president, Stephen Yokich, who headed the Ford department for several years, explains, "In the old days we went to Ford's offices, or during some difficult negotiations we'd agree to meet on neutral grounds. They never came to us. And the managers of a local plant wouldn't consider stepping foot inside a union hall. It was enemy territory. Both sides are acting more like adults today. If I want to see Pestillo, and if he's going to be on this side of town, he doesn't hesitate to stop in to see me, and vice versa."

It was the desire by both sides to seek solutions to common problems that led to an unusual mission to Japan. In 1981, Pestillo and Donald Ephlin, a retired UAW vice-president who then headed the Ford department, arranged to send members of the negotiating teams to Japanese Mazda plants for a two-week period so that they could observe Japanese efficiency firsthand. Ford agreed to pick up the tab for both sides. It marked the first international travel venture undertaken by management and labor. In the past, Ford had rarely sent union leaders anywhere to receive education or training.

During a meeting with a Mazda vice-president, who was introduced as having a similar position to Pestillo, the Ford executive inquired; "How much time do you devote to labor relations and how much to personnel?"

The Japanese manager gave a quizzical look as the question was being translated. He responded, "I do not separate the two functions."

"I learned a valuable lesson from his reply," Pestillo explains. "He meant that he didn't do union relations, but instead, did 'human relations.' *He did people.* In other words, he didn't segregate problems by saying, 'This is union and this belongs in personnel.' From my experience, union relations is impersonal and legalistic. What's more, it is overly concerned with precedence. 'If this is done, then that is the way it will have to be done tomorrow and thereafter.' So it is not what is right for this particular situation but what are the implications for future problems of the same nature? However, when something is kept on an individual level, it can be fixed without being blown out of proportion and getting you bogged down. With this approach, we can avoid the bargaining process and are lighter on our feet in our response to workers' legitimate needs."

The trip also served as a good opportunity for union leaders and Ford managers to become better acquainted. Included were several union members who represented the next generation of leadership, and it was a particularly good occasion for them to spend some time with Ford managers. "It was a small enough group so all of us had dinner together each night," Ephlin mentions. "By being together for two weeks, we really got to know each other. It was the casual, informal conversations that let you discover how your concerns are the same as the other guy's. You share the same interests about such things as baseball, or that your kids are both in Little League, and, of course, you chat about the problems that the company has. By communicating on an informal basis, you discover that our [the union's] objectives for the company are in the same ballpark as theirs."

It was better communications that led to the negotiation and eventual signing, in February 1982, of an unprecedented 2.5-year agreement between Ford and the UAW—a contract that was not due for renewal until eight months later. "We needed some relief in the cost of living adjustment (COLA) provision of our agreement with the UAW to keep our expenses from raising," Phil Caldwell explains. "Now Doug Fraser could have easily said, "Don't talk to me. I have a contract," and there would have been nothing we could do except wait until the contract expired in September. The UAW didn't have to open the negotiations at the beginning of the year, but they knew we needed some relief and they were willing to work with us. It was not an easy course for Fraser and Don Ephlin to take."

UAW leaders were aware of Ford's staggering back-to-back billion dollar annual losses and were agreeable to accepting some wage concessions and foregoing some cost of living increases. In exchange, they bargained for some voice in plant closing decisions and more job security. Most important to Ford was an agreement to defer the COLA that would have occurred during the upcoming nine-month period. The UAW consented, but with the stipulation that it be restored in December 1982. Paid personal holidays and bonus Sunday payments were also eliminated. (Workers were previously entitled to receive ten days of paid absence allowance.) In return, the UAW demanded a 24-month moratorium on any plant closings as the result of outsourcing the product manufactured in a Ford facility. The UAW also negotiated—and received—a guarantee that, in the event of a future layoff, eligible workers with 15 or more years of seniority would receive an income guarantee at the rate of 50 percent of their hourly wages. Under certain conditions, this income would increase up to a maximum of 60 percent and be paid by the company until workers reached age sixty-two or on retirement, whichever occurred earlier. This Guaranteed Income Stream (GIS) benefit stipulated that an eligible worker must be able and available for work and accept any reasonable employment arranged by the company or a state agency. Another clause in the agreement included a jointly governed program for training and retraining current and displaced workers.

A first-ever provision in the contract called for profit sharing with all U.S. Ford employees receiving a share of the company's earnings as sales of cars and trucks returned to the higher levels enjoyed in previous years. At the time, the rank-and-file worker was not particularly impressed that he or she would someday be sharing in future profits. Instead, having a job was a much higher priority. And with back-to-back losses running into the billions, it was anyone's guess when Ford would recover and generate even a meager profit.

As Don Ephlin explains, "The workers were not excited about profit sharing, but I knew sooner or later we were going to be rewarded. The company would eventually turn the corner, or else there wouldn't be any Ford Motor Company."

When Ford began operating in the black, its workers did indeed share in the profits. In 1983, every eligible Ford salaried and hourly employee in North America received a profit-sharing check of $400. The following year, they received profit-sharing checks for $2,000. These checks kept arriving on an annual basis as Ford continued to prosper. While the annual payment dropped to $1,200 in 1985, it rose again to $2,100 in 1986. In 1987, when $3,700 was paid, it set a world's record for profit sharing paid in a single year by a major corporation. During the first six years of this program, profit-sharing payments totaled $2.1 billion, with the average eligible Ford employee receiving a total of $12,200.

"We've paid out $2.1 billion in profit sharing since 1983," explains Peter Pestillo, "and I maintain it's the best money we have spent because it gives the people an interest in the business that they've never been invited to have before. They care about the company's success. When you talk to workers today, they talk about quality, and productivity and profits are no longer dirty words. They have become businesspeople, and that's what we want them to be."

While a large profit-sharing check is a bonanza during the boom years, in times of calamity and massive layoffs, job security is a worker's biggest concern. "There is really no way to understand the agony of being laid off unless you've gone through it," Fraser says. "To anyone who is ready, willing, and able to work but without a job, it is the ultimate frustration. We have studies on workers who lost their jobs during the 1980–1981 period that show alarming increases in alcoholism and wife and child abuse, and there are even cases of suicide. Workers with as many as 20 years seniority were laid off—which, until then, was unheard of. Imagine the macho guy who has never allowed his wife to work, and he's unable to fulfill his role as the breadwinner, so she's forced to get a job to support the family. It is a shattering experience and it destroys the poor guy."

"Union members have said to me, 'But you don't know what it's like, Doug.' But how well I do," Fraser recalls. "Back in 1938, I was working at the DeSoto plant and was laid off for 11 consecutive months, and at the time, I had a young wife and we were starting our family. It was a shattering experience, and I will never forget the worry and painful feeling of destitution I had. I can imagine what goes through the mind of a worker with a wife and six kids."

When the word gets out that a plant shutdown is in the works, it always causes near panic throughout the premises. During the spring of 1980, it was heard through the grapevine that the Cleveland Stamping Plant, located in Walton Hills, Ohio, could be shut down at any time. The reasons were threefold: First, the company was burdened with excess stamping capacity as a result of the automobile depression. Second, the company had announced that quality would be the criterion to determine what plants were shut, and the workers at Cleveland Stamping produced inferior products. Third, the plant had been an embarrassment to the company ever since it opened in 1954, having perhaps the poorest rela- tionship between management and the union in the entire Ford organization. The plant's inferior quality performance was a reflection of its pitiful labor relations.

The plant went into production in 1954, Local No. 420 received its UAW charter the following year, and from the beginning a cold war existed between workers and managers. Much of its original 3,500-person work force consisted of transplants who found their way to Cleveland from the coal mines of West Virginia and Pennsylvania—men with deep battle scars from the harsh treatment they had received as miners. They were consumed with contempt for anyone in a supervisory position. The company tackled them head-on by bringing in its toughest, hard-nosed managers, along with others who were not in the good graces of those in power and so were sent to "Siberia." It is no wonder, then, that the plant had an environment filled with the stresses and tensions found in a combat zone.

Ron Wallace, who was sent to Walton Hills as plant manager in 1977, explains, "It was not one of my favorite places. Nobody wanted to go there because the odds were that you just don't survive at the Cleveland Stamping Plant. I was told, 'If you survive there, then you will be successful in the Ford Motor Company, and if you don't, then what have we lost?' Managers and union members were constantly at each other's throats. Instead of stepping in and fixing a problem, everyone took the position that it was easier to fight and blame the other side for what was wrong."

"It didn't take much for us to strike," says Joe D'Amico, Local No. 420's president. "We'd strike at the drop of a hat. Once we walked out when somebody got fired. Another time, we went on strike because a foreman spit on a committeeman. Then there was the time we shut down Ford nationwide in protest for not having doors on the restrooms—but we got our doors! As soon as we'd get one strike settled, we'd start compiling data to come up with a reason for the next time."

Local No. 420 was, indeed, busy. In addition to the UAW national agreements with Ford, each local union negotiates an agreement to determine local work rules. Then too, there are some unwritten work rules that are not included in the contract but are still followed. Over the years, with the constant threat of a strike hanging over management's head, Local No. 420 leaders chiseled some of the most expensive contractual commitments Ford had ever granted workers.

Once such concession dictated that workers did not have to make up for machine downtime. Another permitted workers to quit for the day after reaching certain production goals, thereby making it possible to leave work perhaps two or three hours early on a daily basis. This meant that if standard production was set at 100 pieces an hour, once the production total reached 800 during an eight-hour shift, workers called it a day. The union made sure its members had it both ways: If a machine breakdown caused the line to shut down for two hours, the workers only had to produce 600 units on that work shift. Still yet another provision permitted workers to quit ten minutes early at the end of shift to clean up—a seemingly minor perk to each worker, but ten minutes per person on a daily basis throughout the year totals an enormous amount of payment for no value received to the company. And there was even a union mandate that required a "walking millwright" who walked along-side a forklift vehicle, under the pretense that it was necessary for safety reasons. Little by little, the union had burdened the plant with work conditions that handicapped its ability to compete in the market.

"The day I walked into the plant, there were 4,500 racks of reject material that could not be shipped," Wallace reflects. "With 25 to 30 doors per rack, that's more than 100,000 units that had to be either repaired or scrapped. Talk about having inefficiencies. We were riddled with them!

"I met with several groups of workers and supervisors and asked what they thought went wrong at the plant. The general consensus was, 'Management and the union could never get along here. So, management retaliates against the workers by taking out its frustrations on them and vice versa. That's just the way it's been here for 30 years.' "

Poling had already begun his drive to cut expenditures by closing plants across the country, and if ever there was a likely candidate to be shut, it was the Cleveland Stamping Plant. So in the spring of 1980 when negotiations began with Local No. 420, it was obvious that the union did not have much bargaining power. After all, it could not rely on its big gun—a threat of a strike—as it routinely did in the past. As the local's president, Joe D'Amico opted to discuss strategy with Ken Bannon. Bannon had served as the UAW director to Ford since 1947. He had started his career at the age of twenty-two on the assembly line of the Rouge plant in 1936 and was an in-plant organizer years before the signing of the first UAW-Ford agreement in 1941. Bannon was scheduled to retire in mid–1980 from a job he held for 33 years, a UAW record that will certainly endure.

Following a lengthy discussion, D'Amico joined Bannon in Dearborn to meet with Poling, Marvin Runyon (a top manufacturing executive who later retired from Ford to become the head of the Nissan plant in Smyrna,

Tennessee), and a handful of other top brass. Upon being told that the plant was scheduled to be closed, Bannon made a request: "I would like to have one more shot at it. If I fail, then you can close it. Give me this opportunity as my last assignment before I hang up my shoes." It was agreed that Ford would give the plant another chance if the union would give up some of its burdensome work rules, and then only if there were substantial improvements in quality.

Following the meeting, Bannon pulled D'Amico aside and said, "Will your members go along with this?"

"It's gonna be a tough selling job," he replied.

At a daylong meeting in Cleveland with the local union's bargaining committee, D'Amico explained the conditions set forth at the Glass House in Dearborn. They were appalled that the company was asking them to make work rules concessions. Not one person favored going along with D'Amico and Bannon.

"I don't think it's right for us to decide the future for the membership of this union," D'Amico said. "I'll send an announcement out, and we'll put it to a vote."

The following week, the full membership of 2,000 workers showed up at the nearby Northfield Race Track, the only facility available for renting in the area to house such a large turnout. D'Amico explained the company's take-it-or-leave-it offer to a hostile crowd. As he spoke, many of the members booed and hissed.

"Strike, strike," some chanted. Others sang, "Let's go out in a blaze of glor-r-r-y!" the lines from Kenny Rogers's popular song.

"We've been threatened with plant closings before," he assured them, "but we could always tell when they were bluffing. Hell, all of their stamping plants had more work than they could handle. It didn't take much brains to know there was no way they were going to shut us down. They always took us for being stupid and didn't give us credit to know what was right in front of us.

"It's different this time," he continued. "You've all seen the trucks hauling dies out of the place every day. They're moving our jobs to other plants. And as it is, we're down to 2,000 from a previous high of 3,500 jobs. Ford stamping plants are working at half-capacity, so the handwriting is on the wall for any of you who want to read it. Things are not the same any more. We're in a different world."

"Do you want to know what has me so convinced?" he confided to his audience. "Even more than all that's happened with the economy and the Arab oil embargo? This is the first time that they put it in writing. They sent us a letter, signed by a company official, saying that if we don't buy their package, we'll be phased out of existence by the end of the year. In the past, Ford has made all kinds of verbal threats at the bargaining table, but they have never put anything in writing that they weren't willing to back up. They couldn't because they'd lose credibility.

"They aren't bluffing this time," D'Amico continued. "They've already shut down other plants, and I think we have no choice but to go along with them. Right now, our average age bracket in this plant is fifty years old. Let me ask you something: Where you gonna find a job if this plant goes down? You will be out of work. Period.

"Nobody likes give backs. I don't like them dictating a contract to us that you elected me to negotiate," D'Amico said, lowering his voice. "I see two options. If we want jobs, we have to vote for it. If you don't, then vote against it. If it doesn't pass, make no mistake, they'll close us down by the end of the year. I'm voting to accept it. I don't like it, but that's the way it is."

After a long pause, D'Amico said, "Now, I don't want you to vote today. First, go home and talk to your families, and we will vote on it three nights from now."

The other members of the union's executive board did not endorse D'Amico's recommendation. They feared it would end their union political careers. After all, it was a hostile crowd, and they were the same people who turned down the last two master agreements, and both with substantial gains for the workers. The air was filled with confetti from torn contracts and smoke from others that were burned. D'Amico was discouraged, but he persisted.

"Had it been put to a vote that night, they would have felt I rammed it down their throats," D'Amico said later, "and they would have voted against it. I wanted them to sleep on it and make a rational decision."

Three days later, 87 percent of the union voted to go along with his recommendation.

That same day, D'Amico approached Ron Wallace to discuss how the new agreement would be phased in. The plant manager welcomed it as a breakthrough that would put an end, once and for all, to the self-destructive labor relations that had existed. Working closely with D'Amico, Wallace arranged to conduct mass meetings in the parking lot during each shift, with executives from Dearborn attending to explain the new contract. Together, Ford managers and union leaders fielded questions. It was agreed that the revised work rules would be effective following the plant's July 4, 1980 vacation shutdown.

In the meantime, even though the union had accepted the agreement, workers continued to be laid off in Walton Hills. "It was scary," D'Amico explains. "We were down to 1,500 people, and the possibility still existed that the plant would be shut down." This frightened workers and supervisors alike and provided the incentive for the two sides to meet regularly to resolve differences. "We tried for win-win solutions," D'Amico says, "and with both sides cooperating, we started to see some daylight."

However, many union and company people were used to the old ways of winning their positions by being tough and unbending. "They didn't trust us and we didn't trust them," D'Amico states. "I mean, how do you convince a union officer that he can be elected again by working cooperatively with management? Don't forget he's the same guy who was elected for his hard-nosed stance in the past. And how do you tell a man who started on hourly and worked his way up to a supervisory position by kicking ass and taking names that that's not the way to do it any more? There's a natural tendency for people to resist change, so it took a while for both sides to bend and work together."

Each week, D'Amico and Wallace toured the plant together, an unprecedented move in the automobile industry. In the past, the only time plant management and union leaders were seen publicly together was when they disagreed—and engaged in a shouting match. On a tour, D'Amico was often accompanied by his bargaining committeemen while supervisors followed Wallace. As they stopped to chat with workers and foremen, each would ask questions about problems. When an on-the-spot solution was possible, the difficulty was fixed immediately. Those problems that could not be quickly resolved were delegated to someone in a position to remedy them.

"To eliminate from the plant years of the adversarial feelings," Wallace explains, "my attitude was that Joe and I were partners. As a partnership, he had his job to do as the union president, and I had mine as the plant manager. We met on a daily basis to ensure open communications, and there wasn't anything I'd keep from him. Sometimes, in fact, he'd know what was going on before some of my supervisors did. But it wasn't a bed of roses. There were some union old-timers who berated us for being so close and claimed we were destroying the collective bargaining system. That was absurd. Both of us believed in collective bargaining, and the truth is that it was strengthened because we were able to get rid of the petty stuff that the union and management had always quibbled over on a daily basis."

There were still those who resisted the notion that the union and management could work together. In fact, during the 1981 Local No. 420 election, a former union president campaigned on a platform that denounced D'Amico, accusing him of being in bed with management and destroying American unionism. D'Amico won with a 95 percent plurality and eventually served as president for an unprecedented four terms of two years each.

What helped implement a nonadversarial attitude at Walton Hills was the provision concerning EI that first appeared in the 1979 UAW-Ford master agreement. Working together, Wallace and D'Amico selected two EI coordinators, a salaried employee and an hourly worker. These individuals were responsible for instructing others on how to form EI groups. It was essential for EI to be a joint venture of labor and management; if one side didn't go along with it, it would fail.

"At first, both sides were suspicious," says Julius Sabo, the plant's industrial relations manager. "Managers thought EI would diminish their authority and union people feared it was their road to oblivion, a way to manipulate workers and break up the union. It took a while for people to feel comfortable with it, but Wallace and D'Amico were so positive that their enthusiasm was contagious. Then, as we had some successes, it began to pick up momentum. We were soon leading the country in EI participation."

"A foreman used to say, 'Go do this,' and no matter if it was right or wrong, you did what he told you to do," D'Amico explains. "There was no use even trying to discuss anything with him because of his 'I'm the boss, and that's it' attitude. But even those hard-ass foremen started to move with the flow once EI was in progress. What the hell, why shouldn't they? It makes their job a helluva lot easier. And when you get a worker involved and he cares, he feels a sense of ownership. That's bound to improve efficiency and quality."

Once it was certain that the plant was running efficiently and making vastly improved products, Wallace announced to Ford's top echelon in Dearborn that the Cleveland Stamping Plant wanted more production work. More work would mean more job security for everyone at the plant, and to Local No. 420, it would also mean increased membership. He let it be known that the plant would take any job, no matter how difficult, and with the support of the entire work force, Cleveland Stamping could do it at a profit. One particular job for which Wallace lobbied—and which he got—was the production of sheet metal components that were being outsourced to the soon-to-be-closed Budd Company plant in Gary, Indiana. In addition, more work was assigned to the plant as other Ford stamping plants were closed. With more orders, more people were hired, bringing the present work force to approximately 2,500 workers.

In 1982, Wallace and D'Amico met with the mayor of Walton Hills, and the three men addressed a letter to Caldwell requesting that he officially change the plant's name to Walton Hills Stamping Plant. In the letter, they stated that it was time to bury the 25-year stigma attached to the Cleveland Stamping Plant image. The request was granted.

About the same time that Walton Hills was faced with a shut down, Ford's transmission plant in Livonia, Michigan, was also in danger of going out of business. For years, it produced automatic overdrive (AOD) transmissions, a fuel-efficient transmission in its day but made only for rear-wheel drive. The industry was downsizing, so in the future, the demand would be shifting to small cars with front-wheel drive. The rumor mill had it that, at best, the plant had a life expectancy of five years.

After many sleepless nights, plant manager Marvin Craig got together with Robert "Red" Little, the head of the UAW's Local No. 182. They mutually decided the only hope of saving the plant was a team effort that would result in substantially improved quality while sharply reducing costs. Craig decided to deliver a state of the plant speech to all employees.

Craig made the speech to groups of several hundred workers at a time. He explained that there was a way out. The plant could produce a front-wheel overdrive transmission (AXOD) for medium-size cars (the 1985 Taurus and Sable). It wouldn't be easy because it meant competing with Mazda, in which Ford owns a 25 percent interest. "Mazda is a formidable opponent," Craig stressed to the workers. "This plant can have a future, but I can't make it without you. Damn it, we've got to quit arguing about whose job it is to get the job done. Those boys across the pond are beating you in quality and they're beating you in cost. Either we work together as a team and do the job or it will be a case of the last guy out, please turn out the lights."

He received a standing ovation for his speech.

Quality was given precedence over meeting production schedules. Craig proved he meant business when he received a call informing him that there were some flawed pistons on the final assembly line and he gave the order: "Shut the line down." The dead silence of the nonmoving assembly line got everyone's attention. The line had broken down in the past, but it had never been shut down because of a bad part. Actions such as this that made believers out of the Livonia workers.

When employee involvement was introduced, 80 committees were consisting of more than 700 members. Each week, each committee chairman met with the plant's management to cite everything that went wrong in its department, and the following week management reported back on what had been corrected. The Livonia workers were delighted to see that management was responsive, and it was reflected in the quality of their work. In the past, 23 out of every 100 completed transmissions were in need of repair; soon this number dropped to 11. In 1979 absenteeism was 6 percent; it dropped to 3.8 percent in 1981. As a result of EI, suggestions poured in and hundreds of small cost-saving changes were made. Perhaps most significant, as a team, the workers and managers were able to implement methods to upgrade some of the existing machinery and thereby eliminate the need for a complete retooling of equipment for the switch to a new product. This alone saved more than $1 billion.

Coupled with the quality improvements, Poling was convinced that the plant was capable of manufacturing a quality product. But still, it would have to make a competitive bid for the AXOD to get the work. The bid was submitted, and for weeks, everyone waited.

On November 12, 1981, the office of John Betti, then vice-president of Ford's Powertrain and Chassis Operations, called Craig to say that Betti would hold a press conference at the plant later in the morning.

In front of television cameras and scores of reporters from the press, Betti announced that the plant had underbid Mazda. Within minutes, the news had traveled throughout the plant and the place was in an uproar. "We beat the Japanese," Craig declared on a loudspeaker. "When we work as a team, there's nobody we can't beat!"

"What happened at Livonia was a real shot in the arm for all of our plants," Betti declares. "It demonstrated that Ford could compete with the Japanese, and we *can* win."

One provision in the 1982 contract called for a jointly governed program for training and retraining current and displaced workers. At the time it seemed insignificant, one of those clauses members skip over during a first reading of a proposed labor contract.

When Ford agreed to establish the UAW-Ford National Education, Development, and Training Program, the rank-and-file worker viewed it as only an afterthought, like the profit-sharing plan. And why not? It didn't put any money into their pockets, nor did it provide job security.

"The 1982 agreement did not contain any details about the program, and nothing was mentioned about the bricks and mortar for the National Center building," explains Ken Dickinson, Ford's coexecutive director of the program. "There was only a letter of understanding between the union and management. The letter stated the following objectives should be sought. (1) To educate, train, and retrain Ford's active work force; (2) to retrain and assist in the reemployment of laid-off workers, who, in turn, could find jobs with other companies; (3) to establish funds for the program as well as other UAW-Ford joint programs; and (4) to engage in research to improve the industrial environment and quality of life in general of Ford employees."

The company agreed to fund the program, nicknamed the "nickel plan," by contributing five cents for every hour worked by union members. It set up an autonomous entity operating as a nonprofit corporation and reporting to a governing body consisting of eight members—four UAW persons headed by Don Ephlin, and four Ford persons currently headed by Peter Pestillo. While the program began operations immediately following the signing of the agreement, it was not until May 1983 that a ground-breaking ceremony dedicated its official location. A modern 10,000-square-foot building was constructed on the grounds of the Henry Ford Community College campus in Dearborn. It was not long thereafter that its success demanded more space, and a 50,000-square-foot addition was completed in 1988, including a 400-seat auditorium, a 50-seat lecture room, conference rooms, 38 offices, a library, and a teleconference room that broadcasts live and prerecorded television to every Ford facility in North America.

In 1979, Ford employed more than 200,000 UAW workers; by the end of 1982, the number in the United States had dropped to slightly less than 100,000. So in the beginning, the training center's top priority was to relocate laid-off workers. "We focused on helping these workers during a very traumatic transition in their lives," Dan Vergari, former UAW coexecutive director, observes. "The program provided counseling, educational and training opportunities, and the funds to obtain these services from outside sources. In addition, we ran a series of workshops conducted by members of our staff as well as noncompany professional advisers. Up to $5,000 was made available to each worker to cover costs for tuitions and other related expenses, to aid in his or her development for relocation. This amount was later increased to $5,500."

"When the company announced it was going to close the San Jose plant," Vergari adds, "there was considerable concern that the quality of its production would drastically drop following the time of the announcement to the actual closing. There was even some concern that workers would sabotage the plant. But because the company openly communicated about why the shutdown was necessary and simultaneously demonstrated a genuine concern for the workers' welfare, there were no repercussions. And what was done at San Jose established a pattern for early intervention at every plant scheduled to be closed."

"From 1982 to 1984, the program's primary concentration was to assist the 100,000 plus workers who were laid off," Dickinson explains. "Since then, Ford's work force has been increasing, so today, the program focuses on developing and assisting our active workers. It offers education and training on such diverse subjects as health and safety in the workplace, the employee involvement process, product quality, and assistance for workers with serious personal problems such as alcohol or other drug dependency and other emotional illness. Workshop sessions range from such topics as retirement planning to money management. Educational programs cover the gamut from overcoming illiteracy to providing assistance for workers pursuing college degrees. Our work force in the year 2000 will consist of about 80 to 85 percent of its present workers, and without continual improvement of their skills, they could become obsolete in the job market. Our estimates are that the average worker requires some retraining every five years or so."

While the training center is headquartered in Dearborn and presently employs 56 people, training is available in 90 locations at various plants and parts distribution centers in 20 states. A joint committee consisting of both Ford and UAW people work on a volunteer basis and manage the program at these Ford facilities. Teams of full-time traveling representatives assist in developing programs at these learning centers operated by the plant volunteer groups. Ford and the UAW each have 20 people on loan working full-time at the Dearborn center, including coexecutive directors Ken Dickinson and Libby Jemasks.

After-hours education programs of this nature in U.S. industry as a whole average around 2 percent participation; 53 percent of the Ford workers participate in their program, with an estimated annual total of 20,000. The program demonstrates how Ford and the UAW work together as a team to the mutual benefit of each.

Yet, even with the obvious gains that have resulted through improved labor relations since the early 1980s, there are UAW members who criticize the "jointness" efforts as "a new way for management to speed up the line." As one dissident says, "Management is trying to place everything on the team. When there is a problem, now it is *our* problem, instead of their problem." Some union dissidents insist, "To be a cooperative adversary is a contradiction in terms. As union leaders we can't be concerned about the corporation's agenda."

UAW president Owen Bieber stated a different point of view, however, in his keynote address at the 1989 triennial convention: "Our participation in joint programs is motivated by only one consideration, and that is the universal desire of workers to have a more satisfying and secure situation at work. That's not and never has been a response to the corporate agenda or a reflection of a weak union."

Interestingly, Don Petersen indirectly assisted the UAW in its 1982 negotiations with General Motors. Ford had announced its plans to close its small plant in Northville, Michigan, when the local union asked Petersen to reconsider the shutdown. He agreed to reexamine the original decision, but without giving a commitment to reopen it. In the meantime, UAW president Doug Fraser called Don Ephlin and explained, "It would be very helpful in our negotiations with GM if Ford would reopen the Northville plant." By this Fraser meant that since GM had been closing plants too, it would be helpful for him to be able to cite that Ford was reopening some of theirs.

As a consequence, Ephlin called Petersen to solicit his help. "It will strengthen Fraser's position with GM."

"While I can't tell you what products we will make there, you have my word that we'll do it," Petersen replied.

The UAW quickly arranged for a press conference in Northville to announce that there would be no layoffs in the small community after all. Although the plant employed only 100 workers, it was the largest local employer, so the news was well received. Petersen's act was viewed as a token of good faith, and Ephlin called it, "a concrete sign to our members that the new relationship with Ford was paying dividends."

The last day of Phil Caldwell's 31-year career with the company illustrates the changes in labor relations that had evolved during the past decade. While Caldwell had caused some anger among UAW leaders during the previous year when his $7.3 million in pay, bonuses, and stock options for 1983 was announced, on this special day marking his retirement he received a hero's welcome at the Rawsonville plant, just west of Dearborn. As Caldwell and his entourage of Ford managers and union officials walked through the plant, workers cheered. In a speech, he urged them to continue along the path that had saved the plant and helped Ford make its turnaround. And he noted, "There are 380,000 employees in the Ford Motor Company here and all over the world. This is the last day that I shall be one of them." He then asked for one final request of them: "For what you have done here at Rawsonville, I can project you as a symbol and a part of what we have all done these past five long, hard years. I urge you to take the fine example you have set and spread it . . . get even better."

After Caldwell completed his prepared speech, David Curson, a member of the UAW's National Ford Department, made an unusual presentation. He handed a union card and sweater to Caldwell, declaring him to be the first CEO of a U.S. automobile corporation ever inducted into the UAW. He stated that it was a unanimous honorary gesture by the 3,100 members of UAW Local No. 898. Then, in reference to Caldwell's large salary, Curson made the tongue-in-cheek remark, "Of course, this means you will have to pay union dues on your salary." Curson's line received a big laugh, and after a pause, he added, "But relax, Phil, beginning tomorrow you will be a retired member of the union, and retirees don't have to pay dues."

Proudly putting on his new sweater, Caldwell's voice cracked as he spoke. "I wasn't really prepared for this. It wasn't in my notes. I don't even have a speech to throw away. I am proud, very proud." He added, "And when you say it was the unanimous vote of the membership, I am overwhelmed."

Others have that pride. Steve Yokich, UAW vice-president who formerly directed the Ford department before moving to head of the General Motors department in 1989 has strong union roots. Both of his parents as well as his two grandfathers were UAW members. A grandmother also worked for Ford. Yokich recalls when union members did not have much pride in working for a Big Three company, but he admits that times are different now. "The other day, I ran into my cousin who works at Ford and was wearing his blue Ford jacket. Kiddingly, I said to him, 'Jesus Christ, can't you afford a jacket?' I was joking, but there was a time when it wasn't a laughing matter. At one point it would have been considered treason."

But times have indeed changed and it is reflected in television commercials and in newspaper and magazine ads. One Ford advertising campaign is geared around how the joint efforts by the company and union have resulted in dramatic improvement in quality. Starring in these ads are Ford workers. The sincerity of the workers comes across on television. "The workers love to look for their buddies in these commercials and you should hear them brag about their 'movie stars,' " Ephlin says.

Today's relaxed labor relations has produced a far different environment than that which had existed for so many years. Now it is a relationship based on trust and cooperation—gone is the adversarial environment that bred suspicion, contempt, and confrontation. A sign of good faith was displayed by both sides in September 1987, when the negotiations on the three-year Ford-UAW contract continued past the expiration date. What occurred was something that would not have been remotely possible in the old days. For the first time since the signing of the original agreement in 1941, UAW members worked at Ford *without a contract.* There were no walkouts—business went on as usual. What's more, there was no name-calling or accusations that the other side was trying to win an advantage. It was a far cry from the days when paid thugs beat up union sympathizers and UAW workers would strike simply as a matter of course.

6

TEAM TAURUS

O n a hot, sticky September afternoon, Lew Veraldi was working in overdrive, in preparation for the introduction of the 1973 Mustang. He was too busy to return the several calls placed to him by Philip Caldwell, then executive vice-president of Ford's International Automotive Operations. About 6:00 P.M., Caldwell finally got through. "Get over here right away," Veraldi was told.

During the five-minute ride from NAAO to world headquarters, the chief engineer of Ford's Automotive Assembly Division wondered what was so urgent to warrant such a call. "Perhaps it is just Caldwell's nature," he surmised.

Veraldi entered Caldwell's office and received a cordial greeting. Then Caldwell got down to business: "I'll get right to the point. We want you to go to Europe."

"I'm right in the middle of launching the Mustang. I can't go anywhere."

"We want you to go," Caldwell firmly repeated.

Veraldi shut up and listened. He knew that when it was put this way on the 12th floor of the Glass House, you did what was asked.

The next day, arrangements were made to get passports for the entire family. None of them had ever had a passport, including Veraldi. It would be his first trip abroad, and he was not looking forward to it. "We have six children and none of us had the least interest in moving to England," Veraldi remembers. "It meant the kids would have to give up their activities—football, cheerleading, and scouting—and their friends. The company was uprooting us, and we didn't like it."

As Veraldi now recalls, "It turned out to be a fantastic experience. We traveled all over Europe during the 3.5 years we were there, and our children became quite international in their thinking." After a brief pause, he adds, "We're really appreciative about how good life is in America. Since we've been back in Detroit, we've had an American flag waving in front of our house 24 hours a day. That's a vow we made, and we've kept it."

Lew Veraldi was only fourteen when he enrolled in the Henry Ford Trade School in 1944. Upon graduating, he joined the army but returned to Ford after one year to become an engineering file clerk. While working at Ford, he also graduated from Lawrence Technological University with a degree in mechanical engineering. His career was mainly design engineering until 1971 when he began a three-year stint in the company's manufacturing group. This assignment provided him with an awareness that a design engineer rarely possesses. It provided him with keen insight into what happens during the manufacturing process *after* the engineering process. Traditionally, U.S. car manufacturers have separated the two functions. Not only were manufacturing people and engineering people prone to snub one another after hours, they also blamed each other for whatever went wrong. With such poor communication, things rarely went right.

During his three years in manufacturing, Veraldi learned to appreciate the dedication of the people who worked in this end of the business. Once, for instance, he witnessed a fire that gutted the Ford's paint department in Dearborn on a Friday night, posing a threat to Mustang production at a time when demand was far greater than supply. He observed in awe how the managers and workers labored around the clock for the entire weekend to guarantee production by Monday morning. The incident inspired Veraldi, and soon he was seen appearing on a regular basis on the plant floor. "I wanted to be out there rather than in my office," he explains. "I literally worked night and day in what was a two-shift plant. This allowed me to pick up manufacturing experience twice as fast."

Don Bastian, who was general manager of Ford's Automotive Assembly Division and Veraldi's mentor, once told him, "I hate engineers, but if I had to pick one engineer that would make a manufacturing guy, you're the guy." Veraldi considers this to be one of the highest compliments he ever received.

The word spread around the company that Veraldi understood both the engineering and the manufacturing viewpoint and process. He was familiar with how things got on paper and how and why they were designed. Veraldi also knew why those things often failed to work. "When I went from a pure engineering function to a manufacturing function, I became the receiver of information that I had worked over as an engineer," Veraldi explains. "I would go to the plants and they would say they couldn't put a part together because it wasn't designed right. Traditionally, when you engineer a car, you design it, release it, give the drawing to the manufacturer, and say, 'Here, go make it.' It was always a sequential process—everything was done in segments. And every time you handed off a design or released a drawing, the next area down the stream always had trouble with it. Complaints such as 'Why did you make it this way?' and 'I can't assemble or service it this way' were voiced with such regularity that they'd go in one ear and out the other. Ford was no different than most American companies: If you were a designer, you didn't worry about the engineer. If you were an engineer, you did your piece, handed it over the the manufacturer, and he did his piece and passed it on to the assembler. Finally, the marketing people got the product. It's what we used to call, 'tossing the baton over the wall. I'll design it and toss it over, you're in manufacturing, you figure out how to make it.' Nobody ever talked to anyone else. We tended to work in chimneys rather than together."

Veraldi's exposure to engineering and manufacturing, and his earning respect in both areas, appealed to Caldwell. In Europe, Ford was initiating the most costly clean sheet car (brand new model) program in the company's history, the Fiesta small car project. The Fiesta had a hefty budget of $870 million. Since the Fiesta's conception, the company's European engineering and manufacturing sectors had been bickering and, as a result, the project was foundering. It was into this scenario that Veraldi, the peacemaker, was summoned. Conditions had deteriorated to such a degree design engineers were not even allowed to enter the assembly plants.

Originally, the Fiesta was a small car designed in Detroit under the code name Bobcat. Veraldi's team did a complete redesigning job, adapting it to European driving conditions. Since the Fiesta was a clean sheet car, Veraldi had total design freedom. This was an opportunity for which he had been long waiting.

"In the old way," he explains, "the engineer wouldn't even talk to the manufacturing people until six months before it was time for them to make it. With the Fiesta, we got the manufacturing people to actually design things that the engineers would normally do. Why? Because, they had the best experience to be able to do it. In effect, we brought the downstream people upstream into the design process. They were told, 'Before we put this design on paper, how do you, the manufacturing and assembly people, want us to proceed to make your job easier?' While this doesn't sound like a radical change today, back then it was a first for Ford."

The entire process was executed simultaneously and, as Veraldi explains, "It decreased later changes that were normally made and, in the process, we were able to save a lot of money. The Fiesta was probably Ford's first car that not only made its business return, but bettered it. It came in under $800 million, and it even met its profit objective. We sold 5 million of those babies before we changed the model!"

Veraldi recalls one specific item in which he takes particular pride: "The Capri, which was built previously in Europe, had a third door similar to the Fiesta's back door. It used to leak like crazy under water tests. Naturally, we feared that the same thing would happen with the Fiesta, so, at one meeting I announced that I wasn't going to let our engineers design it. Instead, I told our manufacturing people, 'You guys are going to design it yourselves.' After they did, our engineers drew it up and released it. The thinking was pure and simple: Let the right people bring their expertise to the party. The results were amazing. Not a single one of the 5 million Fiestas we built ever leaked!"

As a result of his Fiesta success, upon his return from Europe in 1976 Veraldi was named vice-president of Advanced Vehicles Development (AVD). In this capacity, he assumed the task of creating advanced cars in hardware, not just on paper as was the norm. Veraldi's first challenge in this new capacity was the Taurus, and its sister car, the Sable.

Although the Taurus project officially began in 1979, it actually got its start in 1977. It was originally designed to be marketed in the mid–1980s, when the cost of fuel was projected to be $3 a gallon. Thus a small five-passenger car with a four-cylinder engine approximately 170 inches long made sense. Conceptually, Ford sought to supplant the larger model LTD and Mercury Marquis with the Taurus. Later, however, when fuel prices began to stabilize in the $1 to $1.25 gallon range, the Taurus grew into its present form—a six-passenger six-cylinder car, 188 inches long. Size was not the only alteration. During a series of strategic planning sessions, its original code name, Monica, was changed to Sigma, and finally to Taurus.

John Risk, who was the Taurus program manager, explains, "We hedged our bet by building it as a midsize car so we could go either way.

If the cost of fuel skyrocketed, the Taurus could become our large car and we'd make more small, fuel-economy Escorts. In all probability, had a fuel crisis occurred, the Taurus would have done quite well because it would have been the only full-size interior package on the market with decent fuel economy. Even after our tooling had progressed to the point where we were committed to building the car, we still had the option to go with the Taurus to replace our luxury cars. Then we could have offered it if the market dried up with the Lincoln Town Car and the other big cars. As a hedge car, depending on environmental factors and market conditions, it provided us with flexibility."

The style of the Taurus was closely tied into Ford's search for ways to improve fuel economy. Fuel efficiency was what prompted Jack Telnack, then NAAO's chief design executive, to make the design conform to the principles of aerodynamics, the way wind acts against bodies in motion. "It was a return to the notion that form follows function," Telnack explains.

In an industry that spends millions of dollars on technology to gain an extra tenth of a mile in fuel efficiency, an aerodynamic body would add as much as three or four extra miles to each gallon of gasoline. "By aero streamlining the car," Telnack asserts, "we were able to significantly reduce the drag force, or air resistance. For example, a 10 percent reduction of drag force results in a 2 or 3 percent improvement in gasoline mileage. Isn't that incredible? That's equivalent to reducing the weight of the car by 10 percent. And it's all free! It doesn't require major technical development programs. You have to shape the metal anyway, so why not shape it right?"

Telnack recalls one particular incident in the early spring of 1980 that changed his career and, most likely, the destiny of Ford. Shortly after Don Petersen was named president, he visited the design center to review some proposals with the youthful, silver-haired designer.

"Petersen is a real car person," Telnack says, "and the designs that I presented to him were extremely traditional, very boxy and very angular."

"Are you really proud of what you're doing?" Petersen asked. "Is this really the best you can do?"

Telnack hesitated, and Petersen continued, "Do you really like that sort of thing?"

"No," Telnack replied.

"Well, why are you doing it?"

"Because this is what was requested."

"Why don't you show me what you can do?" Petersen said. "Better yet, show me what you would *like* to do."

"Well, I have some sketches on the wall here," Telnack responded with caution.

The designs were soft and futuristic. Petersen studied them and asked, "Why aren't you doing that?"

"There are people in this company who don't want this kind of design."

"What would you like to have parked in your driveway?" Petersen questioned.

At first, Telnack didn't know how to react. He remembered those times in the past when senior management approached him and said, "Reach out, reach out." Then, when, the young designer would present a nontraditional design, they'd say, "You've got to be kidding." Over the years, Telnack learned to play the game conservatively. But he sensed that there was something different about his meeting with Petersen, that he really meant what he said. So, again, Telnack pointed to the wall at the sketches of the cars.

"Let's do it!" Petersen said.

Telnack requested a few weeks to touch up his sketches and get back to Petersen. Later that month he met with the president and a handful of other senior managers. Telnack made his presentation, and the reaction was mixed. "It was a fifty-fifty split on the design. Some loved it," Telnack recalls, "and some hated it. But with that kind of a reaction, we knew we had something that was really different."

In his presentation, Telnack emphasized that "it's okay if you feel somewhat uncomfortable with a new and daring design. In the car business, if you see an old friend, it's a sign that the design will lack longevity." Telnack understood well how, as a designer, he had to condition top management to the look of the future. He knew that what might compete with existing cars in the early 1980s would not necessarily be viable at the end of the decade or in the 1990s. He added, "We have to live in the future if we are to pick designs for the future." Upon being asked if there are any limits to the aero look, he replied, "Absolutely not. All birds are aerodynamically designed, and yet they are as different as the canary and the eagle. The same goes for cars."

Telnack also pointed out that aerodynamics emphasizes simplicity. "That's the message it sends to the buyer," he adds. "In these days, when microwave ovens look like the instrument panel of a space shuttle, it doesn't hurt to look simple."

The introduction of a new car with a radically different look always involves some risk. Would the public like the way the Taurus looked? Ford couldn't afford to gamble and lose. The stakes were far too high.

Those who opposed it recalled how the Edsel had an entirely different look, and how there were some who had believed it would have succeeded if not for the fact that it had been ahead of its time. Could it be that Telnack's aero styling was also ahead of its time?

"We were willing to explore any avenue that would improve fuel efficiency," Caldwell states, recalling the trying times. "While our engineers concentrated on reducing the weight of the car, our designers worked feverishly to cut down the wind drag. Sure, we were able to come up with good numbers confirming the savings in fuel, enabling us to measure how the aero styling contributed to function. But, what about the aesthetics? Well, we knew it was time for a change. Too many of our new models were what I call 'cold alligator-shoe cars.' But how would the aero look be accepted by the public? This is not something that can be determined by mathematical equations. It's a matter of taste. While I felt quite comfortable with the Taurus's looks, this business cannot be run on personal tastes. By walking through a styling studio, I was able to get a better feel for what we had because I could sense the enthusiasm of the troops. Then too, we got some positive feedback from our marketing people who were conducting focus groups to survey the public's reaction to it."

These focus groups made Ford executives keenly aware that the company had no real identity in the market. For years, the company had been playing follow the leader with General Motors, rarely taking the lead with styling innovations. The company's huge losses hammered home the fact that breaking into the more profitable middle and upper-middle market segment was imperative. "We weren't leaders in that segment, in fact, Ford was very much behind with the LTD," Veraldi observes. "There was total agreement that we wanted to be world-class leaders in that segment."

"We had made so many mistakes in the past by following this or that trend, this or that competitor," Petersen notes. "Finally we realized that we should not be driven by other people's choices but by our customers."

"In the old days," Telnack explains, "Ford was a top-down oriented organization. It was very frustrating for me to work in an autocratic-structured company, and this was not a fun place to be a designer. I can remember how management would say, 'This is what we want you to do,' and we would design it their way, even though it wasn't the quality of which we could be proud. Beginning with the new management regime under Caldwell, Petersen, and Poling, we were given the freedom to express ourselves because we had management's support. I can't emphasize enough how much it meant to have them behind us, knowing that they really wanted us to do something different. Without their support, we could have produced a *Mona Lisa* every hour on the hour, and it wouldn't have mattered."

Telnack recalls that William Clay Ford, who served as vice-chairman of the board and chaired the influential design committee, was also support-ive. As one of the largest company stockholders, William Clay Ford had, perhaps, the most to lose if the aero look was a bomb. "Having his backing meant a lot."

When Telnack graduated from high school in 1954, he bought a 1941 Mercury, worked on it, and then drove it out to Los Angeles where he attended Art Center College, majoring in transportation design. Upon finishing college in 1958, he came back to Dearborn to work for Ford. Telnack confesses that he wasn't particularly happy with his job. He was given designs to draw that he didn't respect and sometimes felt as though his creativity was being stifled. He was frustrated to the point that he moonlighted by designing powerboats, and for a while, considered leav-ing the car industry. His first assignment was to do preproduction detail work on the rear end of the 1960 Ford. "There was considerable detailing in the rear ends in those days," he reminisces. "We had grilles on the rear as well as on the front. Those cars were an expression of our culture at the time. America had won the war. We felt like we could take on the world—and we could! There was an energy in the country, and our designs expressed this."

Rarely does anyone get to Ford's upper echelons today without some overseas experience. In 1966, at age twenty-nine, Telnack was named chief engineer for Ford of Australia, a position that he held for three years. "I learned a lot about Europe when I was in Australia," he points out, noting the similarities in culture and in taste between the Europeans and Australians.

In 1969, Telnack returned to Dearborn and was appointed design executive for the Mustang and Pinto. In 1973, he was promoted to vice-president of design for Ford of Europe. This stint in Europe, where gasoline prices were quite high, was a crucial influence in his application of aerodynamics. One important reason why Telnack was chosen as the chief designer of the Taurus was because he had worked closely with Veraldi on the Fiesta in Europe. Today, he is vice-president of design, and in this capacity he runs Ford's design staff worldwide.

Now working in Ford's design center, Telnack has traveled around the world only to return home to his birthplace. Coincidentally, he was born in the Henry Ford Hospital. What's more, his father, John Telnack, worked as a maintenance man at the Rouge while moonlighting as a musician. "As a small boy, my dad used to take me to the Rotunda when the new cars came in," Telnack recalls. (The Rotunda was an exhibition building in the 1939 Chicago World's Fair that Ford disassembled and reerected in Dearborn.) "It was the 1941 Continental that kicked off my love affair with cars." A dyed-in-the-wool Ford man, Telnack says, "It's always been my dream to be a Ford designer. I don't think I could have drawn a Chevy if I tried. Sometimes, I think I was born with a blue oval on my chest."

In the late spring of 1980, Veraldi, Telnack, and other key members of the Taurus team made a presentation to senior management on the merits of the new car. Among those attending were Philip Caldwell, Don Petersen, and Red Poling, the company's top three. It was a meeting in which decisions were made about such things as the car's specifications, designs, and, naturally, its budget. Of prime concern was whether to go ahead with a costly, radical, clean sheet design presented by AVD, or, considering the company's huge losses, which by this time were in the billions, to opt for a low-investment program. The easy route would be to liberally borrow componentry from the Tempo and Topaz scheduled to come out in 1983 and thereby lower the ante by a couple of billion dollars. In his presentation, Veraldi stated that Ford had reached a crossroad: "The company could play it safe or go with something radically different and become a world-class leader in a key segment of the automobile business."

Senior management supported the clean sheet project. "Having a muddle-through, parts bin car that took something from this car and something else from that car," Caldwell explains, "would not have represented any forward movement. It was a matter of believing in our business and its future. Did we think it had potential to be a good business, or should we get out? We couldn't just piddle along. We decided that since we were going to compete in the market, we'd better do it right."

At this critical meeting, it was agreed that the management team, now referred to as "Team Taurus," would implement the concept of concurrent rather than sequential car design and development. A budget for the Taurus was set at $3.25 billion. Veraldi would have the distinction of having played key roles in the two most expensive car projects in the company's history. The vote of confidence was a gutsy move on the part of Caldwell, a man who had become chairman of the board only a few weeks earlier. Veraldi praises his courage: "Caldwell is sometimes portrayed as a plain vanilla–type guy, but in my opinion he probably had more guts than any CEO in the history of our industry.

"Senior management's approval at the 1980 meeting was not a final approval, however, but rather permission to work on the project in earnest, and no matter what we came up with, it would ultimately need final acceptance by the board. It was then that we started to work together as a team, bringing people in during the early stages so they could participate in the initial decision-making process."

By December 1980, a prototype of the Taurus was built. "It was a car with running hardware," Veraldi explains, "and I drove it home just before the Christmas holiday. I will always remember that day as the most devastating day of my career. The car was horrible! I was so demoralized I actually cried that night. I kept repeating to myself, 'Three and a quarter billion dollars and this is what we will get?' "

The next day, Veraldi conducted a meeting with his Team Taurus members and major revisions were instituted. "If we had not had a team in place, with everybody knowing what was going on, and why, we probably would have had delayed Job One by a couple of years," Veraldi points out. "It was exhilarating to see how everyone cooperated. If you're a supplier, for example, and you are privy to why a decision for change is made, then you're more than likely to get behind it. The old way of doing things was that you'd fight it. As a team, we were able to expedite major changes including changing to a fully automatic four-speed transmission. A floor shift was changed to a steering column shift. We enlarged the trunk; a 2.3-liter, four-cylinder base engine became 2.5 liters; and we increased our V-6 from 2.8 to 3.0 liters. Additionally, we made major revisions in the architecture of the car."

On October 2, 1981, Phil Caldwell, Don Petersen, and Red Poling arrived in Paris. The triumvirate was to meet with other members of Ford's board, already in Europe, where they would decide whether the company should go ahead with its ambitious plans to produce the Taurus. On the same agenda was a $2 billion investment recommendation for new plant technology and product improvements on other Ford models. Even during the best of times, $5 billion is an enormous commitment.

Among those board members present was the aged Henry Ford II. Although no longer a company executive, he served as chairman of the finance committee. In this capacity, Ford had enormous influence on the company's major money-spending decisions. As the family patriarch, he had the responsibility to vote according to what he thought was in the best interests of the Ford family. However great the temptation to reduce spending, Ford stuck to his commitment to leave the management of the company to the professional managers. "There were many times when

Henry could have stepped in and said, 'We are not going to do this,' or 'We will not do that,' " explains Caldwell. "But he didn't do any of that. He played his role perfectly, and by doing so, gave us his vote of confidence."

During the course of the Paris meeting, the board members pondered the company's future. It had become clear to all that the Ford LTD and Mercury Marquis would not succeed in the middle segment of the market.

Several other proposals that required far less investment were hashed through, but it was decided that if Ford were to leave its mark, it would have to leapfrog the competition and produce a vehicle that was truly different, one that would set the company apart from other automakers. It soon became apparent that there was only one course to take and the most pressing issue was no longer whether to make the Taurus, but whether to make it front-wheel drive or rear-wheel drive. The cost of front-wheel drive would run approximately $1 billion more, and while studies had shown that this feature was superior for small cars, rear-wheel drive was still more suitable for large cars. The Taurus could go either way. "A billion dollars was an awful lot of money, and the board was split on which way to go," Caldwell recalls. "But General Motors had a huge promotion going that extolled the virtues of front-wheel drive, which meant we might not have been able to convince the American people to go with the Taurus as a rear-wheel car. Besides, the aero look projected an image of the car of the future and, at the time, the public thinking was that eventually all cars would be front-wheel drive. This thinking prompted us to go the more expensive route, even at a time when we were looking for ways to cut costs."

Giving the go-ahead to build the Taurus and its sister car in the Lincoln-Mercury Division, the Sable, was one of the most daring decisions in the annals of American industry. David McCammon, currently vice-president of finance and treasurer, who served as vice-president of corporate strategy at the time, recalls, "The Taurus/Sable program had a $3.25 billion budget, and we had to make the decision at a time when we were incurring staggering losses. To put this figure in its proper prospective, the previously most expensive car program in the history of the company was the Fiesta, which, in comparison, was a paltry $800 million."

"Making a decision on the Taurus/Sable program when we were losing billions of dollars demonstrated a tremendous commitment to our business," Red Poling states. "Sure, it would have been nice to have known from its conception that the program was going to be a winner. But the Taurus had a new styling theme and there were no guarantees that it would be accepted. If it had failed, God only knows what would have happened."

Upon the board's approval to forge ahead, a casual one-on-one meeting between Caldwell and Veraldi took place, which set the pace for the entire program. At this time, Caldwell proposed a simple and direct question, "Why should anybody walk across the street to buy our car?

"The answer to this question, Lew," Caldwell told the team captain, "must be continually addressed throughout the implementation of the entire program. With each aspect of the program, keep asking, 'What are we doing different to make sure we can come up with a winner and not a loser?' Let's set up the organization so that each member of the team keeps this question in mind."

"From then on, 'Why buy Taurus?' became our battle cry," Veraldi explains.

"It was so inspiring." Veraldi recalls, "to know that the three top men of the company were 100 percent behind Team Taurus. They made us feel as though we had a mission to accomplish, and the future of the company depended upon its success. When management is able to instill its people with a feeling of such strong purpose, it's a tremendous motivating force."

It would be four years before the actual production of the Taurus and Sable, and during this period, "Why buy Taurus?" was repeatedly addressed in scores of meetings. Other questions heard often were "Why would this car be a success?" and "What would Ford have to do to make the car absolutely world-class in terms of quality and customer satisfaction?" The questions provided direction and their answers, consistency of purpose.

All Team Taurus members reported to the Car Program Management Group headed by Lew Veraldi. John Risk was car development planning director; A. L. Guthrie, chief engineer; Jack Telnack, chief designer; and Philip Benton, vice-president of North American sales. These were the key players who worked closely with the estimated 150 vice-presidents, directors, and managers from all areas of the company, such as manufacturing, component engineering, service, legal, and sales and marketing. "The idea was to have people who were in the mainstream of the company on Team Taurus, but not remove them from their regular work," explains John Risk. "In the past, task forces were set up as special groups and tended to work in isolation. As a consequence, their work was not acceptable upon its completion. In this new program, people reported to the program manager as well as their regular boss, but they were truly dedicated—it was as if 'Team Taurus' were emblazoned on their fore-heads. Then there were countless meetings held that were specific to subsystems such as the front end, brakes, suspension, chassis, body, glass, and so on. These meetings were quite intensive and everyone attended who had responsibility for the specific part in question. In addition to the subsystems meetings, we conducted mass meetings that every key team member attended. Here, we'd review the total vehicle objectives. Then there were plant meetings where the workers would attend and give their input."

Veraldi describes Team Taurus as "a kind of *ad hoc* group with program managers who functioned as team leaders in their respective areas but, rather than working separately, they worked together within the entire process." Veraldi points out the team approach, based on the success of the Fiesta, laid the groundwork for Team Taurus. "Unlike the Fiesta, this program was done in total, and there are two reasons for it: (1) we knew the team concept was a good premise so we expanded it and (2) the stakes were so high we had to give it our best shot. Team Taurus would include all the disciplines involved in produc-ing a car right from the beginning. As the natural extension of the Fiesta program, we said, 'Why not include the service people?' 'Why not the sales and marketing people?' 'Why not the dealers?' 'Why not the cus-tomer directly?' This is how Team Taurus evolved. Everybody becomes involved in the project before one line is drawn on a CAD computer screen or one pencil is sharpened in accounting. What results is that events are forced to happen simultaneously rather than sequentially. And all input is received from every direction before plans are formalized."

From its inception, each team member shared the common goal of producing a truly world-class car in its segment, and throughout the program this objective was never compromised. To implement this ambi-tious goal, a "want list" was developed. All constituencies were asked to express what features they wanted to include in the car on which Ford was betting its future. To make certain that nothing became prematurely etched in granite, the list was compiled early on. Representatives from all groups who would be involved with the Taurus were asked to voice opinions. A memo went out with the question: "Considering the kind of car we're planning, what would you want to see included, changed, etc?" Everyone was invited to express what he or she thought should be included in the new car. Opinions were sought from the expected sources such as designers, body and assembly engineers, line workers, service people, marketing managers, dealers, and suppliers. But then Team Taurus took the extra step, contacting ergonomics experts, UAW leaders, independent service people, consumers, lawyers, and insurance experts.

Insurance experts were asked how the car could be designed to ensure better accident coverage. At the same time, Ford's Service Manager's Council made valuable recommendations on what would make the car easier to service. Independent repairmen and insurance companies were asked to suggest changes and additions concerning bodywork, and as a result splices were installed in places where cars are most frequently damaged in a collision. Advice was also sought about where to cut the car to provide the correct structural integrity after an accident. "We did as we were advised and sure enough, shortly after the car went on the market," Veraldi tells, "Allstate and State Farm offered substantial discounts to Taurus and Sable owners."

Ford attorneys were questioned about what laws were likely to be legislated after 1985 which, in turn, could affect the Taurus. The legal department projected high-mounted stop lamps would be mandated (which they were in 1986). Also recommended was the installation of larger windshield wipers, which are still not mandatory but have been a good selling feature. "Because the cars were expected to be on the market for seven or eight years," Veraldi explains, "we asked our legal and safety people to tell us what changes or additions to anticipate with emission and safety regulations so we could 'bake in' complying features to the design and specifications of the car. The car was also built so it could be easily adapted to the European market."

All in all, the response to the want list was phenomenal. As suggestions poured in, the list eventually spawned 1,401 ideas of which 68 percent were incorporated into the Taurus. Many came from the Atlanta Assembly Plant, the lead plant—the first to build the Taurus and Sable. Six months later, the Chicago plant also assembled both cars, and it, too, was a source of many suggestions. This was the first time top managers from Dearborn visited a plant to get input from production workers, and *their visits were 4.5 years before production started.*

"Layouts were put on the wall," Veraldi remembers, "and I announced, 'This is the car we want to do.' After the hourly employees and foremen looked things over, I told them, 'Now I'd like to have you guys tell us all the trouble you're currently having so that, before we design this thing, we will know what not to do.' I made several trips to Atlanta to conduct other meetings on the plant floor, and we took notes on every single suggestion. In fact, while half the Taurus Team resided in Atlanta, the rest of us were from all over, and we spent months living in hotel rooms down there over the course of a 4.5-year period.

"On subsequent visits, people approached me and said, 'Boy, you mean that you put my idea in? I can't get over it. Nobody ever listened to me before.' Workers were so excited, they'd slap me on the back and gave me hugs when I'd visit them. It's amazing what esprit de corps results when you communicate with people and let them know what you want from them. If people are permitted to be part of the equation, they'll be in the boat rowing with you, rather than trying to tip it over from the outside."

Some of the improvements that resulted from the Atlanta workers' suggestions are

> Formerly, nuts and bolts came in many sizes, which made it more time-consuming and tedious to fasten interior moldings. Workers had to keep changing the heads on their screw-torquing power tools. Today, however, a single standard size is used. The same change was made with the nuts and bolts that were fastened underneath the car.
>
> The number of body side panels was reduced from 12 pieces to 2 pieces, which greatly reduced the likelihood of outside noise and water leaks from door openings.
>
> The interior plastic trim pieces were enlarged, which made them easier to install. Not only did this result in a better fit, but the appearance also was improved.
>
> Previously, after doors were affixed to the body of the car, workers would install the trim to each door. Workers had to climb into the car and crawl on their hands and knees to make the installations. Door trimming is now installed as an off-line assembly operation, before the doors are put on the car.

The above are representative of the many suggestions provided by the Atlanta workers. While each by itself may seem insignificant, in total, there was substantial improvement as well as a marked increase in morale. It had been common for 10 to 15 cars of every 100 assembled to be taken off the assembly line for repair. This number dropped to 1 per 100 cars and the present goal is to improve quality so that *no cars need to be repaired*. Also, the plant is more flexible so it is now possible to convert from the production of the Taurus to the Sable and from station wagons to sedans each hour on the hour, if necessary.

Although robots have been installed, the real gains are from people. As

Petersen asserts, "Eighty-five percent of the gains are attributed to managing smarter and only 15 percent to new technology."

Suppliers were also asked to participate early in the game, and a new program called "Must See Before" was instituted that required suppliers to show parts they made for the Taurus well in advance of production. The parts were examined to make certain they fit properly, functioned correctly, felt right, and looked attractive. "Suppliers were accountable for quality and fit before they began production," Veraldi explains. "We began sourcing parts 42 months before Job One. On average, sourcing was completed 26 to 29 months before production, which let suppliers plan their production and quality programs. Because suppliers were required to make long-term commitments, we went as far as making loans to certain ones to help them get ready. Long-term contracts were signed with suppliers that, I believe, demonstrated a mutual trust.

"As an added incentive," Veraldi continues, "we set up 'system sourcing' for purchasing whereby suppliers received bigger-than-normal jobs. For instance, instead of having different companies supply, say, interior trim moldings, only one company supplied all the moldings. Likewise, all the plastic went to one company, which meant that colors and grains were all the same, and most important, they fit. We even had all the tools made by one supplier. Everything was more efficient because confusion and difficulties were reduced in resolving fit problems.

"We said to our suppliers, 'Give us your ideas.' " Veraldi adds. "Sounds so simple today, but this was never done in the automobile business. And did they ever respond with some wonderful ideas! For instance, Prince Corporation gave us a dual sun visor. Now doesn't it make sense to seek their expertise? After all, who knows better than they about sun visors? They make tens of millions of them every year. In another situation, Massillon Corporation, a carpet supplier, figured out a way to index carpeting so that napping would match in the interior back end of the Taurus station wagons. So, for the first time, the napping was consistent. Again, a small touch, but certainly an improvement."

The team did an in-depth study of cars built by Ford's competition. This was accomplished by purchasing hundreds of domestic and foreign cars for the purpose of identifying 400 of the world's best-designed and engineered automotive features, ranging from sun visors to steering systems, and incorporating as many as possible into the Taurus. Every major car in the world in the same class or market niche was studied to get features that the customers really wanted. These cars were methodically reverse engineered to reveal how they were designed, manufactured, and assembled. Every detail, no matter how minute, was scrutinized. What became known as "creature comforts," or "CC's" included easing the effort it takes to crank a window or to open a door. Touch controls were installed for operating electric windows and the radio, so that the driver could feel when they were on or off without looking. The diameters of the necks of windshield wiper fluid bottles were enlarged to make it easier to pour the fluid, reducing spillage. Other CC's included a net in the trunk to secure packages, a built-in compartment to store a garage door opener, more foot room under the front seat for backseat passengers, map pockets, a container to store coins, a picnic tray on station wagon tailgates, adjustable dual sun visors, depressions to hold beverage containers, oil dipsticks painted in bright yellow for quick identification, and concealed drip moldings.

Repeatedly, Caldwell's question "Why buy Taurus?" was asked. "The question was addressed throughout the development of the car," John Risk explains. "We asked it with everything we designed, and again with everything that got approved. 'Why would a customer want it this way?' 'Is this better than the competition?' 'Is this a new feature, something that the customer will really appreciate or is it just a trifle?' Not only did we borrow from the best, but we added many innovations, such as flush glass, aerodynamic headlights, and flush door handles."

The best-in-class philosophy was a sharp departure from Ford's previous practice. "The old philosophy was 'We don't want to be too rich in content for middle America,' " notes Caldwell. Such an arrogant attitude toward the American consumer was no longer tolerated by Team Taurus members. Naturally, how much a best-in-class feature cost was always a consideration. Too many extra items would increase the Taurus's price tag, eliminating its competitive edge, especially when there were 400 under consideration, but 80 percent of these features were incorporated into the Taurus and Sable.

While the board approved a $3.25 billion budget, the program actually cost slightly less than $3 billion. One major savings resulted from the design changes following the start of production; they cost only $35 million compared to the usual $150 million. The team concept enabled Ford's biggest car investment to come in under its budget, an unusual feat in the automobile field. Veraldi attributes this to "how well everyone communicated with each other. By talking to each other, we were able to come up with constructive changes. It's interesting that with Team Taurus we didn't set up incentives, but instead relied on one's pride in workmanship. We discovered that most people want to do the job right when given the chance. People were motivated because they had an equity in the product, a feeling created by listening to everyone carefully. Furthermore, each team member understood our objective was to provide maximum value and all efforts were directed toward producing the best product. When costs exceeded budgeted variable costs, it was up to the individual to measure himself. And when you measure yourself, you're going to be a lot tougher than your boss. An atmosphere was created where it was okay to have arguments. Conflict and bargaining were permissible—as long as they increased the quality of product. As the process went on, we were constantly improving it, each time asking what could be done to make it better, even if it meant starting over again from scratch."

While the commitment to Team Taurus started at the top, it filtered down to the workers on the assembly line. "I saw a dedication I had never seen before," Veraldi adds, describing what he observed at the Livonia plant where Taurus and Sable transmissions were made. "The workers stayed on until 8:00 P.M. to show me how they were building parts. At each station the workers had small charts on easels or taped to desks— they were all different—and they would say, 'This is how we are going to manufacture this part at this station—and this is how we are going to make it perfect.' They all had their own way of showing how they did statistical process control. The methods were common, but their individual applications differed since the plant manager had given them the latitude to run their own businesses in the way they thought best."

At one time, Ford cars and their sister Lincoln-Mercury cars were produced separately. The Taurus and the Sable, however, were purposely developed by the same team and manufactured at the same plants in Atlanta and Chicago. "By doing them together," explains Risk, "we could make sure there were maximum differences. It was a matter of having your left hand and your right hand at the same place so they didn't end up too similiar. Otherwise, we would have had the same problem GM has, where everyone thinks all GM cars come out of the same tube. With that in mind, we spent over $200 million making sure that the Sable was different from the Taurus."

While the two cars are virtually identical mechanically, there are a few distinguishable design differences. The Sable has a more sporty style and plush interior that appeals to younger, chic buyers whereas the Taurus is designed more for family-oriented buyers. The Sable is 2.5 inches longer and has an extra 1.5 cubic feet interior space.

Naming a new product plays an important role in projecting the right image, and in the automobile industry considerable time and money is generally spent making this decision. For instance, more than 18,000 names were submitted before the name "Edsel" was chosen, and the Thunderbird was picked from a selection of more than 5,000 names. It is a worldwide market; an acceptable name in the United States can have a bad connotation in other countries. For instance, when GM shipped its Chevrolet Nova to Mexico, it did not realize that *no va* in Spanish is "no go."

Yet the naming of the Taurus was quick and simple. One day in early 1980, during a casual conversation, Veraldi and Risk discovered that both of their wives shared the astrological sign Taurus. They submitted the name to marketing and when a consumer survey revealed positive reactions, the car became the Taurus. The fact that the Taurus is the sign of the bull, suggesting brute power and tenacity, also worked in its favor. The higher-priced Sable was appropriately named after the small, sly animal that inhabits northern Europe and Asia, desired for its rich, elegant fur.

Marketing played a different role in the development of the Taurus and Sable than it did with previous Ford products. In the past, marketing people were brought in after the fact. Once cars were designed and manufactured, they were told, in effect, to put together a marketing plan. Ray Ablondi, retired executive director of market research, labels the former way of doing things "report card research." He explains, "We were told, 'Here it is. How good a job did we do?' Then they'd ask, 'Now, what can you do?' But the car was already done so it was too late to change anything."

This time market research people worked side by side with designers and engineers. Throughout the development of the Taurus and Sable, market research was continually conducted, in fact, more so than ever before in American automobile industry history. Martin Goldfarb, a marketing consultant headquartered in Toronto, played a major role in conducting research with focus groups. Goldfarb and his staff carefully analyzed what was expressed during these interviews and made recommendations to Team Taurus. In the beginning, focus group members were shown designs, then clay models, and later on, prototypes made to scale. By January 1985, 11 months prior to shipping Tauruses and Sables to dealer showrooms, preproduction units were viewed by small numbers of people during focus group sessions. It was the first time that Ford had ever revealed *real* cars to the public so far in advance of an introduction. It was also the first time that the company had ever taken a final product to the public to do marketing research, and it came back with some changes prior to Job One. For example, there was a woman in Florida who was inspecting underneath the car's front dashboard and asked the question, "I could never find where to release the hood. Why don't you make it yellow so I know where it is?" So the Taurus has yellow hood releases.

In California, the nation's bellwether for new trends, the radically new aerodynamic look was well received. However, in more conservative markets, such as Boca Raton, Florida, there was an entirely different reaction. For instance, when one elderly, retired woman was interviewed, she commented, "I love the car, but I am concerned about what my neighbor will think."

Market research revealed that the Taurus and Sable would be accepted by people receptive toward trying a new product, but there were others that Ford designers affectionately label "Johnny Lunchbuckets." These people aren't quite so daring but perhaps might buy a year or two after they have become accustomed to the new look. Others in the "twilight market" vacillate between owning a domestic and foreign car, or own one of each. These potential customers are receptive to both quality-made and newly designed cars and could be convinced to buy an American-made car only if it were exceptional. It was imperative that Ford educate the American public on the uniqueness and extraordinary qualities of the Taurus and Sable prior to revealing them in dealers' showrooms.

In early 1983, David Scott, then director of NAAO public affairs, gave out an unusual assignment when he named Chuck Gumushian as the project launch manager for Scott's office. Gumushian joined Team Taurus with the specific task of developing a launching strategy. Nobody in the history of Ford had ever had such a job description. But never before did the company have so much riding on the introduction of a new car. As Gumushian explains, "It was a do-or-die proposition, and Scott's orders were that we had to come up with something big." Scott set a goal that the marketing research people felt was vital to the success of Team Taurus: 50 percent of the public must know about the new cars prior to their arrival at dealer showrooms.

Following his meeting with Scott, Gumushian formally joined the team; for the next eight months he learned everything he could about the project. "Prior to my meeting with Scott, Taurus meant nothing to most of us in public affairs, other than a sign of the zodiac," Gumushian notes, "so I spent a major portion of my time doing research."

With orders to create the splashiest introduction of any Ford car in history, where else could Gene Koch, another member of the public affairs team, go but to Hollywood? On January 29, 1985, almost a full year before the Taurus went on sale, the public affairs group arranged a world premiere at the MGM Entertainment Company in Culver City, California. Rogers and Cowan, the large West Coast public relations (PR) firm that specializes in the entertainment field, was hired, and MGM's huge Studio 37 (used for filming *Gone with the Wind* and *Ben Hur*) was rented to house the event. Robert Jani, who played a key role in the television production of the 1984 Olympics in Los Angeles, staged a gala evening program that was attended by an estimated 400 media people from around the world. Also present at the festive gathering was a bevy of VIPS including Ford executives, politicians, and show-business people. Some reporters compared it to the Academy Awards. At a stately banquet, Philip Caldwell made a brief after-dinner speech, which was followed by a dramatic unveiling of four cars—a sedan and station wagon of both the Taurus and the Sable. As giant-size cones raised each car into view, there was a hushed silence that soon became a standing ovation. "It was quite emotional," recalls Scott. "I don't ever recall such a reaction to a new car, especially from the usually skeptical members of the press."

"The industry had been so lethargic during the eighties," Gumushian says, "that the media couldn't believe what they were seeing. They couldn't imagine that we, Ford Motor Company, were really going to build this car. They kept saying, 'These are concept cars, aren't they?' They couldn't get over the fact that these cars were actually scheduled to come out in ten months."

To keep the momentum going, the Taurus and Sable were taken to the Chicago Auto Show, America's most prestigious auto show, in February 1985. There they would have to share the limelight with other cars from around the world. Generally, concept cars are exhibited at this show, not next year's models. And while perhaps a thousand people saw the cars in Culver City, more than a million visited the Chicago exhibit. Here, too, Ford used spectacular stages to display the cars, and again, received sensational reviews.

With the Chicago Auto Show under its belt, efforts were needed to keep the ball rolling. At a brainstorming publicity meeting, Bill Peacock, a longtime Ford PR man, listened intently to a discussion about the difficulties that were so common in the introduction of a radically new car. The discussion centered around how Ford's aerodynamic styling seemed too far ahead of the market, and how, to have a successful launching, the car had to remain in the public eye until October when dealerships would begin receiving shipments. Peacock commented on how the company had 200,000 employees in the United States and even more people worked for Ford suppliers. "Let's send out photographs of the Taurus to these people," he suggested, "and start a word-of-mouth campaign across the country."

"By the time the meeting had adjourned," David Scott says, "we came up with a plan to take the Taurus on a road show across the country to visit suppliers' plants, an idea we had actually come up with two years ago. By doing this, we'd kill two birds with one stone because it would also be a great morale booster for the employee involvement program. Most important, we didn't want to lose the momentum we started in California and at the Chicago Auto Show. Chuck Gumushian was put in charge of operating what became known as 'the caravan.' "

There were actually two caravans. Each had two vans that transported a Taurus and a Sable along with a team of four or five Ford people—a public relations person, an engineer, a designer, a company executive, and, of course, the van driver. For a 2.5-month period, beginning on March 11, a total of 110 communities were visited. A caravan arrived by 8:00 A.M. at a plant and pulled out by 3:00 P.M. to head for the next town. The selection of the participating suppliers was made by the purchasing department. Those with Q1 ratings were on the top of the list. Gumushian orchestrated the road show, working closely with local Ford regional managers who, in turn, worked with the local media to generate publicity.

"The suppliers were very enthusiastic and supportive," Gumushian explains. "Each would receive a letter stating the time of our arrival, plus a kit with suggestions on what to do, including how to involve the local newspapers, television and radio stations. I wanted to create a carnival-type atmosphere in the parking lot or garage where all the supplier's employees could attend. I suggested setting up a tent, having a platform so a few brief speeches could be made, and even providing a small band to liven things up. Most of the time we went to suppliers in small communities in which they were the towns' largest employers. In fact, I never before heard of most places we visited. The caravan was a major event for the town, and not only did the local media give it lots of coverage, but often the local dignitaries were present, such as the chamber of commerce president, the mayor, a state senator, a congressman, the bank president, and so on.

"The reception was always terrific," Gumushian continues, "but in some cases, it was spectacular. For instance, A. O. Smith in Granite City,

Illinois, which makes the front subframe for both the Taurus and Sable, really went all out. There were about 3,000 people in the crowd, and a large stage was constructed for a formal presentation. A chef provided a giant-size cake and a large ice replica of the Taurus.

"In addition to the publicity, the caravan was great for morale," Gumushian adds. "I remember one woman, who worked for a carpet supplier, examining the car with a great deal of pride and declaring 'Now I know where this carpet I've been making is going!' The caravan visited our Atlanta plant and I overheard a worker say to his buddies, 'Hey, guys, look here at this. By golly, they finally listened to us!' "

The caravan ended on May 14, 1985, and was followed by the annual two-week technical news conference in June. During this time, the long lead media were invited to visit Ford in Dearborn to review new models. About 150 writers for automobile and trade publications attended the event. Normally, this would have sufficed until Job One rolled off the assembly line, which was originally scheduled on July 31, 1985. (Once Job One occurs, it takes about two months for cars to be delivered to dealer showrooms.) However, the consensus of Team Taurus was that the level of quality was still not high enough, so Job One was postponed for approximately two months. It was Ford's longest delay ever for Job One. The delay put more pressure on the public affairs office; the momentum could be lost. As a result of the caravan's success, it was decided that the two teams would be sent to another 110 suppliers' plants beginning on August 11 and ending on November 4. Gumushian states that the cost of the caravans was relatively low, considering the exceptional goodwill that was generated. "While senior management was initially skeptical of caravanning, it is now a standard precedure for the introduction of a brand new car."

Meanwhile, there were several problems faced by Team Taurus. The biggest reason for Job One's delay was a result of advanced automation procedures at the Atlanta plant. "The sheet metal for our prototype cars was not made with our production tools," Veraldi explains, "and we discovered that with a different metal used for actual production, the interior moldings did not fit properly. They had to be redesigned. Unfortunately, we were unaware of this until it was too late and this postponed Job One. Today, we get the production metal ready much earlier.

"Then, too, we learned from experience that it's wise to build at least 300 preproduction models and quickly get them in the hands of users prior to Job One," Veraldi continues. "I learned this trick when I visited IBM. They built 1,200 of a particular typewriter model a year before putting it into production so they could get feedback from users. This enables a manufacturer to get the kinks out of a new product *before* mass producing it. It boils down to having more time to discover what the problems are before the production start date.

"There were several little problems that we discovered after the car was on the market that resulted in subsequent recalls. All in all, there were eight recalls that affected a relatively small number of cars. For instance, the ignition key could be withdrawn when the car was not in park. This was a result of a manufacturing mishap by the vendor, and one that was easily corrected. And the glass of the quarter window of the Taurus station wagon was prone to break because it had not been properly tempered. Then there was a rotten egg smell generated by the platinum coating on the catalyst. This had to do with temperature and other environmental factors, and it, too, was not difficult to correct, but it did cause some bad press."

Donald Jesmore, general manager of Ford's Body and Assembly Operations, explains, "The job of Team Taurus ended at Job One, and then new teams of engineers and manufacturing people came in to make improvements in the quality of the Taurus and Sable. We conducted surveys with new-car owners and concentrated on a list called 'Things Gone Wrong.' These small teams specialized in specific problems. For example, there was a squeak and rattle team, a ceiling team, a door fit team, an interior trim component fit team, and so on. By doing this, we were able to implement changes in the production of the Taurus and Sable. It also enables us to find better ways to design the cars that will come out later in the 1990s."

There was considerable confidence among the team members that the new products would be smashing successes. Its designer, Jack Telnack, who was positive it would succeed, says, "Deep down inside I was totally convinced that the aerodynamic design was a winner. I believed this because I knew inherently that it was right. It was an idea whose time had come. In fact, when Iacocca and others in the industry started poking fun at the Taurus after the Chicago Auto Show and called it 'the jelly bean car' and 'the flying potato,' I knew their remarks were just sour grapes because we beat everyone to the punch."

William Clay Ford concurs: "I chuckled to myself when I first heard them call it those names. Their ridiculing convinced me of what I had felt all along—that we had a real trendsetter. Personally, I remember seeing a model of the Taurus when it was all dressed up with the chrome and wire wheels, and after looking at it, I thought, 'Boy, I would like to own that car myself.' I can recall my feeling of disappointment when I then realized I'd have to wait until it went into production. The car had so many good points that, by comparison, it made the competitor's designs look archaic. I knew they'd eventually copy what we had, and it was a nice feeling to be out in front."

While Telnack and other Team Taurus members appeared not to worry, there were senior managers whose optimism was guarded. "We were certain that the Taurus was an outstanding car," Allan Gilmour notes, "but no one yet has ever produced a car that was *too* good. Furthermore, even if you bring out the best car in the world during a recession it won't sell because people can't afford to buy cars. Fortunately for us, 1986 happened to be a very good year."

In addition to a healthy economy, it also takes favorable reviews by the prestigious car magazines to inform the public that a new vehicle is really all its manufacturer says it is. The opening of a Broadway show serves as a good analogy. No matter how good the play's investors, producer, director, and cast members think their production is, if the critics pan the show, its chances for success are minimal. And even with rave reviews, *the audience* has to like the play. So nobody started popping champagne corks before the reviews were in, the buying public had made its firsthand inspection, and, most important, the cash registers started ringing.

After the long delay of Job One, the Taurus and Sable finally made their debut on the day after Christmas 1985. This, too, set a precedent because the holiday season was always considered a slow time for the automobile industry. Cold weather and Christmastime festivities meant people tended not to buy cars. But with the Taurus and Sable, it was a very good time to buy. As the automobile magazines gave their highest marks and as the word of mouth spread, orders began to pour in before the cars arrived at dealer showrooms. All in all, more than 150,000 advance orders were taken.

The following spring, *Motor Trend* named the Taurus the 1986 Car of the Year. The Sable was runner-up. By 1987, the Taurus was the number one selling car in the United States. Ford's $3.25 billion gamble had paid off. In spades. While a return of 8.5 percent had been projected, Ford realized more than an 11 percent return.

Ford's reputation for "Following the General" in price and styling of domestic automobiles was no longer valid. For the first time in decades, Ford was the leader. Team Taurus generated a new confidence within the company, a vital ingredient that had long been missing.

THE COMPANY IS CUSTOMER DRIVEN, OR THE PRODUCTS ARE NOT

When the automobile industry was still in its infancy, Henry Ford's obsession was to mass produce affordable cars. It was a noble ambition. An exceptional value, the Model T had captured an astounding 48 percent market share in the United States by 1914.

As a young entrepreneur, Henry Ford was customer driven. His cars were built for the customer—pure and simple. Ford cars were excellently made, and, for a while, the company had a lock on the automobile business. When the industry became more competitive, however, other automakers, notably General Motors, began to cut into Ford's market share by offering innovative features not available on the Model T. Bit by bit, these competitors gnawed away at Ford's market. As America built better roads, people wanted more speed, and technological advances made it possible for cars to go faster. Cars also came equipped with more comfort and styling. Yet Henry Ford continued to make the same Model T, refusing to alter the decade-old design or offer any color other than black. When his marketing people complained that the company was losing ground to the competition, he glibly remarked, "As far as I can see, our only trouble with the Ford car is that we can't make them fast enough." The man referred to as the father of the automobile industry continued to build cars that *he* wanted to build rather than what the customer wanted.

However proficient in the manufacturing end of the automobile business, Henry Ford had ceased to be customer driven. He wouldn't accept the fact that the customer wanted a car for reasons other than merely transportation. While Ford was comfortable with the idea that "a Ford will take you anywhere except into society," the customer expected his car to do just that—take him into society.

In the mid–1920s, General Motors offered installment financing, and Edsel attempted to convince his father to do the same. "They're styling their cars better than ours," he pleaded, "and what's more, they're offering financing to provide the customer with the means to purchase a car." To placate the company's dealers, the stubborn founder finally agreed to provide a finance program, but only if it was done his way. His way was for the customer to pay $5 a week for three years, and *after* having paid the last payment, only then would the company manufacture and deliver the car! It took five years for him to realize that the American public wasn't interested in buying cars on the layaway plan. Only after General Motor's financing arm, GMAC, was proved a huge success—and already had a running start—did Ford consent to offer installment financing.

Ford Motor Company was a classic example of what can happen to an industry leader that ceases to be customer driven. The company foundered during the 1930s and only after Henry Ford II became CEO did the company begin to regain some of its lost market share. Had it not been for the pent-up demand for cars following the World War II shortages, the company might not have survived. The 1950s were golden years for America and the Big Three prospered with virtually no outside competition, having only each other with which to contend. During the 1960s, the domestic automakers continued to prosper. It took two energy crises and formidable competition from the Japanese automakers to bring the automobile industry to its knees in the early 1980s.

Ford's monumental cost-cutting program during its back-to-back years of billion dollar losses was important but not enough. Nor did it suffice to continue production only at those plants with the best quality. There was also a pressing urgency to provide quality cars that would sell and to provide service to customers so they would continue to buy Ford products. To achieve a competitive edge, it was Petersen, Ford's *car guy,* who heeded Peter Drucker's advice that quality is "not what the supplier puts in. It is what the customer gets out and is willing to pay for. Customers only pay for what is of use to them and gives them value. Nothing else constitutes quality."

This is not to suggest that Ford has abandoned its "Quality is Job One" philosophy. Instead, Petersen expanded the philosophy so that Ford's goals became "to be accepted as the manufacturer of the world's best-quality products and for that line of products to be truly driven by what the customer is asking for.

"It was not just severe financial difficulties in the early 1980s that made us reexamine our product line," Petersen points out. "We were experiencing a free fall in market share. The nature of the automobile industry is cyclical, and we had suffered through bad times in the past. But this time we were not only losing large sums of money, our products were being rejected by customers.

"Downsizing our entire line of products in the United States was a definite requirement for us," Petersen adds. "We had no choice. We were faced with the fuel economy laws coupled with fact that the demand for our larger-size cars had disappeared. We recognized that it was mandatory for us to continue spending to come up with new cars, and it was essential to make them appealing to the customer."

Phil Caldwell, Petersen's predecessor, says, "I inherited [from Lee Iacocca] a whole fleet of cold cars. He liked to bill himself as one of the great car men of all time, but he left a legacy of cold cars. They were cold alligator-shoe cars, and the market said they weren't any good and the customers didn't buy them."

It was with this in mind that Petersen gave his now-famous order to Jack Telnack in 1980 to "design the kind of cars *you* would like to drive." Petersen explains that "we had made so many mistakes in the past by following this or that trend, this or that competitor that it dawned on us we shouldn't be driven by other people's choices except for our customers."

Becoming proactive rather than reactive was a new way of thinking for Ford. More than 50 years had passed since Ford was the trendsetter. Both Ford and Chrysler avoided daring changes in styling that might not sell; almost always they let General Motors be the first to test the waters. Petersen was determined to change Ford's follow-the-leader role. "To break away from this pattern," he insists, "required coming up with a better way to listen to the customer because what we were doing just wasn't working."

The company turned to Martin Goldfarb, the founder and president of Goldfarb Consultants, a Toronto-based firm. His background included teaching anthropology and sociology at the high-school level. Goldfarb later attended graduate school at the University of Toronto and became a staff member. Joined by his wife, Joan, in 1966 he founded his consulting firm. Two years later, after publishing a series of marketing research articles, Goldfarb was approached by some executives from Ford of Canada.

In the beginning, the Goldfarb firm conducted qualitative research to analyze Ford's advertising in Canada, and in particular, to assess its effectiveness. "Our qualitative research was based on studying people in group sessions. We'd have 10 to 12 people in a group, and we'd conduct two-hour interviews with them," Goldfarb says. "What happened is that we would develop dynamics similar to what goes on in group therapy, but our focus was on advertising. After conducting enough group interviews in which we'd test, say, five commercials, we'd take the two most promising ones and with the recommendations of the groups, run them by as many as 150 people in what we refer to as mall intercepts. We'd stop people in mall shopping centers and ask, 'Are you the principle driver of a vehicle?' If a person was, we'd ask him or her to fill out a questionnaire to score our advertising. Then we'd evaluate these reactions quantitatively and the results would serve as a measuring device." Goldfarb's work in measuring customers' reactions to advertising was noticed by Ford's marketing research office in Dearborn, and soon he was doing similiar research for NAAO products.

Today, Ford is convinced that Goldfarb's insights from focus groups are accurate. Goldfarb describes his thinking as "very anthropological in structure. Our thesis is that a car is an artifact, and as an artifact, it has a relationship with the consuming public that is cultural. That artifact fits into the way of life of society, and we attempt to understand a cultural variable and apply it to motivate consumers so they will want to come into a dealership to look at Ford products."

John Vanderzee, advertising manager of the Ford Division, says, "Through focus groups, we can make quantitative advertising studies to determine how customers respond to our messages. We give them enough alternatives to determine which ones work and which ones don't. When a company thinks it's so smart that it doesn't have to ask the customer what he or she likes, it ends up with an Edsel."

In 1980, Louis Ross, who at the time headed product development, and Ray Ablondi, executive director of marketing research, brought Goldfarb in again to conduct pulse research. This time the Toronto consultant would seek the public's opinions about the company's cars, and then he would analyze them. What was interesting and different about Goldfarb's work from NAAO's past marketing research was that he would attempt to find out what customers thought about Ford cars *before the fact*. This meant bringing in his consulting firm during the early stages of product development.

"I had my own intuition about what was wrong," Ross explains, "I knew what *I* didn't like, however I wanted to get a firmer sense of what the customers thought. We had Goldfarb set up some pulse groups in Chicago to find out how people reacted to our cars in relation to General Motors cars. To accomplish this, we converted some space in an obscure warehouse into a showroom and displayed some of our cars. We felt that in order for the pulse groups to be effective, we shouldn't reveal ourselves as Ford representatives; instead, the Goldfarb organization was introduced as an independent company conducting a public opinion survey. This way we figured there'd be no pulled punches. Goldfarb served as a discussion provoker, and we sat in the background to observe.

"We asked questions to Ford car owners such as: 'What do you like about your car?' and then we came back with 'What do you dislike about your car?' Well, they told us that our cars weren't quality, and furthermore, didn't look like quality.

"When we were through asking questions about our cars, we conferred among ourselves, 'Well, nobody has what they're complaining we don't have.' Then we replaced our models with GM models and invited some GM car owners in and asked them the same set of questions. To our dismay, they weren't nearly as critical about GM products."

Pulse groups will often consist of people who are considered "interesting"—individuals such as architects, designers, interior decorators, or perhaps script writers. "We invite them," Goldfarb explains, "because we think they are more sensitive about the world around us than the average person. Often groups are either all male or all female. This sexual homogeneity allows men to express themselves in their own language, which we think differs from women who are so much more sensitive and for the most part, tend to have a better command of the language. I'll sometimes even separate age groups because young people have different verbal skills than older people."

One of the keys to a successful pulse group study was to invite back some of the interviewees who gave the best and worst ratings. These people were then asked more in-depth questions, and their comments were carefully analyzed. Each time, the results were the same: GM cars had clearly made mincemeat out of Fords.

It was a rude awakening for Ford executives witnessing these focus groups. Ablondi recalls an incident that, today, makes him smile, but at the time, made him wince. "Lou Ross was sitting in the back of a room," he remembers, "listening intently to members of a focus group voice their opinions about Ford products. Lou said to one of our executives sitting next to him, 'I didn't catch what that man said. Did he say, 'It looked like a Chevy?'

" 'No, Lou, he said that it looked shitty.'

"It was no laughing matter at the time, but thank heaven, we can laugh about it today."

Following these first focus groups in Chicago, Ross informed Petersen of the findings. "One of our problems is how we try to compete in every segment of the market like GM and with the same products," Ross points out. "Why do we try to appeal to one-third of the market segment? After all, our market share is hovering around 17 percent, so doesn't it make more sense to come out with a product that makes a solid appeal to about 30 percent of the market? If we do this, we'll do considerably better with this 30 percent, and so what if the other 70 percent doesn't like it—they never did! At the time, the 1980 Thunderbird had lost market share in what was previously a profitable segment. So we were now in the process of regrouping for the 1983 T-Bird with three years' lead time to make changes. We then used focus groups to identify *who* would buy the T-Bird. On a numerical score of 1 to 10, with 10 being the highest, it rated a shade greater than 6, which is nothing to get excited about. But when we studied the data and discovered that there were large numbers of people who gave it a 9 and other large numbers that gave it a 2 or 3 rating, we said, 'Look at how this one-third of the people like it strongly. Do we have the guts to go after this market segment only and write off the rest?' That's what we did and the car was a smashing hit."

Following the Chicago experiment, more pulse groups were conducted in Atlanta with foreign cars, specifically Honda owners, followed by Toyota owners. These people were asked what they liked about their Japanese cars. "This was when I discovered an appreciation for the creature comforts," Ross notes, "the little things like having a spot to store a garage-door opener, which is really just a nickel item, or a coin holder, a map holder, and so on. We counted 20 of these little storage spaces that Honda provided, and this was what led us to accumulate our list of 'tremendous trifles' for the Taurus."

It was a simple matter to induce people to come in and participate in a pulse group. In addition to receiving a free dinner, a $25 gift certificate, or, perhaps, a contribution to one's favorite charity, "people like to give their opinions," Ross explains, "and especially about cars. During the early 1980s, the American public was angry with the domestic automakers.

They felt as though the American auto industry let them down. So even though we didn't identify ourselves as Ford representatives, they knew we were conducting the focus groups for the automobile industry and they wanted to express their opinions."

One interesting pulse group study was conducted in Marin County (an affluent bedroom community just north of San Francisco) and the Silicon Valley area in Santa Clara County. The selection of these counties was based on the unusually high sales penetration made by the Japanese automakers and the low market share for Ford. Ford viewed the inroads made by Japanese in this area as a magnification of the rest of the country. These pulse groups were made up of consumers who owned cars and were considered upscale people—one group consisted of community leaders, another of engineers, another of psychologists, and so on. What was particularly disheartening was the *lack* of opinions that these northern Californians had about Ford Motor Company. For instance, at one particular session, Goldfarb wanted to get a response from a Ford car owner, so he asked the question, "Do any of you own a Ford?"

"No."

"Do any of you have anyone in your family who owns a Ford?"

"No."

"Do you have any neighbors who own a Ford?"

"No."

"Has anybody been in a Ford lately?"

"No."

Each member of the group turned to one another, waiting for somebody to reply yes, but there was silence. Ford officials sitting in the back of the room squirmed and remained silent, and even the group members appeared to be slightly embarrassed that they were unable to voice an opinion about Ford products.

Somebody asked the question, "Have you seen a Ford commercial lately?" Again there was no response.

"We didn't exist," Ross explains. "It had a jarring effect on us. It was important to us to know what these people thought about Ford because we view California as a pacesetter in styling, and as such, a barometer for how the rest of the country will eventually react. So we took these reactions to our products very seriously. We didn't simply shrug our shoulders, and write off Marin and Santa Clara as two insignificant, offbeat counties."

The northern California findings were brought back to Ford headquarters in Dearborn. "We presented a report to top management that contained excerpts of some stories people told us," Albondi comments. "For example, we reported how eighteen and twenty year olds said, 'I have never been in a Ford.' 'Nobody in my family has ever owned a Ford, and I don't have any friends who own a Ford.' In the beginning, when we presented our report, there were some people in management who didn't want to accept what we told them. They'd say, 'You can't say that in a Ford meeting,' and I'd reply, 'Who says I can't? This is what the people are telling us, and it has to be said.' "

Films of focus groups were then presented. "These films showed people shaking their fists at the camera," Albondi says, "and scenes like this relayed messages that no written report could. Anyone who viewed the films could sense that the customers felt as though we had let them down. Following the films, we presented graphs that showed that our market penetration in California was going off the chart—downward. Then the mood of the meeting shifted and the reaction was, 'My God, what are we going to do?' "

"Much to the credit of Petersen and Poling, they didn't shoot the messenger," Albondi adds. "They made a commitment that the company would be customer driven, and they were determined to listen to what the customers were saying. When we suggested that they come out and observe firsthand what went on in a focus group, they consented."

"It wasn't enough to read reports or view a film," Goldfarb explains. "It was imperative for Petersen, Poling, Benton, and other top executives to understand the dynamics of consumer hostility, which meant attending focus group sessions. After all, the Ford Motor Company was so out of the mainstream that, if it wasn't careful, the company could go out of business. So we convinced them to spend several days sitting through a whole series of focus groups, not only with Ford car owners but GM, Honda, and Toyota owners as well."

Goldfarb believes his work with Ford was effective because "it had support from the top of the company. In the beginning, Phil Benton, while at the head of sales for North America, was our first sponsor. Immediately, Bob Rewey, serving as general manager for both the Lincoln-Mercury Division and later for the Ford Division, bought into it and announced, 'I want every one of my guys to attend these sessions and listen to what consumers are telling us.' For a while, Benton, Petersen, and Poling were coming to all of our sessions. They set the example and made it clear that nobody in the company could think he was too important to listen to what consumers have to say. Eventually, managers in design, marketing, engineering, finance—in all areas—were participating in this research process. It was a real breakthrough for Ford, and I believe that the dynamics of interaction between the product, the consumer, and management is what separated Ford from the rest of the pack."

Petersen recalls what it was like for him to attend a focus group session: "I sat in the back and just listened, and it was quite a sobering experience. It's one thing to read a research survey but quite another to observe people who acted as if the company didn't exist. Sure, there were previous times when we went into the field to seek public opinion, and we'd give a clipboard to people, telling them to look at some of our cars and write down their opinions. Afterward, we'd give them a little gift and thank them for coming. But this was different. These people were engaged in a heated conversation about our products. Then they'd discuss to what extent some of the subtle elements of an automobile were important to them, and how it affected their opinions of one car as compared to another. Later, Goldfarb would get people to talk about their driving experiences with different cars. They'd mention little, seemingly insignificant points about what it felt like in one car, while another didn't feel comfortable. 'The seat didn't seem to be right,' or 'I didn't feel comfortable with where the controls were,' or 'The steering wheel seemed too high.' These are the kinds of comments that you have to hear in person to appreciate.

"Much of our past marketing research was too superficial. The old way of thinking was for a transmission engineer to deliver an assessment about the subtleties of shifting gears. There wasn't much to be learned from the customers when it came to evaluating a car's technology as it related to the needs of the car owner. I remember talking with one engineer who was puzzled about the negative customer reactions to a particular kind of transmission. He assumed that the way the transmission had been designed and manufactured would guarantee a quality product. But after he went out driving with some customers he understood what quality really meant. The customers would point out to him what they didn't like, maybe a little stumble or a slight hitch. He then understood that the customers' reaction was what refined quality, not only the refinement of gear-tooth cutting. So it was a great light dawning on our engineers when we started sending them out to go driving with customers on a routine basis."

David Hagen, general manager of Ford's Engine Division, observes, "The domestic automakers thought we knew exactly what the American customers wanted, and so we stopped asking. But in the 1970s, when

Toyota, Nissan, Mazda, and Honda were just entering our marketplace, they assumed we had an advantage over them because we had so many years of experience in dealing with our customers. The Japanese carmakers didn't know what the customers wanted, so they went out and asked them. Ironically, we had to learn from them that we must go out and ask the customers too. We can never assume that we already know."

Another eye-opener, rarely practiced by top-ranking Big Three executives, is now routine for Red Poling. When he's not on the road for business, he drives different types of cars—Ford's and the competition's—to and from the office. "It's the best way I know to spot the little things customers notice when they're behind the wheel," he states.

Of course, there is considerable risk when an automaker changes the style of a model, and it was particularly risky to introduce a radical design like Ford's new line of aerodynamic cars. While a newly designed car might be well accepted at the time of its introduction, its popularity must have longevity in order for the company to recoup the huge costs required to develop it. So it wasn't enough to evaluate a general collective consensus—the company had to find out what new products "leading-edge-style buyers" would want. These buyers are the kind of individuals who want to be the first on the block to own something new. To find out what will sell in the future—as far as ten years—group interviews were conducted with the "leading edgers" who were, in turn, questioned on very specific details. Tom Moulson of Ford's marketing research was the individual who devised methods to ask specific questions and, most important, to evaluate the responses of the interviewees. For example, opinions were solicited on what people thought about a hood cap, a headlight, the shape of a window, the angle of a mirror, or, perhaps, the visibility of a back window.

"We have a highly sophisticated way to ask certain questions of customers during research for new designs so that we can separate style progressives from other kinds of customers and consequently come up with different readings," Benton explains. "A style in this instance is a level of acceptance, and while it may start off with poor acceptance, it soon catches on, and over a long period of time, it peaks and then disappears. In this respect, it's like a long-term fad. Now, if everything goes right, at the time we're planning a car its acceptance is low, but by the time it comes out, it's on its way up the curve. We have to be careful not to bring it out at the top of the curve because, while first year sales would be great, we have to sell it for several years. As I mentioned, it's a very sophisticated concept, and it's come a long way since we started going out and asking Joe Blow, 'Do you like the looks of this car?' "

William Clay Ford, who served as chairman of the company's design committee, played an important role in the process of approving the aerodynamic styling. He was well aware that its radical look would have some initial resistance. "It's human nature to resist change," Ford points out. "People have a natural resistance to anything that's a radical departure—it makes their backs go up. We anticipated this reaction before we introduced our aerodynamic cars. But as our focus groups revealed, people thought it was a very pleasing look. So we knew these cars would take some getting used to, but the public would eventually accept them."

In 1982, a few months before the the new Thunderbird and Cougar were released, the company again conducted some focus groups in Marin and Santa Clara counties. These cars were designed based on what Ford had learned by listening to its customers. The response was wonderful. In effect, the Ford executives were told, "These cars look terrific, and if they are manufactured as well as they look and hold up in service, we'll consider Ford products again." These people also indicated they wanted to hear how good the cars were by word of mouth. Ford had lost its credibility and the consumer had little faith in the company's advertising.

Market share for the Thunderbird was so low in Marin County, the company gave away free three-day loaners to be test-driven by customers. High-profile people were selected to test-drive the Thunderbird. The loaner plan was simple. The car was delivered to the person's home, and the person could drive one car for a full week, or one model for three days and another one for the rest of the week. At such time, a Ford representative would pick it up. No dealers contacted the person because the company didn't want anyone to think he or she was being pressured to buy a car. The company wanted to learn what the consumer thought about the car (a questionnaire was completed), and it wanted the car to receive exposure. There were no strings attached. "Our objective was to create some interest in our products," explains Tom Wagner, vice-president and general manager of the Ford Division. "Our reputation was so poor we didn't think advertising would get people into a Ford dealership. Soon, for the first time in years, people in the community were talking about Ford. Somebody at a cocktail party, for instance, would say, 'You wouldn't believe the experience I had today. I went out and drove a new Thunderbird, and it is something I would never have anticipated coming from Ford. It's really a special car,' We felt this word-of-mouth campaign was more meaningful than all the advertising we could have run on television."

Goldfarb says, "Our objective was to get exposure. We wanted to get our cars into the neighborhoods, the airports, the golf clubs, the beaches, and the ski resorts where they'd be seen."

The car loaner program helped Ford turn things around in Marin County, where imported car sales exceeded 70 percent of the market share. Ten percent of those people who test-drove a Thunderbird bought one within a six-month period. The results were good enough to encourage Ford to repeat the program in other communities with the Tempo and later with the Taurus and Sable. Today, import car sales enjoy around 50 percent market share, but Ford is the top seller followed by Honda and General Motors. Ford and Lincoln-Mercury, which had a combined market share under 10 percent at the beginning of the decade in California, now can claim 24 percent.

Other focus groups were conducted to include dealers, who, like Ford executives, sat in the background to observe customers expressing opinions about everything from advertising to dealership servicing. Customers would be asked, "How are you treated by your dealer?" and dealers would hear replies such as, "Well, John Smith Ford screwed the hell out of me" and "It's impossible to get your car fixed right the first time in their shop." General comments ranged from complaints about impolite treatment by salespersons to dissatisfaction with the initial service experience. Dealers' reactions to focus group results were similar to those of Ford managers. Listening to customers got the message across far more effectively than reading reports of complaints.

"We made a concentrated effort to keep our dealers informed about our problems," Bob Rewey explains, "and they appreciated the fact we were leveling with them. We told them that the cars introduced in 1979 and 1980 had not been properly researched—in fact, some were never researched at all—and we were paying for our mistakes. We confessed to them that we had built cars for years that customers didn't want and even built more cars than they [the dealers] wanted. The cars were made the way Ford wanted them to be, and that's the way it had been for 70 years. But now the market has changed, and our dealers couldn't sell those cars. Just the same, we kept putting cars in their showrooms, and they were filled with eternal hope that the business would turn around. But the depression hit.

"They could see how the company was laying off people and closing plants to reduce costs," Rewey continues. "The dealers knew about the company's drop in market share, and they had firsthand experience with the stiff competition brought on by the Japanese automakers. Everyone realized there was enough blame to pass around to everyone; so it was agreed that instead of fighting among ourselves, we should work together to solve our mutual problems. To the credit of our Ford dealer organization, our dealers rallied behind the company."

Ford executives were told to "tell it like it is," even when the news was bad. At the 1980 national dealers council, Phil Caldwell gave it to his audience straight when he said, "Gentlemen, the reason we're in trouble today is because we haven't been giving the public an honest product, one with integrity. It's going to take us three years to turn it around, and we're committed to doing that. In the meantime, we're going to lose a lot of our net worth, but we believe we have enough to hang on. Our message to you [the dealers] is that we're going to lose some of the dealers, but if you can hang on, hang on, because the rewards will be there. For a while you may have to fend for yourself."

Harry Lum, in Independence, Ohio, and past president of the Lincoln-Mercury Dealers' Council, recalls Caldwell's speech. "It was the most direct and honest admission I ever heard an automobile executive make that the products were not timely and in keeping with what the public wanted. Because the product cycles are so long, we understood that it would take a minimum of three years before we'd have some competitive cars. There were 19 dealers present, and, while there was a feeling of despair, we knew he was exactly right. Our future and the company's future rested on what the product line would be like down the road. I was shaken up by what he said because everything I owned was invested in my business. If the dealership failed, they were going to come to take my furniture out of the house along with my kids' bicycles. But at the same time, I felt relieved to know Caldwell was telling it to us like it was."

Caldwell talked about the new Taurus program and its potential, but at the same time, he explained that the company was doing some drastic cost-cutting, and how much he appreciated the dealers' cooperation and support. The dealers expressed their concern about having high inventories at the end of the model year and how high carrying costs could hurt them. Caldwell gave his assurance that the company did a reasonable planning job and, in fact, there was not an overproduction. As things turned out, his assessment was correct.

"As vice-president of sales, I spent a lot of time with dealers in the early 1980s," Phil Benton recalls, "and it was saddening to see what these people were going through. Typically, an automobile dealer is highly leveraged, so when the bottom drops out, they don't have much of a reserve to fall back on. Some dealers came up to me with tears in their eyes, expressing how their life savings were going down the drain. Some were hostile and others were frightened. They'd corner me at dealers' affairs and plead, 'What can you do to save me?' That's how desperate they were. At world headquarters, you'd see some short tempers, but out there, you'd see desperation."

In the past, Ford dealers were invited to attend meetings in Detroit, and there were district and regional conferences at which top officers addressed large groups of dealers. As one dealer remembers, "They were like kings. They'd come in and everyone was expected to bow down to them. They'd speak to us from a podium in some rented theater or hotel ballroom, and their limousines would rush them back to the airport and they'd take off in their private jets."

Another Ford dealer recalls when Iacocca came to his city: "The regional sales manager always had a box of his favorite cigars waiting for him in his hotel suite. He was surrounded by an entourage of people, so I could never get close enough to him for a personal conversation. He'd deliver a speech, mention that he had to be in another city later that afternoon, and they'd whisk him out of there."

"Prior to the 1970s, Ford representatives were dictatorial, and even up to the 1980s, they were 'Big Daddy,'" notes Harry Lum. "They told us what they wanted us to do, and it was a one-way conversation. We did what we were told. Under the auspices of Iacocca, there was a lot of show and little substance. When gas was cheap, we were selling big cars like there was no tomorrow. The company's attitude was, 'Hey, we're bullet-proof, and we don't have to listen to anyone. We're operating at full capacity and selling everything we can build.' The sad thing was that I would sell a car and knew when it was delivered that I'd see it back in two weeks for repair. I was remanufacturing cars after I delivered them! While I was reimbursed under the warranty by Ford, the customer who buys a new car doesn't want to have to bring it back for reassembly. The quality control was in the hands of the customer when the company should have taken care of it before the customer got it."

The new regime was different and the dealers started to take notice. The long-winded speeches were replaced with short talks followed by lengthy question-and-answer sessions. "In 1980, we knew it was going to take several years, and it wouldn't be until 1984 or 1985 when we'd have appealing cars for our dealers to sell," says Ross Roberts, vice-president and general manager of the Lincoln-Mercury Division. "So during those bad days, we talked to our dealers about the future. I mean, back in 1981 and 1982, we had nothing. Zilch! We kept asking them to sell the same bad cars that put many of their friends [other Ford dealers] out of business and had put many of them on the brink of bankruptcy. It was tough because all we could talk about was our dedication to the future. We'd show them some brief sneak previews of what was coming down the road, which was just enough to whet their appetites. Yet, the vast majority had confidence in us and said they were only here because they believed we would have the product."

Ford's dealers believed in the company because, for the first time, they were given the hard, cold facts and when they asked questions, they got straightforward answers. It impressed them to see top executives like Petersen, Poling, Ross, and Benton travel across the country, taking time out to speak to groups of dealers, and, most important, to listen to what they had to say. This new breed of Ford executives always carried notepads in their breast pockets, and they wrote down inquiries and complaints. Then, after they returned to their offices in Dearborn, they'd follow up. It wasn't always what a dealer wanted to hear, but the response was prompt. The top brass routinely visited out-of-town dealerships whenever their hectic schedules allowed it.

Ford representatives at the district level worked daily with dealers, giving advice on the right cars to carry and in the right quantities. The district offices worked closely with dealers on promotions, introduced expense controls, and helped in the hiring and firing of people. "The district also had the responsibility of making sure morale was up," Tom Wagner points out. "This, of course, was the most difficult task because many of them had their lives on the line. We didn't want anyone to give in to the pressures of the day and be dragged down to the point where he couldn't function."

Wagner notes that the turnover of dealerships occurred mostly at the bottom half of the organization. "It's always been like this during the tough times. The top half is fairly stable and they were able to weather it. The number of Ford dealers in the United States dropped from 5,500 in 1980 to today's 4,500. There are 850 Lincoln-Mercury dealers, down from around 900, and about half of them own a Ford dealership, too. In most cases, we didn't replace the dealers we lost because our volume per dealership is significantly higher. While there were some dealers who decided to retire during this period, for the most part it was survival of the fittest, and our present dealers are better businesspeople than those who failed. Consequently, we sell more cars per dealership today."

When the quality of Ford products improved and the new Fords were able to compete in the market, its dealerships began to realize sizable profits. "I got a lot smarter when our products were accepted in the market," Lum says. "Today, I'm making a lot of money with my Ford and Lincoln-Mercury dealerships, and I'm losing a lot of money with my Oldsmobile dealership. I'm applying the same business principles. So why am I so smart with the two and so dumb with the one? The fact is my success is closely tied in to product acceptance, and the manufacturers control that."

But product acceptance is also affected by quality service. In the past, American consumers had to accept inferior service. Typically when an individual purchased a new car, he drove it for a few weeks and jotted down everything that wasn't right about it. When it was time for the first checkup, he'd come back to the dealership with his "laundry list" of problems. A discriminating customer might have two dozen or so things that needed to be repaired. When his list was presented to the service manager, the two of them would haggle over what items were legitimate complaints. If a customer didn't like a paint discolorment, for example, he might be told, "Don't worry about it, nobody will notice it. If we try to touch it up, it's liable to look worse." If the complaint was about a squeaky door, the serviceman might say, "Don't worry, you'll get used to it. All the doors on this model squeak a little. Besides, there's nothing we can do about it." After some horse trading, the service manager would whittle down the list and repair only a small number of the customer's problems.

The word *mottainai* plays an important role in the Japanese culture. Its definition is "all things are precious, and to waste is a sin." Japan has a population density of 318 people per square kilometer, about 15 times that of the United States. To succeed, Japanese companies must offer extraordinary service. Those companies that do not, are doomed to fail. It is common for an automobile salesman in Japan to call a customer when it's time to have a tune-up. He will pick up the car at the customer's house in the morning, have it serviced, and return it that evening. Although many American companies are fond of using the slogan "The customer is king," for the most part it is only lip service. In Japan, people refer to the customer as *Kami-sama*, or God.

Not every Japanese company excels in service. But the ones that do are far more successful, particularly in the highly competitive automobile industry—when as recently as the 1960s, there were ten automobile manufacturers in Japan. The most successful of these companies—Toyota,

Nissan, Honda, and Mazda—expanded their market and came to America. And when they came, they served their American customers with the same commitment extended in their homeland.

With an acute awareness of the Japanese automobile invasion, Ford management knew well that quality products had to be coupled with quality service. Company employees and dealers have become acutely aware of the potential value of a single customer. It is a constant goal to convert each new sale into a long-term relationship. The sale of one car represents a single transaction, but a satisfied customer who buys a Ford product may mean several hundred thousand dollars in future business. In addition to repeat sales, a satisfied customer will generate word-of-mouth advertising, referring many relatives and friends to the Ford family. "When you consider that it costs several hundred dollars in advertising expenses just to get a single customer to take a demonstration ride," says Ross Roberts, "it's essential to take very good care of every customer. Note, too, that a satisfied customer will tell 8 people and a dissatisfied customer will tell 20 people."

In the past, service departments rarely provided anything other than repair work. For years, the emphasis had been placed on the selling effort at the dealership level; the service end of the business was a neglected stepchild.

"When we made our 'Quality is Job One' commitment," explains Phil Benton, "it had to be followed up with the same commitment to service. This was a natural sequence because, while a company may sell a quality product, the customer will only be satisfied when he's treated properly during the entire ownership cycle. It boils down to people perceiving that they're receiving value for the money they're spending. The person who ultimately determines the acceptability of our cars and trucks is the customer—the person who turns the key and starts the engine and drives to work every day, and to the kids' soccer game, and to the theater, and back again. While it's certainly not a new thought, one that we've come to appreciate as being so critical is that *the customer is always right.*"

In 1982, Quality Care (QC) was formed. QC is a series of programs designed to help dealers improve the level of customer satisfaction throughout the ownership cycle. To help implement the program, Dick Lockridge, a Boston consulting firm, was hired and consequently established Partners in Customer Satisfaction, a program in which the company and its dealers would put more emphasis on taking care of customers *after the sale.* Under the QC umbrella, the education training program was put into gear, a program in which dealers, salespeople, and service technicians could enroll in courses to improve their skills in customer relations. Ford dealerships have had an estimated 25,000 people receive training from this program. Other programs were also set up to educate service-people in today's rapidly changing automobile technology.

Another QC program is the On-Line Automotive Service Information System (OASIS). OASIS helps the service technician at a dealership to diagnose difficult service problems quickly and accurately in a way that would have seemed like science fiction only a decade or two ago. Today, a service technician transmits a vehicle's symptom and identification number to the main OASIS computer in Dearborn through a telephone-linked terminal in the service area, and seconds later, a printout is produced with an index of available technical data, listing probable causes and the latest repair information specific to that vehicle's particular problem. To further assist service technicians, a service bay diagnostic system makes it possible to connect a computer in Detroit to the car's instrument panel and to get a readout of the solution. Coming up in the near future is a devise similar to a flight recorder used for an airplane, whereby a module will be inserted in a car to record problems not detected at the time of service. The car operator only has to turn on a switch and when he returns to the service department the problem can be diagnosed.

Ford now has a service loaner program that provides customers with free service loaner vehicles during the times their cars are being repaired. To encourage dealers to participate in this program, the company shares in a portion of the cost.

As the quality of cars continued to improve, Ford introduced broader warranties; for example, in late 1985, a 60-month/60,000-mile power train transmission and engine warranty was brought out. A lifetime service guarantee was also made available to Ford customers. This contract provides free parts and labor if the same repair must be repeated during the lifetime of the car. Excluded are wear items ranging from brake pads to windshield wiper blades.

A new emphasis was put on outstanding service of all types. Attention was given to making sure customers received a friendly greeting when entering a showroom, that they were not kept waiting for service, and that repairs were made on schedule. One nicety that every customer receives today is a free full tank of gasoline with the purchase of a new car. A small touch, yet one that sets the tone for what can be expected.

Taking care of customers *after* the sale has made a significant difference. Each year since 1980 customer satisfaction has increased, and at a considerably higher rate than the rest of the industry. A 1988 survey of

Ford customers shows that, when recording things gone wrong per 100 vehicles, since 1980 there has been a 67 percent reduction for cars and a 70 percent reduction for trucks. "We must realize that customer acceptance of our products isn't simply a matter of the fewest things gone wrong," Benton emphasizes, "but, rather, the most things gone right."

One of the most innovative and best-received selling concepts is Ford's price-point merchandising, the brainchild of marketing vice-president Bob Rewey. In brief, by purchasing a car in a dealer's showroom instead of with unusual options, the customer receives a substantial reduction in price. The showroom packages consist of the most common options, and the cars come in a variety of colors. What's more, the customer doesn't have to wait for a custom-made car to be built. It's a blessing to the dealer, too: No longer is a large inventory of, say, 45 Thunderbirds required, all having different equipment and prices. Instead, for example, a dealer might carry three different packages, each consisting of 15 Thunderbirds, identical except in color. The company's image has also improved by price-point merchandising because fewer stripped-down vehicles (known as "stripos") are sold. And not only does the customer drive a car with more options and in the process receive more enjoyment, his trade-in value is increased because the car is fully loaded. Here too, the dealer benefits because the traded-in car is easier to sell than the stripo.

The salesperson benefits too. He or she doesn't have to become familiar with every car in inventory with an endless combination of optional equipment. The salesperson can also make a better presentation because he or she is more familar with how every piece of equipment in the package works.

Price-point merchandising is a radical departure from the traditional manner in which domestically made automobiles have been custom ordered in the United States. While custom-ordered cars are still available, most buyers realize the advantage of purchasing a car already in inventory. Today only 15 percent of all Fords sold are on a custom-order basis. As a result of higher repeatability on the assembly line, this manufacturing approach also results in improved quality and productivity.

Point-price merchandising can make particular option packages available in certain parts of the country. For instance, in California people wanted an Escort with a rear window defroster because this feature came as standard equipment with most of the imported cars. Styled steel wheels are popular in California and are consequently included in the "Western States" package. "In the New York City area, people don't want cars with flashy exteriors to drive into the city," Rewey explains, "they would rather have a stereo sound system inside and forget about the clear coat paint. Again, by talking to our customers around the country, we make cars that they want, not what we want to sell to them."

Ford dealers can also locate a particular car that they don't have in their own inventory via a computer program that gives them access to the central system in Detroit. Acting as a clearinghouse, the company maintains precise records of all daily sales and thereby can track what is available across the country at any given time. A dealer who has a request for a red Mustang GT with certain equipment is able to get a readout on his computer terminal of all such cars in inventory at all other dealers' locations. Once the car is located, the two dealers horse-trade and the car is transported to the buyer. The customer also benefits from this service because the exact car he or she wants becomes available.

"By automating our communications with our dealers," explains Wray Haack, director of marketing systems and communications, "we were able to streamline our process for distributing our product and scheduling orders. At present, there are approximately 90 people working in our customer support center who handle and process dealer inquiries on the status of their orders. The center also provides dealers with data pertaining to accounting, inventories, and warranty claims. Back in the early 1980s when Phil Benton and Red Poling approved the project, its $5 million price tag seemed expensive; however, not only has the service to our dealers and customers improved tremendously but the realized annual savings is in excess of $400 million."

Once management was assured that its products and services were indeed substantially improved, the consensus was that it would be appropriate to send this message to the public via its advertising. Doug McClure, who served as the Ford Division's advertising manager from 1979 until being named corporate advertising director in 1984, recalls, "It was difficult to advertise our cars when I first became advertising manager because we had lost credibility; but by 1984, our quality had vastly improved and we finally had a story to tell. Of course, we couldn't very well have our message say, 'Boy did we make a lot of bad products up until now, but we reformed and have taken a pledge not to drink anymore.' Instead, we simply said, 'Have you driven a Ford lately?' Through our advertising focus groups we were confident this message was a good one. We learned that we couldn't just say, 'Have you driven a Ford?' because everyone has driven a Ford. But 'Have you driven a Ford *lately?*' had the message we wanted to get across."

Ford has a three-tiered advertising program consisting of the company, the dealer association, and the dealer. Simply put, the company's message says, "When you are in the market for a car, consider a Ford," and it tells why a customer should do so. At the dealer association level, local dealers pool their money with a central fund that is supplemented with additional funds provided by the company. Here the message is "Now is the time to buy a Ford." The individual dealer's message is "Buy a Ford from me and here is where I am located." Because each dealer is in competition with other Ford dealers, this level of advertising might stress such things as dealer rebates, exceptional service, or perhaps special financing.

Unlike much of the advertising by other automakers, Ford rarely knocks the competition. "By mentioning a competitor in one of our ads," John Vanderzee, the Ford Division's advertising manager, says, "we provide them with free exposure. It also acknowledges the competition to be in the same league. Furthermore, I think many people today frown upon taking digs at the other guy."

Vanderzee also points out that Ford advertising rarely uses a "borrowed interest" to promote its products. "We don't use celebrities to endorse our cars," he states, "instead, we want the car to be the star. Here too, today's consumers know that Joe Schmo will say anything if he's paid for it, so we don't use testimonial advertising. Sure, we did in the past and in fact, with the combination of Farrah Fawcett and a cougar our Lincoln-Mercury ads were terrific. But that was before Farrah became a star, and today, it wouldn't have the same effect. Then too, we feel there's enough interest in our new car products today that we don't really need the borrowed interest. The car stands on its own."

One individual who appears to be an unlikely candidate to hold a senior management position with a giant industrial corporation is Joe Kordick. His first day on the job, in April 1985, after becoming general manager of the Parts and Service Division, he spoke on closed-circuit television via satellite to thousands of employees in his division: "The most important thing in my life is my relationship with God. I love you very much. I sense that there are a lot of people out there who are hurting. I just want you to know there's now a guy sitting in the corner office, who would be willing to help you in anyway I can."

Joe Kordick does not hesitate to pull out his Bible during a high-level meeting or to let troubled employees know that both his office and his checkbook are always open to them. "The Japanese philosophy about business is very basic," he says. "They don't have a lot of natural resources, so they must think long term. They don't worry about short-term profits or about meeting the demands by Wall Street for higher stock prices. Instead, the Japanese concentrate on meeting customers' needs. With our Judeo-Christian ethic in America, we should know more about loving our fellow human beings than anyone else in the world. Yet we had to go to Japan to find out how to take care of our employees and customers. But to our credit, Ford, as well as some other American companies, were able to recognize there was a better way, and fortunately we did something about it. The company had to lose an unbelievable amount of money and prestige to finally get back down to the grass roots and start listening to the customer and producing quality cars. It was no easy matter to turn a company's culture around, however. I think what Ford did during the first five years of the 1980s is analogous to taking the *Queen Mary* through the Panama Canal, stopping her, and turning her around 180 degrees. It's incredible but we changed the entire process, and, frankly, I don't think Ford will ever go back to its old ways."

Not only does Kordick tell employees that he loves them, but he tells them to love customers. "I believe that love is a legitimate business strategy," he insists, and refers to the Bible when Apostle Paul spoke to the Christians about how love is not listening to bad things but being willing to trust others. "For five years I told dealers that we have to trust each other, and I told them that it has to start with me since I was the guy who administered the warranty policy. In this position, I had the power to change how customers were handled when they came back with a problem about their car. For years, the company operated a system designed to protect us from getting ripped off by the customer. This meant that we did business with our customers on the premise that they weren't trustworthy. So when there was any adjudication of a warranty claim, the company would refuse it, and rather than the dealer eating the cost, he'd pass it back to the customer by being less benevolent and less caring.

"Well, I contended it wasn't good business and we should build around the majority of our customers who are good, honest people. To change the system, we told our dealers, 'We will open the gates to you. There will be no more hassling over claims and we're not even going to audit you. We will even give you some money to hand out to customers at your own discretion.'

"Once this new way was in place, the dealers treated customers with a different attitude, which was 'I trust you.' In effect, a dealer saying, 'If you come in and tell me that your engine has blown, and you did everything according to the owner's manual to take care of it, I believe you.' Of course, if there is some overriding circumstance that suggested the customer isn't being truthful, the claim is denied. It naturally took a lot of cultural adjustment to implement this new way of handling customers, and some dealers have not changed. But the majority have.

"Will customers rip us off by treating them this way? Of course, it's inevitable that some people will try to take advantage. But will we increase customer loyalty, repeat sales, market share, and bottom line? I think this is inevitable, too. My point is that a company should not alienate the majority of its customers to save a few dollars on a small deceitful minority."

Ford reserves warranty and policy funds that are used to compensate a dealer for the cost of a borderline claim. "Under the old way," Kordick explains, "a customer who came in after 18 months and complained about a broken door handle was told, 'Sorry, but your 12 months is up.' But to a customer, it didn't make any sense for a door handle to break after 18 months. Today, at the discretion of the dealer, the customer might be told, 'It really isn't covered, but we will take care of it for you.' Each dealer is allocated x amount of money based on a formula with his car sales, and it's up to him how he uses the money because he knows his customers better than we do. When this was first initiated, there were certain members of management (who shall remain nameless) who accused me of having an open checkbook policy in this department. However, our budgets are tightly controlled, and we haven't engaged in a profligate spending spree. The dealers are prudent about it and are delighted with the confidence placed in them. Consequently, they have exerted a strong effort on their peers to make sure they don't ruin it by ripping off the company. As a safeguard, our computers print out average performances, and if a dealer is far out of line, we'll meet with him and point out the disparities. We don't make any accusations, however, because it could be a legitimate situation whereby the dealership has sold a large number of a particular car with a specific problem."

Kordick points out that Rich's Department Store in Atlanta has had a no-questions-asked policy with returns for years. "A customer might bring back a pair of shoes that are three years old and complain they didn't wear well. So Rich's gives them a new pair of shoes. Not only does this create exceptional goodwill, but the vast majority of people don't take advantage of the store. What happens is that a business eventually sheds itself of the bad customers—they don't feel comfortable doing what they want to do so they go elsewhere."

In early 1988, an angry woman called Kordick to complain that her dealer refused to pay for a valve job for her 1977 Maverick with 280,000 miles on it. "Why would you expect us to pay for an 11-year-old car with so many miles on it?" Kordick asked.

"Well, I had a 1964 Falcon that had 350,000 miles and I never put a nickel in it," the woman said.

Kordick thought to himself, "I will do unto her as I expect her to do unto me, and I said to myself that I would never have made the call." He pauses and adds, "I would like to have a happy ending to this story, but I didn't help her because her expectations were unrealistic. This is the only time the golden rule breaks down."

At a conference consisting of Ford's top 400 executives and their spouses held in Tucson in 1988, Kordick made a speech that will probably be talked about for years. He was one of the last speakers to address the audience who had attended the three-day session and knew that it would take something special to capture its attention. "I could see people were growing restless and as I approached the podium I kept thinking of something I could do to keep them from falling asleep. So I said, 'It's loving and caring time. Everybody on your feet.' I glanced over at Petersen and Poling and thought to myself, 'Oh well, it's only a career, so here goes.'

" 'Now everybody hug the person next to you.' Absolute chaos ensued. But when they sat down, they listened very carefully about what I had to say about being a customer-driven company."

Red Poling recalls the incident and adds, "Everyone was startled and surprised. But then they did it. Joe's one of the few people who can get away with that."

In January 1989, after 34 years with the company, at age fifty-seven, Kordick again did the unexpected. A devout Methodist, who once considered being a minister, Joe Kordick retired. Joe Kordick, a poor Czechoslovakian kid from a Chicago ghetto, walked away from a vice-president's title and a $500,000 salary and bonus to work for free in a hospice in Stuart, Florida. In this capacity, he is one of 38 members who are assigned to dying patients at the Martin County Hospice. "I've always had a great desire to serve society outside the economic milieu, where I can honestly say I'm working for nothing," he says. "I remember how my mother died, and I wanted to help others so they didn't have to go through what she did."

Lee Miskowski, who succeeded Kordick as head of the Parts and Service Division, shares his predecessor's views on how to treat customers: "Two things we repeatedly stress to our dealers are 'Take care of the customer, because it's the right thing to do,' and 'It makes a lot of business sense to do so.' "

In 1985, Ford started Quality Commitment-Performance (QC-P), an owner follow-up communications program in which customers let the company know their thoughts about their vehicle and dealership on an ongoing basis. This is achieved by a 30-day customer survey, a 12-month customer survey, as well as in-between surveys conducted semimonthly and monthly. The company furnishes quarterly reports to provide dealers with feedback on what levels of customer satisfaction they have achieved. The reports rate dealers' performances on a scale of zero to ten. "QC-P is more than a device to measure dealers," Miskowski explains, "it helps dealers and the company improve the sales and service efforts because excellent feedback is provided."

QC-P surveys reveal that customers who are completely satisfied with the handling of service complaints have a 71 percent loyalty rate, meaning that they expressed their intent to purchase another Ford product. Those who feel the handling of their complaints is acceptable express a 54 percent loyalty rate, and those who are dissatisfied show only a 22 percent loyalty rate. These numbers indicate how important good service really is. "A company can engineer in all the quality in the world and the quality circle teams at the manufacturing plant can do the same thing," notes Bob Rewey. "But if the vehicle isn't sold and serviced properly, the customer doesn't separate out who let him down. For instance, if a customer purchases a brand new Town Car and on his way home from the dealership his radio doesn't work and his power windows are defective, he's not concerned about whose fault it is. To him, it was Ford that failed him."

As a major incentive for dealers to attain a high QC-P rating, Red Poling founded the President's Award. The prestige associated with the President's Award is on a par with a supplier achieving a Q1 rating. Each district is divided into three groups consisting of large-, medium-, and small-size dealerships, and the top dealer in terms of customer satisfaction becomes a President's Award winner for that group.

"The more sales volume a dealership does, the harder it is to score high marks for customer satisfaction," explains Richard Strauss, who owns a large Ford dealership in Richmond, Virginia. "The dealers in the small group outscore the rest of us for two reasons. First, when volume is low, a dealer can give more personal attention to each customer. Second, a low-volume dealer in a small town personally knows the majority of his customers, so even when somebody is a little unhappy, he or she is reluctant to complain. In a large dealership, you can do 600 cars a week, and even with a 98 percent customer satisfaction, there are 12 people who are mad at you that week. In my business, we work six teams of mechanics and each team has an assistant service manager. We do everything we can to make our customers happy, but with such large numbers, there are always some who will be disenchanted with the service, or the price they had to pay for it, or the time it takes to perform it. Of course, we're working hard to continually improve, and while there are 30 dealers in my group in my district, my people are working hard to win the President's Award."

In addition to the actual award, the awardee receives a lot of publicity throughout the Ford organization as well as in his or her local community. It's a wonderful tool to use in sales promotion. Each year, President's Award recipients are invited to attend an annual black-tie affair held for a few days at a fine resort. In 1988, out of a combined total of 5,700 dealerships, an elite group of 119 Ford and Lincoln-Mercury dealers and their spouses attended an all-expense paid President's Award conference in Tucson, Arizona.

Perhaps no dealership exemplifies being cutomer driven better than Tasca Lincoln-Mercury in Seekonk, Massachusetts. The Tasca dealership, operated by Bob Tasca and his three sons, Bob, Jr., Carl, and David, are living proof that outstanding service pays off. The Tasca operation, a large-volume dealership, has qualified for the President's Award for an unprecedented four consecutive years. While Seekonk is a small town of 9,000, its marketing area has a population of about 450,000; and while Lincoln-Mercury's U.S. market share is 7 percent, the Tasca dealership captures 15 percent.

What's their secret? "Sales opens the door to service," explains Bob Tasca, Sr., "and service keeps it open to sales." At the Tasca dealership, this is more than a clever slogan. The dealership has 16 salespeople, and it employs 49 servicepeople, split into two shifts, working from 7:00 A.M. to midnight and all day on Saturday. "My eldest son, Bob, Jr., is the president of our company," Tasca says, "and he's in charge of QC-P. So the commitment is from the top down. We budget $100 for each car to make sure the customer is happy. This means we'll replace tires, repaint cars, *replace* cars—whatever it takes to make the customer happy, we do. I've discovered that with a happy customer, the chances are better than 90 percent that he'll come back and buy again, but with an unhappy one, the percentage is less than 20 percent. So by making customers happy, we guarantee our future."

Tasca, who started in the business as a mechanic and also developed performance race cars, hasn't forgotten his roots. "I can take a car apart and put it back together again, and I've trained my three sons to do it, too. We know the cars, inside out, backward, and from top to bottom. We're successful because we know our product and how to fix it. I believe it's better to build a better product going in than to build a mediocre product going in and then trying to buy loyalty after the sale. To accomplish this as a dealer, we give our customers a car that doesn't have any problems, to eliminate the cost factor. On a scale of 1 to 10, we take cars that are a 6, and we'll work on them so they're a 9.5 before we deliver them to our customers.

"We're fanatics in preparation. There's no company in the world that knows how to build a car better than I can deliver to the customer after I get through with it. Say a car comes in to me with a margin anywhere from 2.5 millimeters to 9 millimeters in the way the door fits, you know, the space between the door and the body. It may be a 6- or 7-millimeter gap on the top and 2 millimeters at the bottom. The match is not right, and the pieces don't look like they match each other. The doors don't close easily, or they have to be slammed. I don't care what it is, if the car doesn't satisfy me, we're going to work on it until it does. We prepare our cars so they're better than anything on the road. When we're through with a car, its TGW [things gone wrong] is three times better than the best of any automobile manufacturer in the world. For every four cars we sell, only one comes back for a defect in 90 days."

Tasca's service technicians are paid on a team basis, and all earn considerably more than the going rate for mechanics in the area. "We pay them bonuses based on our earnings, and we earn more than other dealerships. Contrary to what some dealers must obviously think, excelling in the area of customer satisfaction doesn't take away from the bottom line, it adds to the bottom line," Tasca declares. "Incidentally, their bonuses are based on QC-P."

Tasca claims that his dealership spends about $225 to prep each car, and it's money well spent. "There's no end to what we will do to make a customer happy," he says. "We've *got* to make the customer happy. Right now, I estimate we have a 99 percent loyalty factor, which is probably the best in the world. Still, we continue to push ourselves—we want to do better."

Today, it seems natural for customers to be treated well. What is most interesting, however, is how Ford employees who have no direct contact with dealers or consumers treat other people within the company as customers. Morgan Whitney, who heads Ford's robotic center, comments, "Our work here at the center encompasses such things as robotics, machine vision, simulation, artificial intelligence, and integrated manufacturing, all of which we do for operations. In fact, the center's whole purpose is to develop manufacturing technologies to improve productivity and better ways to make quality products. Just as it is stated in the guiding principles that dealers and suppliers are our partners, we, too, at the robotic center are partners with operations who also happen to be our customers."

"An interesting phenomenon has happened here," explains James Bakken, retired vice-president of quality. "Today, when we talk about quality at Ford, we're not just talking about cars and trucks but about every process having an output [product] that goes to someone. This means, that within the company, there are internal customers. And each individual seeks to deliver a quality product to his or her customer. For example, a designer's product goes to an engineer, and an engineer's product to a manufacturing person and the manufacturing person's product goes to the marketing person. Similarly, public affairs people have internal customers, and so do the accountants, the attorneys, and so on. With this mind-set, everyone strives to produce a quality product and everyone is customer driven."

COMMUNICATION— A TWO-WAY STREET

I n the mid–1970s, a Ford plant manager was thinking about giving a state-of-the-plant speech to his employees. As a matter of routine, he ran his idea past the head of the accounting department. "With fringes, we're paying an average cost of $20 an hour," protested the accountant. "If it takes an hour from the time they stop the line, assemble, hear your speech, and get back on the job, that's a total of 5,000 hours, and at $20 that's 100 grand." The speech was never given.

In sharp contrast, during the months of August and September 1988, a series of two-hour meetings was conducted at every Ford plant in North America—no one calculated how many production hours were lost nor did anyone put a price tag on how much it cost. These meetings were jointly conducted by Ford managers and UAW leaders, each focusing on what could be done so the company could maintain its competitive lead. The workers were told, "We made a great comeback, and we've had record earnings, but being on top is being a moving target. There's always somebody behind us trying to knock us off. There's no room to feel comfortable; to keep our momentum going will require everyone's support." Following each speech, small group meetings were conducted during which time people were solicited for their ideas.

There was a time when a manager would issue an order: "This is what I want you to do. Just do what I say. I've got to get my production out of the door." Direct and concise orders were believed to be the best form of communication—and it was always one-way communication.

Today, promotions in the plant are given to those individuals who possess people skills as well as proficiency in the manufacturing process. During a rap session at the Executive Development Center, when Petersen was asked what he thought were important leadership qualities, he replied, "Communication skills are crucial, and I mean in both directions—not only to have the ability to articulate, both in writing and orally, but to listen."

Developing an awareness of the need to communicate is the most crucial challenge, particularly in an organization with 370,000 people scattered around the globe. In retrospect, the manager who allowed himself to be talked out of making a state of the plant speech could very well have had the communication skills to give it. What was lacking, however, was a corporate culture that placed a high enough value on communicating to justify its cost. The difficulty at Ford was compounded by nearly eight decades of corporate culture that advocated an autocratic style of management.

Today, high-ranking executives and scores of managers carry the "Mission, Values, and Guiding Principles" card in their suit pockets, and it is also common to see enlarged framed cards hanging on office walls. But, explains Peter Pestillo, vice-president of employee and external affairs, "The one flaw about our MVGP card is that it's just a card. Until what's on that card is executed hourly and daily, we don't have anything. Just having people carrying it around doesn't prove anything. If they have to read it, we've got a problem with it. So while it's fine for a company to have its mission, values, and guiding principles on paper, until people are applying those fine ideals in their daily work, they are meaningless."

To bring about a culture change required a concentrated effort to communicate throughout the organization. Yet implementing effective communication, particularly in the case of Ford, required a simultaneous change in its culture. One could not happen without the other.

"An autocratic management system predominated at Ford during the first 20 or so years that I worked here," explains Phil Benton. "The old Ford Motor Company was top down, drive-it-down-through-the-system, and promoted a don't-ask-anyone-for-his-opinion treatment of people. We knew there was a better way, but we never chose to do anything about it. The catalyst for our change in management style was unquestionably the horrific downswing we experienced."

Caldwell, Petersen, and Poling recognized the need to get in the trenches with the troops, and they willingly made the rounds to visit Ford facilities across America, meeting with plant managers, UAW leaders, and plant workers. They did the same with dealers and suppliers. And they did it in a manner that took everyone by surprise. They were straightforward in presenting the facts; they talked about the painstaking need to cut costs and how it would necessiate closing plants and reducing the work force. They also stressed quality and how everyone must work together as a team so that the company could once again prosper. And they listened.

Therein lies the real difference. When they communicated, they asked for comments and ideas, and when the workers spoke out to express their thoughts, managers followed up with quick responses that kindled still more actions. Other managers were prompted to emulate what they saw senior managers do. Within time, managers at all levels of the company began to communicate more freely and frequently with subordinates.

This is not to suggest that senior managers had never visited a Ford factory. During the early years of his career, Henry I spent a major portion of his time on the plant floor, developing and then attempting to perfect his mass production theories. There were also many occasions when Henry II made the rounds. But these were Fords, and it was their company. Each, in his time, was the most celebrated business personality in America. Each was a larger-than-life figure. As one old-time employee recalls, "When either of the Fords visited a plant it was as though the whole world stopped."

It was not unusual for employees to seek their autographs and take photographs of the Fords. A stop at a company facility by either grandfather or grandson was a major event that was more than likely to be treated as a publicity tour than a visit by a CEO. Nobody dared to approach them nor would anyone make an attempt to ask a sensitive question. And except for the two Fords, it was considered an unwise and even dangerous practice to have senior executives available at the plants. It would risk having employees approach them and ask for something. "As a consequence, there was a long history when no high-ranking executive walked the shop floors," explains Peter Pestillo, "and because we stayed out of the plants, we didn't know the business."

Those who worked closely with Caldwell on the 12th floor of the Glass House sometimes describe him as a stuffed shirt, but whenever he walked the plant floors he was an excellent communicator. One senior manager comments, "It's interesting how the hourly people loved Philip, and in part, that's because they didn't know him. The salaried people who got to know him felt differently. The general rule was that the more you knew him, the less you liked him. It wasn't that he was disagreeable, inconsiderate, or unpleasant. He simply never seemed to relax and let his hair down."

In any case, Caldwell's willingness to get out of the Glass House and communicate with Ford people on the plant floor was a significant contribution to the company's turnaround. Perhaps he deserves even more credit because to mingle among crowds of people—and, in particular, working people—didn't come naturally for him. Nonetheless, he did it, and Caldwell himself says that, in time, he enjoyed this facet of his executive duties.

Caldwell recalls an incident when he attended the opening of a new automatic transmission plant in 1981 in Batavia, Ohio: "Even though we were closing down plants, we had to build this one for smaller cars because we couldn't convert any of the existing plants that made the big transmissions. I made a speech to the plant workers about quality and challenged, 'I'm waiting for the first time somebody tells me to stop the line because the quality isn't right.'

"After the official ceremony, I happened to be walking by myself in the plant and a worker approached me and said, 'Hey buster, come over here.' I walked over to him and he said, 'I hear you talk a lot about quality. Would you like to know what really goes on in this plant about quality?'

" 'Yes, tell me about it,' I replied.

" 'Well, in spite of all the talk about quality, when two o'clock in the afternoon comes rolling around, and if we're short on our count and we have to ship that day, the foreman tells us to ship what we've got, even if it's a bad part.'

" 'That's not the way it ought to be done,' I said, 'and the next time anyone tells you to release anything that you know isn't right, you call me personally.'

" 'I'm sure he thought what I said was just talk, but about six months later, I got a letter from him. It read, 'Do you remember our conversation? Things are different in the plant now. We don't ship it anymore if it isn't right.' "

In 1982, Caldwell visited the Chicago Stamping Plant. "I met with these big bruiser-type guys whose EI group had come up with a packaging suggestion that saved us about a half million dollars a year," he says. "I listened to them explain how their idea had been implemented and what it had meant to the company. These men were obviously very proud of what they had accomplished, but I became somewhat suspicious when the group's leader said, 'Now we've got one for you.' When I heard that, I figured he was going to say, 'Okay, now where is the handout?'

"Instead, he said, 'There are five or six other plants that are doing what we used to do. What we'd like to know is how can we make sure that they'll do it our new way so those plants can start to save money, too.' It's feedback like this that made it all worthwhile."

While Caldwell isn't a particularly good orator, he is candid, and his sincerity worked in his favor. A prime example of his ability to tell things as they are happened at a high-level meeting with the UAW at the Dearborn Inn. "That morning, just before the meeting, some news prematurely leaked out," Caldwell recalls, "and the *Detroit Free Press* was in possession of a headline announcement telling how Ford had plans to build a new engine plant in Mexico. The article stressed how the company chose to manufacture in Mexico rather than in Cleveland where we already had two big engine plants. The bottom line was that more American workers would become unemployed. This is not the kind of news that promotes goodwill in Detroit, and especially with the UAW leaders to whom I had to speak that morning.

"Well, the only thing I could do was to start the meeting by telling them why we were going to build big engines in Mexico," Caldwell continues. "So I began by explaining the facts of life to them. 'We're dealing with a sovereign nation,' I emphasized, 'and in their country, they are the ones who establish the rules. They tell us that we make a lot of parts and that they sell a lot of those parts for Fords that are assembled in Mexico. Recently we were told that in the future, if we wanted to sell our cars in Mexico, we'd have to equip them with engines built in Mexico. If we didn't like it, we could leave.'

"Then I told the union leaders, 'That's the way of the world.' Naturally they didn't like it, but at least they understood it. When this sort of thing happened in the past, nobody ever bothered to explain what was going on to them. They can understand the problems we have to cope with, but they have to be told about them. Isn't this what communication is all about?

"After the meeting adjourned," Caldwell continues, "we walked out of the conference room and the press people were all over us. A reporter shouted, 'Hey, Caldwell, what did you tell them about Mexico?'

" 'More than they wanted to hear,' I said. Most of the people who had attended heard my reply and they burst out in a big laugh."

Caldwell recalls another encounter with the press: "I was going through one of our plants with an entourage of our people and a group of reporters. 'Why are you doing all of this?' a reporter asked. 'This is just a big dog and pony show. Why didn't you just come down here by yourself?'

" 'I'm not quite sure why you fellows are here,' I answered, 'but I can assure you I didn't stage it, and what you're hearing these workers say is just as I am hearing it.'

" 'No way do I believe that!' he said and kept right on badgering me.

" 'The trouble with you is that you're too cynical,' I said.

"There was a crowd of workers standing around, and the reporter put his microphone in front of one of them and said, 'Look, this is your big chance. All of your life you've wanted to tell the chairman of the board what was on your mind. So, go ahead and tell him, will you?'

"Without any hesitation, the worker said, 'I want to work for a profitable company so I know I will have a job.'

"If I worked for ten years, I couldn't have thought of a better answer. It showed that he understood the whole system. It was so gratifying to hear this worker say that because it let me know how far we had come since those early days when we first started to communicate with our people."

Doug Fraser, retired UAW president, agrees that vastly improved communication is the catalyst that has led to today's healthy relationship between the union and Ford. "Prior to the 1980s, the domestic automobile industry's managers were arrogant and thought they knew all the answers," he stresses. "It was intolerable behavior. But the union was to blame, too, because our perception of management was that it was their prerogative and we accepted it as their role. However, once management started to include labor in the decision-making process, it clearly benefited both sides."

"Today's communication and that of the past, between the union and the company, is like day and night," says Ken Bannon, who retired as the UAW vice-president at Ford in 1980. "I remember one time during negotiations with John Bugas, a company vice-president, telling him that the quality of the 1950 cars was poor and we should do something about it.

" 'Our jobs are at stake,' I pleaded.

" 'Go screw yourself!' he shouted at me. 'We own the company, and we're the ones who run it. You haven't got a goddamn thing to say about the quality of the product. That's our decision, so keep your goddamn mouth shut. The only thing you have a right to do is represent the people. Damn it, man, there's nothing legally that you can say about the product.'

"This was the top industrial labor relations vice-president of the Ford Motor Company talking," Bannon adds. "You can imagine what it was like further down the organization. They didn't want anyone to have a say about anything having to do with the product. They didn't want to lose any of their authority. Well, with that kind of attitude, it's no wonder there was no communication."

Perhaps one of the most celebrated and certainly most elaborate early efforts to communicate with Ford employees was made in 1982, just prior to the introduction of "the Class of 1983." A goodwill tour was arranged to let company workers know that their teamwork was paying off. The proof of the pudding was Ford's new line of quality products, which featured the new aerodynamic Thunderbird. David Scott, in public affairs, and Don Ephlin, the head of Ford's UAW department, paired management spokespersons and workers (selected by the union) into 43 teams. What followed was a three-day publicity blitz with the teams traveling across America, spreading the good word to Ford employees in 125 cities.

David Scott, who organized the tour, explains, "One of the beauties of the tour was its spontaneity. When Don Ephlin expressed his concern about our public affairs people writing speeches for the workers that would impart a company message, I assured him that we had no intention of writing any speeches. I felt this way because, first, it would be wrong and, second, it would be only a matter of time before the media figured out who was scripted and who was not."

One of the 43 teams consisted of David Scott, Red Poling, and Larry Giancomo, who at one time was considered a dissident at the Walton Hills Stamping Plant. This particular team first went to the plants in the Detroit area and then visited Philadelphia and Cleveland. At a news conference in Detroit attended by 75 plus cynical Detroit and national media people, Giancomo was asked if the company prepared a script for him to follow. "No, I haven't been prompted in any way. In fact, they told me they would not tell me what to say and I am on my own."

"Well, what do you think is the difference at Ford these days?" a reporter asked.

"You know, for 28 years I have brought my hands to work and the company has paid me for my hands," Giancomo replied, lowering his voice. "For the first time in my life, they want me to bring my mind as well."

His answer received a round of applause.

Reflecting on the tour, Poling says, "An unexpected bonus was that during the three or four days we all spent on the road, we got to know each other quite well because we had breakfast, lunch, and dinner; stayed at the same hotels; met with the media; and visited Ford plants. A common remark expressed by the plant workers and the management people who toured together was 'We've got a lot in common. He's a human being just like me, who puts on his pants just like I do.' As for me, I had a terrific time with Larry Giancomo. He's a super guy."

Giancomo evidently felt the same way about Poling. When the three-day tour ended in Cleveland, he insisted on riding to the Cleveland Airport with Poling to send him off. Just before Poling entered the corporate jet, Giancomo threw his arms around the executive vice-president and gave him a warm farewell hug.

The 125-city tour received a lot of fanfare and was viewed as a huge success. While those incidents that involved Caldwell, Petersen, and Poling received the bulk of the attention from the press, there was more unpublicized communication that transpired daily. In many cases, it was just a matter of listening. For example, Robert Adams, general manager of the Transmission and Chassis Division, recalls the early 1980s when he was plant manager at the Cleveland Engine Plant: "I started conducting state of the plant meetings every quarter with all of our employees. At first, I'd meet with groups of 300 at a time, but that was too many, so we reduced it to 100 to 150. First, I'd tell them about the state of the company, then the state of the division, and, last, the state of the plant. I'd also tell them what the competition was doing. I felt it was imperative to keep them informed—even when there was bad news to report. And for a while, there wasn't any good news. I believed that when they understood how things were, they would be supportive.

"At first, they were dubious," Adams explains. "When I walked into the room, you could feel the tension. When I'd open up each meeting to questions and answers, invariably, everything gravitated to the problems they were having on the floor. You know, problems about supervisors, what we had to improve, and so on. I recorded every grievance, and if there was a question that I couldn't answer, I'd make sure to follow up and have an answer for whoever asked it. If it was an issue about a problem on the floor, my staff and I would check it out personally, and we responded quickly so the individual wouldn't think we ignored his problem. We didn't always have a solution or what he wanted to hear, but just the same, we always got back to the person.

"For instance, there was this woman working on the assembly line who complained about a line speed change, and because of it, she now didn't have enough room in her area to properly perform her function that involved assembling oil pumps for the 4.9 liter engine. When I spoke to her supervisors, they reacted by telling me, 'Don't pay any attention to her. She's a bitch and complains about everything.' Their comments didn't stop me from investigating further. I had to find out for myself, so along with an industrial engineering manager, a production manager, an area superintendent, and the quality control manager, I went out there to observe her station. She was, indeed, crowded, and it *was* difficult for her to do her job. As a result of the increase in the line's speed, she didn't have enough time to perform efficiently, thereby causing her to let rejects go by. After we discussed it among ourselves, we asked her for her input. The result was that we were able to move another operation farther down the line and thereby give her more room. Eventually there was a substantial reduction in rejects. Not only did we improve the quality of her work, but it served as a shot in the arm for everyone's morale because they saw that we listened and followed through with some action.

"It took some time, but the word eventually spread among the plant that we did care about our people," Adams continues, "and gradually a feeling of trust started to develop. It became particularly obvious at our meetings because soon the tension was gone, and people had an entirely different attitude. In time, a spirit of teamwork and cooperation transpired, something that never before existed in the plant between salaried people and hourly workers."

Joe D'Amico, president of UAW Local No. 420, notes how the Walton Hills Stamping Plant had the same experience: "Once we were able to sit down and talk with management, we were able to solve problems that never got solved before. It's a matter of having open communication. You sit down with the other side and talk. You may not be right, and I may not be right, but if you don't sit down and talk about the issue, it will never get resolved. Even if a problem can't be resolved, and we're told, 'Look, there's no way we can do it at this time,' at least we know they were up front with us. People run into trouble when they try to deceive somebody else.

"For instance, back in 1981, Petersen visited Walton Hills and told us that if the time ever came to put in another assembly line in our plant, the company would get us involved in it. Well, in 1983, another line was added, and true to Petersen's word, a group of hourly workers was invited to attend the layout meeting so we could give management our feedback. There were hourly guys working with salaried guys, and together, we did a helluva job."

Lou Calloway, plant manager of the Dearborn plant that assembles Mustangs, is another believer in communicating with his people. To instill pride in workmanship, he conducts meetings to keep his workers posted on warranty claims made against those cars assembled in the Dearborn plant. "When a customer buys a new car and something goes wrong with it during the first 30 days, the company stands behind it and the cost of repairing it is charged against the plant," he explains. "Each plant is measured on the number of repairs per 1,000 on the cars it makes. I feel it's important for us to let everybody know how we're doing on a monthly basis. We even inform the hourly worker who assembles a particular part so he knows how his work measures up. By communicating this information to the actual worker, it becomes a matter of pride for him to keep down the warranty claims in his specific area. He's especially concerned about how his work is holding up with the actual car owner— this is really the bottom line and something everyone relates to."

Customer opinions gathered by focus groups and passed on to assembly-line workers is also an excellent stimulus. "When a worker is told by an area inspector on Monday morning that the customers said they don't like something about his or her work," Louis Ross says, "the message really hits home." It makes workers realize that customers do notice some little out-of-the-way thing when they are washing the car or changing the oil.

It wasn't just in the plants where managers met with their subordinates. The same kind of communicating was going on throughout the entire Ford organization. For example, two to three times a week, "Coffee with Kordick" meetings were conducted in Joe Kordick's office. There were about 7,000 people in the Parts and Service Division, and on a random basis, both salaried and hourly people were invited to join Kordick for an early morning coffee break. "We'd chat about whatever they wanted to talk about," he explains. "It was a good morale builder because everyone was able to personally express their ideas to me and ask me any questions that were on their minds. From my personal perspective, however, these coffee chats provided me with great input that I would have never otherwise received."

The same sort of exchange has become commonplace at Ford's design studio. "The old system was to do things that the boss would like," Jack Telnack points out. "I'm always asking my guys, 'Do *you* like it?' My job is to create an environment where the entire design staff can freely discuss different ideas and put them to work. There's so much talent on this staff that I've got to spend my time making sure we use all of it."

As chairman of Ford Motor Land Development Corporation, Wayne Doran and his staff work in a building about a half mile due west of the Glass House. Although their work doesn't involve the designing, servicing, or manufacturing of cars, they never feel as though they're out of the mainstream of the company, thanks, in part, to Don Petersen's frequent visits. "Every now and then, I get a call from Petersen," Doran explains, "and he asks me, 'What do you say about you and I getting together with about 15 to 20 of your people for lunch? I'd like to hear what's going on.'

These are informal get-togethers, and Petersen is especially effective at them because he comes across as such a down-to-earth guy."

It's hard to beat direct communication. However, a multinational corporation with nearly 370,000 employees, and thousands more dealers and suppliers spread out around the world, must, on occasion, communicate on a larger scale. To accomplish this, like many other large companies, Ford has its share of in-house publications.

One such publication is *Ford World*, a monthly newspaper, with a 250,000 circulation going out to all North American employees. The 16-page tabloid has a format resembling *USA Today,* complete with photographs and a center spread with a feature story of the month. *Ford World* looks like a newspaper; it's printed on newsprint and even contains display advertising. "People are standing in line to buy ads," explains Gene McKelvey, the associate publisher. "Advertisers include a wide range of firms, excluding, of course, General Motors, Chyrsler, or for that matter, any other automaker. *Ford World* is mailed to employees' homes, so it has an excellent delivery system. While the ads generate revenue, most important, it's the look of an authentic newspaper that we're after. What we don't want is the look of a house organ, full of company propaganda. Why do we do it this way? Because this way, people read it."

Another publication is *Ford Times,* a full color monthly magazine distributed by North American dealers to "friends" of Ford. For the most part, the friends are Ford car owners. Its content mainly focuses on travel-related stories but also features favorite recipes from famous restaurants across the country and, naturally, automobiles. *Ford Times* has a 1 million circulation, by far the largest of any company publication. At the discretion of each dealership, the magazine is sent to its customers with the Ford Division picking up a portion of the tab.

Yet another company magazine is *Dealer World*, a slick, four-color publication distributed to dealers and their employees. And there are several hundred newsletters published by employees at various plants throughout North America.

In situations when it is possible for an organization to assemble all of its employees together at one time, the spoken word is the swiftest and best way to deliver an important message. Small companies can communicate directly; even when employees are located at several locations, they can be invited to attend a conference. Ford, however, is far too large to deliver a "live" message to all its employees. And monthly publications, however powerful, can't cover today's news.

So, in 1981, the company began taping important messages via videotape. The tapes were distributed throughout NAAO with instructions on when they should be played. The tapes served to get a particular message to all plants simultaneously and served as time-savers to already over-worked senior executives. In the early 1980s, it was not uncommon to assemble district managers and salespeople in local theaters and studios in Detroit and other large cities to hear an important announcement.

In early 1983, David Scott, who at the time headed public affairs at NAAO, approached Red Poling to explore better ways in which to com-municate with employees. "One of my suggestions to Poling was a company-operated satellite television system similar to the news confer-ence used to launch cars," Scott recalls. The new 1983 Continental and Thunderbird were introduced to 1,100 media people located in 100 cities across the country with Red Poling and Phil Benton fielding questions via satellite. "About the same time, a white paper on how to improve commu-nications was being prepared by NAAO; however, conspiciously missing in the report was any mention about the use of video. Meanwhile, the company announced a reduction in the medical benefits that would require employees to pay a deductible amount, and many were irate about it. Poling and I concluded that had a better explanation been given about why the changes were necessary, the reaction would not have been so hostile."

In June 1983, Jack Caldwell, a 30-year veteran in the public and educational television industry, was hired by Walter Hayes, then Ford's vice-president of public affairs. Instructions had been given to Hayes to "do something in the area of electronic communications." Al Chambers, an executive producer at NBC, was also recruited by the company for the same purpose. In December 1983, Scott sensed the timing was right for Ford to launch its own satellite television system.

"At an NAAO executive committee meeting, when the subject of how to improve communications appeared on the agenda," Scott explains, "I gave a two-page report on the merits of a Ford satellite television system. 'Here's what we're talking about,' I said, and I started reading. I told them what it would do and how much money it would take. There was only one question asked. 'Now, are you going to tell the truth, good news *and* bad news?' I answered, 'Absolutely. This is going to be freedom of the press within the company.' Everyone was in favor of good employee communication, so it took about 30 seconds to get it approved. It was one of Poling's last decisions as head of NAAO. Lou Ross, who took over at NAAO, was equally supportive."

To a casual observer, such a major undertaking might seem frivolous and perhaps even irresponsible. Yet the company's senior managers clearly understood that if there was a single common thread among its recent successes with the union, the EI process, and its improved relationships with dealers and suppliers, it was effective communication. So even during an austere period when the company was engaged in severe cost cutting, the investment of additional funds to further enhance communication was deemed money well spent.

Shortly thereafter, Scott gave a similar presentation to a policy and strategy committee meeting. It was attended by Ford executive vice-presidents who headed the Automotive Operations, Diversified Products Operations (DPO), and the financial services group. "Their support was terrific and it emphasized how critical communications was to everyone within the top echelons of the company," Scott recalls.

The company invested in hardware such as television sets, antenna dishes, and a small studio. It also leased transmission equipment from a local television station. By buying commercial satellite time, NAAO then had the capacity to send out messages and do teleconferencing within the organization.

Frank Benesh, a former WXYZ-TV news director in Detroit who had considerable technical experience, was recruited by Ford. On his recommendation Poling approved a Textscan program, a closed circuit television system (similar to those used at airport terminals) that projects a scrolling screen on a television set. Poling recognized its vast potential and gave the go-ahead as one of his last acts during his tenure at NAAO.

Today, Ford Communications Network (FCN) is considered the most complete and capable industrial employee communications network in the world. In addition to having its own production studio, it broadcasts news and key issues about the company to 250 different Ford locations across North America. At these locations several thousand television sets pick up the closed-circuit FCN channel. These sets can be found in managers' offices, cafeterias, and break areas on the plant floor. ("If I had my druthers," says Jack Caldwell, "I'd put a set at the photocopying machine, the coffee machine, and the candy machines—anywhere where employees congregate, so while they're in line waiting for a copy or a cup of coffee, they can watch the screen.") Every employee with an interest in viewing FCN can do so during his or her working hours. Beginning at 10:00 A.M. Detroit time, a six-minute live newscast is transmitted every hour throughout the day (with four updated versions daily) to all Ford facilities throughout the United States, Mexico, and Canada. In Mexico, it's translated into Spanish. By the early 1990s, FCN is expected to be expanded to Ford locations throughout the world with appropriate translations.

Frank Benesh originally served as the network's anchorman in the United States. (Benesh has since been promoted to a new job in the United Kingdom to set up the European FCN.) In addition to reporting what's happening within the world of Ford, news on subjects pertinent to the automotive industry is covered. When a news broadcast is not in progress, monthly magazine shows are featured, and videotext information (similar to a ticker tape) appears on the screen. Furthermore, FCN can be used by people in the field for two-way communication with world headquarters. It is also possible to preempt the regular program at specific locations to broadcast, for example, a live or taped message directly to the Glass Division's plants or engine plants.

Although the company is secretive about its investment in FCN, it obviously runs into the millions. Poling justifies its costs by pointing out that "at the time, I wasn't satisfied with the way we were reaching our employees. We weren't telling them enough about important developments taking place in the company. We weren't explaining our policies adequately to thousands of employees scattered across the continent. And our different Ford components weren't talking to each other enough to stay informed about what we were doing. . . . Good internal communication is a vital ingredient of a well-run company. It is important to employee attitudes, job satisfaction, product quality, and efficiency."

Scott emphasizes that "the employee constituency is the first and foremost of all public constituencies. We try to ensure that all public announcements are aired on FCN at the same time the media read, hear, or see it. In fact, we want our employees to know about any significant news before the media. First, it's the right thing to do; second, it ensures that employees know the facts before the media call them for comment, which, in Detroit at least, is a very common occurrence."

Jack Caldwell concurs, "If it's going to be in tomorrow's newspaper, we want to make sure it's on FCN today."

One event covered was the death of Henry Ford II on September 29, 1987. FCN carried CEO Don Petersen's statement to thousands of employees across North America. In part, he said: "Mr. Ford had a strong sense of duty, illustrated time and time again by his unstinting service to Ford Motor Company, his hometown, and his country. On all he left his imprint. He was born to lead, and he fulfilled his destiny."

Another message relayed to company employees via FCN was the 1987 profit-sharing distribution of $636 million, which came to a record average of $3,700 for each eligible U.S. hourly and salaried employee. FCN is always the first to report quarterly earnings, plant closings, work force reductions, increases and decreases in auto sales, how much the CEO received as a bonus, and so on. When possible, important messages are broadcast during a live press conference, such as on November 10, 1989 when Don Petersen announced his early retirement, effective March 1, 1990. It was a surprise announcement, because he wasn't expected to retire until September 1991. He also informed his audience that Poling, who was due to retire in October 1990, had agreed to stay until 1992 and was elected chairman of the board and chief executive officer. He also stated that Phil Benton was named president and chief operating officer and Allan Gilmour was appointed president of Ford automotive group. Petersen assured everyone that his "close relationship with Red Poling for the past ten years provides for a very orderly transition of management and ensures that the strategies we have put into place over the past few years will remain the focus of Ford's efforts into the future."

"Announcements of this nature," explains Jack Caldwell, "should be given to employees *before* they hear it on television or read it in the newspapers. There are certain kinds of information that an employee should receive from the company—good or bad—rather than hearing it from an outsider. It demonstrates that the company cares about him. Then, too, the more informed and educated our work force is about the company and our industry, the better employees they are. Today, we're in several other businesses besides automobiles and trucks. For instance, we're in such diverse fields as aerospace, financial services, insurance, glass, and steel, and recently we've made some important acquisitions including the purchase of First Nationwide Financial Corporation, the nation's third largest savings and loan in 1985 and, in 1989, The Associates First Capital Corporation and Jaguar. The more our people know about what Ford does, the prouder they are to be part of this organization. They have a hunger for this kind of knowledge and it's exciting to them to learn as much as possible about the world of Ford. I think it means a lot to a worker when he can go home at the end of the day and say to his spouse or kids or neighbor, 'You will never guess what I learned at work today.'

"We're delighted to give them accurate information," Caldwell continues, "and we understand that our journalistic credibility is one of our biggest assets. We are not propagandists—we have no interest in that. We are journalists and we report the news. By the way, our research shows that FCN has the same credibility as the *Detroit Free Press* and *Detroit News*. We take pride in our credibility, yet we realize that it can be lost overnight. FCN has played a significant role in what's been going on in the company during the 1980s. There's no magic. It boils down to having people trust the company they work for; with trust they will do better work."

When FCN was in its infancy, there was some concern by UAW leaders that a company broadcasting system would interfere with the union's efforts. Some worried that such mass communication would result in a loss of union influence. "We assured them that we had no intention of broadcasting antiunion information," Jack Caldwell explains. " 'After all,' we told them, 'if this company and its employees are success-ful, then the union will be successful. We're all in it together. Give us some room.' As time passed, we developed a track record with FCN, and today the union acknowledges that the network has never been used to promote propaganda. In fact, union executives occasionally appear on FCN news programs and in *Ford World* articles.

FCN facilities have the appearance of a national network studio in New York, complete with the most modern equipment in the television industry. While the staff has only 21 full-time employees, FCN has doz-ens of free-lance writers, producers, camera operators, and crews available.

From a technological and journalistic viewpoint, FCN is a first-class operation. Employees think, "Just like the cars and trucks we make, this is quality." And as Jack Caldwell puts it, "We'd look silly if we told our people via our network that they need to improve the quality of their work, and, at the same time, the product we used to convey the message was lacking in quality. Since we all work for the company, we must all strive for excellence."

FCN is a source of considerable pride for Ford employees; its reputa-tion as the best of its kind is acknowledged throughout American indus-try. Today, dozens of companies make requests to have their executives visit FCN. So far, however, FCN has been off-limits to outsiders. "We view it as a competitive edge," Scott explains. "Our capability to commu-nicate with our people is not something that we wish to share."

WINNING
IN A GLOBAL MARKET

Worldwide, more than 3,500 companies have manufactured cars, yet less than 100 remain. The graveyard of American automakers is filled with headstones marked Hudson, Studebaker, Packard, Kaiser, Pierce-Arrow, Cords, Willys, Tucker, and scores of lesser-known companies. Two notable failures of the 1980s were John De Lorean's attempt to launch De Lorean Motor Company, and most recently American Motors. Only Chrysler's 1987 acquisition of AMC enabled the AMC Jeep Division to stay afloat. Today, Detroit's Big Three are America's only remaining domestic automakers.

For more than three decades following World War II, Detroit automakers viewed only each other as the competition. General Motors' market share rose to as high as 45 percent, and for a while the company was such a dominant force that its executives hardly even acknowledged Ford and Chrysler as competition. Instead, its divisions competed against each other. Pontiac managers were more concerned about what Buick and Oldsmobile were up to than what Ford and Chrysler were doing. And because General Motors, the world's largest industrial company, had such an overbearing presence, Ford and Chrysler looked at General Motors only. All three failed to take notice of foreign companies.

"I recall senate hearings being conducted on General Motors' monopolistic position in the United States," says Lou Ross. "There was a strong concern about how GM was going to dominate the car industry and we'd end up with a single automaker. With seven Japanese manufacturers now in the United States, nobody even thinks about such a threat today.

Now when there is concern about competition, everyone thinks globally."

In 1989, Japanese car sales in the United States were at an all-time high, having increased by nearly 3 percent over the preceding year, snagging a whopping 25 percent of market share. Furthermore, more than 1 million cars were assembled on American soil in 1989 by Japanese "transplants" (Honda, Toyota, Nissan, Mazda, Mitsubishi, Suzuki, Subaru, and Isuzu), and by the year 1992, this number is expected to surpass the 2 million mark. And Japanese automakers are no longer content to sell only their efficient, high-quality economy and midsize cars in the United States. They have set their eye on producing more expensive cars, those with the highest profit margins, such as Honda's Accura, Toyota's Lexus, and Nissan's Infinity. These cars will directly compete with many of the luxury cars sold in America by the Big Three and the European automakers.

"The automobile industry is changing so rapidly!" notes Robert Rewey. "A few years ago, the biggest threat to the American luxury car business was from the European automakers, Mercedes, BMW, Audi, Saab, and Volvo. Now many of their dealerships are flat on their back. Audi was once selling 100,000 cars a year here and now they can't give them away. It's not that the products are any worse. Actually, like American cars, the quality of the European cars has improved over the past five years. But perceptions change, and, of course, the value of money changes. So while our biggest competition used to be the Europeans, today it's the Japanese, quick to react to change and fierce competitors."

Even though Ford has enjoyed three consecutive years of record profits beginning in 1986, during which time it outearned General Motors (still the world's largest industrial company), there can be no resting on past laurels. In early 1989, after a four-year period of incredible prosperity, the U.S. automotive market started to show signs of softening. Part of the problem stemmed from those preceding years of good fortune when a record 80 million new vehicles were sold. A large portion of these sales were fueled by attractive finance packages, which included easy credit, cash rebates, nothing-down loans, below-market interest rates, and long periods of time in which to make monthly payments. However, the extended car-buying binge had run its course. So many Americans had bought new cars, they were no longer in the market for another one. Some wanted to buy but couldn't. They were strapped with indebtedness from long-term financing and were forced to continue making monthly payments for periods of five years, or perhaps even longer. Some financed cars had negative trade-in values—there was more money owed on them than what they were worth.

Ironically, the improved quality of nearly all cars manufactured in the mid– and late–1980s actually hurt sales in 1989. A new car was simply less necessary. The days are long gone when cars were built to rust out and breakdown after three years. Nor are we likely to see three-year styling cycles in which a model is redesigned for the purpose of encouraging car owners to chuck his or her old one for the latest one. Planned obsolescence would cause the Japanese automakers' market share to skyrocket, and America cannot afford to be a disposable society.

Increased competitiveness led to a new kind of war in the late 1980s—a warranty war. Chrysler's seven-year/70,000-mile protection plan, the industry's longest, was challenged by GM and Ford. Although GM trimmed its coverage from six years to three years, its "bumper-to-bumper and road-to-roof" coverage was hailed as better than Chrysler's warranty, which only covered the engine and transmission. Ford's warranty for the engine and transmission was six years/60,000 miles, but the company also offered free parts and service for anything that required repairing again for the lifetime of the vehicle. There were so many variables in these packages, it became nearly impossible for a consumer to compare them and figure out the best deal; still, the car buyer was definitely better off than before.

The war will be even more fiercely fought in the coming decade. One clear sign of the free-for-all scramble for market share in the 1990s is the record number of discounts, attractive financing charges, and high rebates offered in August and September of 1989 by the Big Three. New 1990 car and truck sales plunged more than 12 percent in October, thereby inducing domestic automakers to cite still more discounts on new models. In the past, such incentives have been used at the end of a model year and only rarely during midseason.

The first rebate program, incidentally, was offered by Ford in 1914 when the sales of the Model T were slow. Henry Ford announced that the company would give a rebate ranging from $40 to $60 to all Model T buyers; however, the offer had the following conditions: While the rebate program would run for the entire year at a price reduction of $60, Ford guaranteed that there would be no further cuts in 1914. Furthermore, unless 300,000 units were sold, nobody would receive the rebate.

Because Ford customers knew that they had to collectively reach the 300,000 target, they encouraged their relatives and friends to buy Model Ts. Newspapers across the nation wrote about the rebate program like it was the greatest thing since sliced bread. One newspaper called it "the smartest marketing plan ever devised by man." The *New York Times,* while admitting it was "well devised," called it "ill-timed" because it happened to coincide with the start of World War I. While the rebate took the public by storm, the country's bankers were furious, crying that Ford was causing people to withdraw money from their savings accounts to purchase cars. Hundreds of angry letters were sent to Henry Ford. One banker wrote that the company was unfair, and stated that since Ford was taking in so much money, some of it should be deposited in his small bank. Sales actually hit 308,000 and the rebates were paid to all buyers of the 1914 Model T.

Basically, discounts, low interest rates (as low as 0 percent), overvalued allowances on trade-ins, and rebates are all the same. Each reduces the cost of the car purchase. And the money essentially comes out of the same pocket—the Sales Division's. If the Ford Motor Credit Company offers 5 percent financing but the going rate is 10 percent, the Sales Division pays the difference.

When sales are soft, attempts are made to generate extra earnings from the financing of the car. For instance, on a car that's financed for $10,000 with a four-year loan at 13 percent interest, the dealer will probably resell the finance contract to Ford Credit at 12.5 percent and receive an immediate payment of roughly $200 from the company. In some instances, the point spread is even higher. Other profits are realized when the customer buys credit life and/or disability insurance coverage, extended warranties, rust proofing, paint sealing, and so on. The total of these extra sources of revenue can provide more profit to the dealership than the sale itself.

Ford was rather slow in entering the finance field. In fact, it was 40 years after General Motors Acceptance Corporation (GMAC) was formed in 1919 that the Ford Motor Credit Company was founded. In 1959, a moderate recession year, the dealers' councils of both the Ford and Lincoln-Mercury divisions voiced their dismay about being at a disadvantage to General Motors. The dealers' dissatisfaction prompted the company to enter the business, and, at the same time, to sell credit life and disability insurance through its dealers.

"Not only do we now provide financing for the car buyer," explains William Odom, chairman of the credit and insurance subsidiaries, "we offer financing to dealers for their floor plan [the dealership's inventory]. We provide these loans at competitive rates, usually with a floating interest rate that changes with the prime rate. While the banks don't mind making these loans, during periods of sharply rising interest rates they don't want to commit to consumer loans with fixed rates. Over the years, the banks have tended to walk away from dealers in droves when interest rates were forecast to rise. As a consequence, the dealers had no source to contract loans for their retail consumers. Understandably, banks also shy away from car dealers when the economy is uncertain. As a result, our financing has become crucial to Ford dealers during periods of downturns such as the late 1960s, the mid–1970s, and the early 1980s."

As a service business, Ford Credit continually seeks out ways to better serve its dealers and their customers. "We realize that today's consumer wants convenience, accuracy, timeliness, fairness, and courtesy," Odom says, "so we've installed the technology to help us provide these service. With our Credit Net, it's now possible for our dealers to have a customer's credit approved in seven minutes. It's all done with computers. All the dealer has to do is give us certain information via his terminal, and Credit Net will furnish him with a credit bureau report, and hopefully approve the loan. In the case of a Ford Credit customer in good standing, the deal will be approved immediately. In the past, the dealer had to fill out a credit application, make some phone calls and have a credit bureau investigation run. Not only does this service make life considerably easier for the customer, it saves time and money for the dealership."

The company's activities in financing and insurance helped offset large deficits during the early 1980s while the automobile business was ailing. As a result of fewer banks being willing to make car loans during the hard times, Ford Credit made more. This also made it possible for the credit company to make many loans at high interest rates since the prime rate hit record levels, as high as 21 percent, during this period. "Because so many banks shied away from making car loans in the early 1980s," explains John Grant, former executive director of Ford's corporate strategy staff, "our credit business was able to increase its share. Later, when the car sales picked up, we had this wonderful idea about making cheap loans to people to buy cars, and this, too, increased our share of the car retail credit business." With more than 5 million customers today, Ford Credit has become the world's second largest finance company, with GMAC in first place. In 1987, Ford Credit had record earnings of $679 million. Although many car owners tend to pay off and refinance their loans when interest rates drop, many do not. Consequently, Ford Credit continued to generate high earnings during the rest of the 1980s when the automotive segment of the company also prospered. Ford's financial services are an important diversification and help stablize downswings in the economy.

When Ford Credit opened for business in 1959, it had 39 employees and one branch in Indianapolis. On its 30th anniversary in 1989, the subsidiary had 9,000 employees in 21 countries. The combined assets of Ford Motor Company's three financial services companies—Ford Credit, U.S. Leasing, and First Nationwide Bank—had combined assets in 1989 exceeding $100 billion, which was more than any U.S. bank except Citicorp. Ford Credit, which accounts for 56 percent of the assets of the Financial Services Group, surpassed the Ford Motor Company in total assets for the first time in 1986.

In addition to being a boon to its automotive business, the company's entry into financial services has enabled Ford to develop its expertise in the capital market. For instance, Ford Credit borrows about 90 cents of every dollar it lends and, at the close of 1988, had $48 billion in debt with outstanding short-term notes of more than $19 billion (nearly 4 percent of the total commercial paper market in the United States).

In spite of these enormous numbers, Ford Motor Company spends more money each year on tooling and facilities in the car and truck business than the entire net worth of Ford Credit. "Ford and the rest of the Big Three automakers have a lot of experience in handling large sums of money," Odom declares, "and some people have gone as far as to suggest that we eat it for breakfast. But the truth is, we invest most of what we have available in the automobile business. Why is this so vital to our business? If you look at the more than 2,000 car manufacturers that have sprung up in the United States since the beginning of the century, and consider that there are only three still around today, it's obvious that the survival rate in this industry is fractional. Sure, poor vehicle quality is an apparent reason for their demise, but so has been the lack of money to finance product improvements. What inevitably has happened with those that have failed is that either their sales were too low, their costs were too high, or they were caught in downturns with no funds to finance new products. Well, as our industry has developed, the survivors have learned the importance of financing and supporting the product. While no company can be better than its products, no product can succeed unless the company provides, on a continual basis, a structure for developing, manufacturing, selling, financing, and servicing them. In this highly cyclical business, it's essential to have a structure that's supported financially through the entire cycle. This is achieved by ensuring that money will come in the door—consistently and in goodly amounts."

Odom points out that the overall U.S. market for retail automobile credit has grown by 10 percent annually since 1960 and now is in excess of $300 billion. "The financing market in Europe is steadily growing too," he emphasizes, "as consumers they are becoming more accepting of an option that they have not traditionally given much consideration. We are now beginning to see countries, historically opposed to free enterprise systems, increasing their involvement in financing in direct proportion to their acceptance of American-style capitalism and consumerism. Conceivably, somewhere down the road, U.S. automobile companies could be financing auto purchases made by customers in Russia and China. There are some major wrinkles that need to be ironed out, but it could happen."

All in all, financial services' profits of $574 million during the three-year period ending in 1982 were a tremendous help in offsetting NAAO's record losses. The biggest lifesaver in the early 1980s, however, was Ford's automotive operations outside North America. The 1980–1982 combined earnings for the company's car and truck activities in Europe, Latin America, and other countries totaled $1.6 billion. Had it been Chrysler rather than Ford with the overseas operations, Ford would have been forced to seek a financial bailout by the U.S. government. Needless to say, there was concern throughout the Ford world that NAAO's staggering losses could bankrupt the entire company. Lee Miskowski recalls being transferred back to Detroit in August 1980 after having worked in Europe for three years. "My European friends with Ford kept asking me how we were doing here. They were concerned about what had gone wrong in the United States, and if the company was going to survive. And if not, would NAAO take them down with it?"

Ford's first international venture can be traced back to 1903 when a small operation in a Detroit wagon factory, staffed by ten people, shipped its sixth vehicle to Canada. A year later Henry Ford incorporated in Canada, operating a plant across the Detroit River in Windsor. In 1908, the first overseas branch was opened in France, and the first Ford national company and assembly plant outside North America were established in England in 1911. Over the next 20 years, Henry Ford opened manufacturing, assembly, and sales operations around the world.

Ford's main reason for assembling cars overseas was convenience. It didn't make much sense to build Model Ts in Highland Park and then ship them to the faraway shores of England and Australia. Therefore, plants were constructed so cars could be made where they were sold. The company was poorly managed during the pre–World War II years, and consequently Ford's performance abroad was no better than in America. After World War II, the first priority was to get the U.S. operations in order, and with the domestic demand far exceeding the supply, Ford concentrated on modernizing and rebuilding at home. It wasn't until the early 1960s that a sustained effort to expand into Europe took place.

Today, the company has affiliates in 23 countries outside the United States, and sells its products through more than 10,500 dealers in more than 200 countries and territories. By 1987, the 40 millionth Ford vehicle was sold in Europe. In 1988, the sale of Ford cars and trucks outside United States and Canada was approximately 2.2 million units, about one-third of the company's total sales. While Ford's 1988 market share in the United States was 21.7 percent and 19.7 percent in Canada, in Europe, the world's largest and one of the most competitive markets, Ford captured 11.5 percent of the estimated 12.7 million car sales. This put Ford in fifth place behind Europe's Big Four—Volkswagen, Fiat, Renault, and Peugeot. Of the estimated 44 million cars and trucks sold throughout the free world market in 1988, about 15 percent of them were Ford products.

As foreign automakers look to the affluent American market, Ford and General Motors are setting their sights on offshore markets for expansion in the 1990s. And while Chrysler also would like to expand into foreign markets to offset the down cycles in the U.S. market, it lacks the overseas operations that both Ford and General Motors have built over the years.

On a worldwide basis, perhaps only two other American companies, IBM and Coca-Cola, have fared as well, and their names are recognized by literally billions of people in all corners of the world, as is Ford's. Internationally, Ford has fared even better than mammoth General Motors, and for the last 24 years it has been the leader of U.S.-based automotive manufacturers in overseas sales.

Henry Ford II was a true internationalist, and his personal love for Europe was influential in the company's activities there. Phil Caldwell recalls an incident at a company plant outside of London in the 1970s. "This particular plant was constructed in the 1920s as a miniduplication of the Rouge," Caldwell says. "As we drove in, Henry said in a low voice, 'I remember when this plant was being built. I was about nine years old and with my father and the fellow who headed Ford of Britain, Lord somebody . . . I can't think of his name. Yes, I remember sitting on a footing that was sticking up in the air.' I said to one of our people, 'See what you can find out about this, will you?' Well, sure enough, somebody found a photograph and there was young Henry in his knee pants, sitting on that footing between his father and the head of Ford of Britain. Henry Ford II grew up in a fashion only few Americans did. As a result, he had a global view of the world. So it came quite naturally to him to set up Ford of Europe in 1967, which, incidentally, is only a legal entity. It actually owns nothing, buys nothing, and sells nothing. In effect, it's a coordinating activity that ties together our European subsidaries such as Ford of Britain, Ford of Germany, Ford of Denmark, Ford of Sweden, and the others. Each of these countries has jurisdiction over the companies that operate within their borders. However, having Ford of Europe in place prior to the common market and years before General Motors set up shop there has given us a strong advantage."

John Grant concurs, "Prior to establishing Ford of Europe, we had a Ford of Britain, a Ford of Germany, and thirteen others that were totally separate entities with separate product ranges, engineering groups, manufacturing groups, and so on. At one time such a structure made good sense since each country had a different national government, different language, different currency and different culture. In the United States, while there are 50 states, we basically have the same culture, language, and government. Because the various Ford companies in Europe were individual entities, they rarely communicated with one another. It was John Andrews, the first head of Ford of Europe, who suggested to Henry Ford, 'It doesn't make much sense for us to do business this way. Our efforts in Europe should be commonized so we approach the common market as an integrated European company.' Andrews's discussion was instrumental in influencing Henry Ford to form Ford of Europe, which is not a holding company but rather a management company that coordinates the activities of the fifteen national companies in each of the fifteen countries. While today this sounds like a relatively simple thing to do, it was forward thinking back in the 1960s."

Since the early 1960s, the Europe market has had a higher growth rate than the United States'. Henry Ford realized the vast potential of this and other markets around the world, and it inspired him to make sure his management team developed an understanding of different markets, cultures, and competitors. Henry Ford II began sending promising executives on the "fast track" overseas to broaden their horizons. A partial list of those with international experience includes Philip Caldwell, Don Petersen, Red Poling, Phil Benton, John Betti, Allan Gilmour, Lou Ross, Jack Telnack, and Lew Veraldi. Ford showed remarkable foresight in this area because this was a time when the domestic automobile market was at its zenith.

Ford also understood that the traditional big American car had evolved because the United States was a nation with plenty of space and wide roads and where nearly every family member who was of driving age drove a car. He understood that Europe had far fewer drivers, its people had lower incomes, fuel was more expensive, and it was a land of narrow roads and faster driving speeds. Although the differences in the American market and European market have lessened, they still differ, and it is likely that they always will to some degree.

"We think that it's very important for our people to have a clear picture of the global nature of our business," explains Allan Gilmour. "After all, we have a global economy today, and everybody is affected by foreign competition. It's no longer possible to be a big business and operate in a single marketplace. To succeed in today's world, a businessperson must know the competition as well as the different markets.

"Of course, when Ford sends its high-potential people abroad," Gilmour adds, "it not only serves as a good training ground but they're given important assignments there."

As a result of its commanding presence in Europe today, Ford is most likely to be in the best competitive position of the Big Three in 1992. That's the year when the European community becomes a single economic entity, and many barriers will come down, completely opening trading among those nations in the Common Market. This will reduce the confusion of dealing with different regulatory requirements of the participating countries. For instance, there will be certain uniform standards in Europe for such things as clean air and safety stipulations and such things as import duties to shipping regulations will he simplified. These changes are certain to increase the number of companies able to compete in Europe. "In time, Europe will evolve into a single marketplace," Gilmour points out, "and we feel that our product development and manufacturing activities are in place there so we can adapt to the changes that the year 1992 brings."

Ford and its Detroit rivals are not the only automakers getting their ducks in line for 1992. Just as America was invaded by the Japanese imports and then by their transplants, similar undertakings are gearing up for the European market. What's more, like the joint ventures between American and Japanese companies, others between the Japanese and European carmakers are in progress, for example, Mercedes-Benz and Mitsubishi, Citroen and Mazda, Peugeot and Suzuki, Adam Opel and Lotus with Isuzu. With these new ventures, it is believed that the European market will be more competitive than ever, especially with the arrival of the new made-in-the-USA Japanese cars. There is now talk of the Japanese boosting their market share in Europe from its present 9.5 percent to roughly the same 25 percent of the market share it has captured in America. At present there are six major competitors in Europe, with Ford in the number three spot with a 12 percent market share.

The intensity of global competition has spawned a new brand of international business relationships. "The rewards for 'going it alone' can be great," Poling stresses, "but so are the risks and limitations. Today, the desire to strengthen our market and cost positions has moved us increasingly into new forms of cooperation and technical exchanges with a variety of business associates around the world."

In addition to joint ventures, large automakers are buying interests in smaller automakers. General Motors, for instance, owns 41.6 percent of Isuzu and 5.3 percent of Suzuki. Ford's principle intraindustry alliance is with Mazda, in which it has held a 25 percent equity position since 1979. While Ford and Mazda have remained independent, the two cooperate on joint projects, sharing technical expertise and resources. There are also certain economies of scale in such areas as engineering, designing, and manufacturing. The Ford Probe, for example, is designed by Ford and engineered by Mazda, and is currently being produced at Mazda's first U.S. assembly plant in Flat Rock, Michigan. To date, the two companies have worked together on five vehicles. Starting in the early 1990s, the partners will reverse their roles with Ford supplying Mazda with compact utility vehicles built at its Louisville Assembly Plant to be sold through Mazda's U.S. dealer network. The company has similar projects with Nissan. These include a joint venture to manufacture a front-wheel–drive minivan at Ford's Ohio Truck Plant, with plans for both firms to market it. Ford also has a 10 percent equity in Kia Motors of Korea, which supplies Ford with the Festiva subcompact car. In Argentina, Ford built the first all-new automotive assembly plant in Latin America in 1922; recently Autolatina Argentina SA was formed in 1987 when Ford Argentina and Volkswagen Argentina merged. In Brazil and Argentina, Autolatina's combined car and truck 1988 market share was 52.8 percent. Other joint ventures by Ford are scattered around the globe from Australia and New Zealand to Turkey.

Ford's most prestigious foreign venture is certainly its 1989 $2.5 billion acquisition of Jaguar, the aristocratic British manufacturer of lush sedans. The purchase was hailed as a victory over archrival General Motors, which had expressed an interest in the elite automaker. In spite of manufacturing cars in an outmoded former aircraft parts plant in Coventry, England, Jaguar has been operating in the black for several years. Still some industry observers believe Ford may have to spend an additional $1 billion to help Jaguar upgrade its products, facilities, and systems to better compete in the prestige car market. Once there, Jaguar would be pitted against such companies as BMW, Audi, and Volvo, as well as the new Japanese luxury models. "By combining Jaguar's heritage and technical skills with our resources," Petersen says, "we think it can grow substantially in the prestige car market." The big question is whether expanding in this market will risk diluting Jaguar's distinctive marque.

Ford is believed to have purchased the British automaker for its snob-appeal recognition. The association gives Ford a viable, high-end luxury brand for both the U.S. and European markets. While both parties have agreed that Jaguars would not be sold through the Ford and Lincoln-Mercury dealerships network, the British firm will benefit from Ford's deep pockets, marketing know-how, and technological expertise. One industry expert says, "Ford had no alternative because, had it lost Jaguar, it would have had to have spent as much as $5 billion to get into the high-end line, and even then, it could take years to succeed—or perhaps—fail. In this respect, Ford made a smart, long-term investment."

In its effort to be more competitive in the worldwide market, Ford has instituted the concept of "centers of responsibility." Instead of designing three or four subcompact cars as different products, the company will select specific vehicles to be designed in specific locations, or centers of responsibility, and then tailor the basic design to fit many different markets. For years, the NAAO and Ford of Europe evolved as if they were two separate companies. This is illustrated by what happened in the late 1970s when Ford attempted to build the Escort subcompact. Responsibility for the car's engineering was divided between the United States and Europe. Each group made considerable deviations from the basic plan, and as a result, the company ended up with two completely different Escorts. While both were successful, there were only two common parts: a water-pump seal and a suspension component.

"We now find ourselves in the somewhat anomalous position of having our European automotive operations," Benton states, "with a complete organization in place for designing, engineering, and manufacturing. What happened was that we ended up with the Tempo made in the United States and the Sierra made in England, Germany, and Belgium, both the exact size with the same mission. So in a simplistic sense, what globalization says is 'Why don't we do that only once!'

"Note, for example, that the Tempo line doesn't have a station wagon," Benton continues, "but there is a Sierra station wagon. Our reason for not having one with the Tempo was because our budget wouldn't allow it.

Had we gone to common engineering, however, both the Sierra and the Tempo could have had a wagon."

"We have a lot of capability around the Ford world," Poling comments, "with two major areas being North America and Europe. By taking advantage of our strengths in both places and focusing on the development of the products where we have the greatest expertise, we're able to realize certain efficiencies. In purchasing, for instance, there's a savings that comes from a supplier's higher volume."

"To facilitate this global development program," explains Phil Benton, "we launched a $77 million computer-based system that links our manufacturing and engineering groups at company locations all over the world. When completed, this network will eliminate language barriers and enable each of the company's 20,000 engineers to exchange information with his and her colleagues throughout the world, providing everyone with immediate access to the same data base. When fully in place, our Worldwide Engineering Release System [WERS] will have replaced six separate and incompatible design and engineering communications networks. The WERS computer base also stores in excess of 100,000 parts and this number continues to grow. Beginning with the 1990 model year, all reference parts are now put into WERS. Not only does this system serve as a reserve bank for parts, it reduces the need to come up with new parts when existing ones are sufficient. I think WERS epitomizes the teamwork and long-term thinking that has been going on around here for the past decade."

According to Poling, "the company is presently doing business in only 40 percent of the world, which means there's quite a lot of room for us to expand." With *perestroika* and the political and economic reforms taking place in Eastern Europe, new territories are expected to open up for the world's automobile and truck market during the 1990s. Granted, it will take years before consumers in these countries are able to afford high-priced cars. Nonetheless, the prospect of expansion into a market with 300 million people is mind-boggling.

"Prior to entering a foreign market," explains Gilmour, "we must evaluate political risks as well as the business risks. This is true with all companies, but in particular, with an automobile manufacturer because we must make such long-term investments that take a long time to generate earnings. While there's no real concern about stability in places like Western Europe, Australia, or New Zealand, there is in certain countries in South America and Southeast Asia. There are questions about what sort of government and social system will exist over an extended period of time. Of course, there's always some degree of risk in any business undertaking; it isn't possible to eliminate it altogether. So it's a matter of weighing the risks and the opportunities."

One major risk of doing business in a foreign country is the exchange rate of currency. In the early 1980s, for example, a weak yen was the cause for Japanese cars to sell at extremely low prices compared to American cars. "We kept hearing angry remarks," Gilmour remembers. "People were whining, 'Those damn fools in Detroit deserve their troubles.' One day I came up with a stock answer for these complainers. 'I've got the cure,' I announced. 'From now on, we're going to put all future plants on aircraft carriers, and we'll float them around until we find a country with a receptive government, friendly labor, and the right currency relationship. Then we'll tie up and build a helluva lot of cars there. Later, when conditions change, we'll unhitch our boats and float away to somewhere else.' "

Of all the markets in the free world, Japan unquestionably has been the most difficult for car exporters to crack. Japan is the world's leader in banking, the largest donor of aid, and in terms of national net worth, the richest country. It boasts a per capita income that has surpassed America's. Its GNP is larger than the Soviet Union's and equal to 60 percent of the United States'. In 1989 the Japanese sold $55 billion more to us than we sold to them. Understandably, this is cause for much concern in America.

American cars are notoriously poor sellers in Japan. For example, in 1978, Ford sold an estimated 10,000 units in Japan; by 1982, this figure dropped below 1,000. While the weak yen had a lot to do with this decrease, the small number of sales caused Ford's distribution network in Japan to collapse. By 1988 Ford exported 2,000 cars to Japan and in 1989, 5,000. From September 1988 through August 1989, there were 2,136,193 cars and 476,403 light trucks exported by Japan to the United States while only 21,058 went the other way. During this period, Japan did not import any U.S.-made light trucks. The dollar value of cars going to Japan totaled $289 million with $20.5 billion of cars coming to America. Japan accounts for nearly 40 percent of the total U.S. trade imbalance and of this, automobiles are 60 percent. This translates into automobiles accounting for one-third of America's worldwide trade deficit.

Many blame unfair trade practices and Japanese laws. There are strict emission control laws in Japan; however, these laws were not written to restrict imports but rather to protect the environment of a very overcrowded country. And because Japan has limited natural resources, nearly 100 percent of its oil is imported.

Others blame poor-quality products and bad management. However, given the improved quality of today's American vehicles and the weak dollar, cars exported from the U.S. clearly represent excellent values in Japan.

According to Jack Eby, Ford's director of public policy issues and business development, "The Japanese have a way of negotiating by throwing the other guy off balance. So, as a matter of course, they complain we don't build the right product, and too often, we react by agreeing with them. For instance, there have been stories about how Ford shipped cars to Japan with the steering wheel on the left side, and this faux pas was the cause for poor sales. Well, the Japanese like to promote this myth, but in truth, a mark of a luxury car in Japan is one with the steering wheel on the left side. Mercedes was concerned about this so they made it an option on the order form, allowing the customer to check off either right-hand or left-hand steering. 95 percent of the Japanese chose Mercedes with left-hand steering—so much for that myth. As a matter of fact, with such narrow streets, many of the Japanese drivers prefer to open their doors on the curbside rather than stepping into traffic."

There's reason to believe that the Japanese lack of acceptance of imported cars is more cultural than governmental. To understand the behavior of its people, one must go back to the rebuilding of postwar Japan. The country was in ruin, and its immense reconstruction was certainly one of the great economic miracles of modern civilization. It was achieved by pulling together the entire nation. The government took whatever measures it deemed necessary to ensure a steady growth of the Japanese economy. This meant that if the government decided that a particular industry had too many manufacturers, it organized a shutdown of some of that capacity. If a particular study group concluded that a certain technology was a key to the future, tax incentives and low-interest loans were granted to expand research and development in that area. In short, business interests were highly protected; all resources as well as economic spoils were directed to the corporate sector. It was a philosophy that also discouraged outside competition—as if national security were at stake. It inspired Japanese consumers to support the country's domestic manufacturers with intense loyalty.

About 40 percent of Japan's population is over the age of fifty and has not forgotten the severe food shortages in the 1940s—or being forced to eat grasshoppers and boil grass to survive. Crops are still scarce in Japan;

its farmers produce only about 50 percent of the food needed to feed its people. As a result of a complicated quota system, the price of a pound of U.S. beef costing $3 here sells in Japan for $15. Farmers are subsidized for growing rice and the government prohibits rice imports, causing consumers to pay a hefty price. Even so, a recent survey showed that two-thirds of Japanese were willing to pay highly inflated food prices rather than see reduced incentives for farmers.

Then, too, Japan is a homogeneous society that, unlike America, consists of one race. This makes the Japanese even more willing to sacrifice to support a national cause.

Also impeding the sale of American-made cars in Japan is Japan's complicated distribution system. Goods must pass through many more channels than in the United States, and this increases the cost to consumers. The Japanese accept this because their companies have long-term relationships with small suppliers, many of which are mom-and-pop businesses, often partially owned by the large corporation and because this distribution system ensures employment of a high percentage of the people.

It has always been extremely difficult for a foreign automaker to establish a distribution network because it couldn't tap into any existing dealers. As Jack Eby explains, "In Japan, automobile manufacturers have exclusive franchises with dealers, which means Toyota can prevent one of its dealers from taking a Ford franchise. In the United States, the antitrust laws don't permit that, so Ford can't stop a Ford dealer from obtaining a Toyota franchise." One way for American companies to break into the distribution system is by forming subsidiaries and collaborations with domestic companies in Japan. For example, vehicles designed by Ford and manufactured in Japan by Mazda are sold through more than 200 dealers of Autorama, the company's distribution network in Japan. Because of the Mazda association, these cars are the best-selling nondomestic vehicles in Japan, with sales of 75,000 units in 1988. Prior to Ford's joint venture with Mazda, its distribution network consisted of such outlets as supermarket chain operators and used-car dealers.

If there is to be a leveling in today's world automotive market, there must be a cooperative relationship between government and industry in America. Governmental bureaucrats must become better informed. Far too often, officials in Washington do not understand automotive technology and consequently make decisions that undermine the nation's automakers. In Japan, highly qualified technocrats are employed by the government to serve industry, not oppose it.

An example of how legislation could tilt the playing field in favor of the domestic automakers is the suggestion that each automaker must boost the fuel economy of its cars, averaged across all models, by the same percentage. This would mean that the Japanese car companies, with high fuel efficiencies that far exceed the Big Three's, would have to work hard to improve theirs even more. It would also discourage the importing of large, luxury Japanese cars that would bring down their company averages. While the Japanese view such legislation as an attempt to erect a nontariff barrier to keep them out of the more profitable luxury car market, supporters claim that the percentage increases would force everyone to push for improvements.

In the 1970s, fuel-economy legislation was aimed at conserving fuel, but today the main concern is the threat of global warming caused by gases such as carbon dioxide engulfing the earth's atmosphere. So while the reason for reducing the consumption of gasoline may have changed, it's certainly still an important goal.

A joint Big Three research effort to deal with these concerns could prove fruitful, and cooperation of this nature does occur in Japan. However, it would require some modification in existing antitrust laws that forbid executives of competing companies from discussing such competitive matters as price and product strategy. In the past, the gathering of Big Three executives has been avoided because such activities could be construed as illegal collaboration.

One way to spread the burden of energy conservation would be with a users' tax on fuel. This would decrease its use and the resulting revenues could then be used to fund environmental clean-up. For instance, a 10 cents per gallon tax on the 165 billions gallons of gasoline consumed in 1988 in the United States would have generated $16.5 billion in revenue. At 50 cents a gallon, it would be $82.5 billion.

Today with public awareness of acid rain and air pollution, Americans realize the necessity of developing alternative sources for power. Nuclear power plants, for instance, would reduce sulfur dioxide levels in the atmosphere; electric utilities, however, are unwilling to make the enormous investment needed to create such facilities unless Congress passes laws guaranteeing operation upon completion of construction. Legislation of this nature would also spread the burden—taking some of the load off the nation's automakers.

Another competitive disadvantage shouldered by U.S. automakers is the nation's existing product liability environment. John Martin, Ford's vice-president and general counsel, states, "because we [U.S. firms] sell a much greater percentage of our output here than the Japanese companies, we incur a proportionately greater degree of the expense of our product liability system in this country. This is only one of the costs—another is the cost of reduced innovation. Engineers are reluctant to attempt to advance the state of the art due to their concern that it will increase the company's product liability exposure. One such fundamental example is that whenever a company adds a safety feature to a vehicle in the United States, it must, first, consider the added liability exposure because the safety device was not available on previously made vehicles; second, there is a risk of being required to recall prior vehicles on a retrofit basis to add the new safety feature. For instance, there are pending lawsuits whereby automakers have been sued for having sold cars without air bags. These suits are based on the theory that the omission constituted a product defect, not withstanding the fact that a long history of government deliberation exists, as well as a conscious decision by the government not to mandate air bags. Instead, automobile companies have been permitted to experiment with a variety of passive restraint devices. The industry doesn't believe there is any basis for saying that a manufacturer has a responsibility to the consumer for including an air bag in a vehicle. From a common-sense and a public-policy standpoint, I don't think a requirement of this nature should be imposed."

Vice-President Dan Quayle, chairman of an administration council of U.S. competitiveness, concurs. In a December 1989 statement, he said, "The current patchwork of liability laws, varying from state to state, generates excessive litigation, inflates insurance costs, and creates uncertainties for American businesses. This is a self-imposed burden on our ability to compete."

Under consideration is legislation designed to impose federal limits on liability lawsuits and curb big product liability judgments. As Martin points out, "In today's legal environment, we're faced with lawsuits involving serious injury where juries must decide whether to deny an award to the injured party or to impose an enormous settlement to be paid by a wealthy manufacturer. What has happened is that the courts have unilaterally expanded manufacturers' liability based on who in society can best afford to incur these costs. This is not justice or, for that matter, sound public policy."

Another handicap of U.S. manufacturers is the nation's runaway health insurance costs, currently at double the rate of inflation. This added expense is estimated to increase the cost of an average car made in

America by as much as $700. The Japanese put this cost in their taxes, and it is then absorbed by the entire society rather than added to the price of their products.

The nation's budget deficit also handicaps the United States. A reduction in the deficit would make more funds available for private investment, bring interest rates down, reduce the need for foreign borrowing, and make the dollar more competitive. At present, one-third of the U.S. budget is spent on defense, which equals about $1,200 for every man, woman, and child in the country. Compare this number to the $150 per person spent on defense in Japan. America today has become the world's biggest debtor—while Japan is the world's biggest creditor. Throughout history, the country holding the IOUs has been able to dominate the world economy.

Over the long haul, it will be the people who determine how this company, or, for that matter, how this nation fares in the global market. Technology has accounted for 40 percent of America's GNP growth and 50 percent of its increased productivity since World War II, but technology is simply one of several tools used by industry. As Phil Benton emphasizes, "It is worthless if its sophistication races ahead of the abilities of people to understand, implement, and manage it. The looming 'people gap' could adversely affect some of America's best-known, most highly respected products and services. Even more basic to the broad issues of America's industrial capability and national competitiveness is the projection that millions of Americans will be without jobs or marketable skills by the year 2000 and that they will have little prospect for obtaining either."

A joint study by the U.S. Departments of Commerce, Labor, and Education indicates that three out of four persons in the U.S. work force in the year 2000 are already out of school, and many of them are ill-prepared to deal with rapidly changing technology because they lack basic academic skills. It's estimated that American industry spends more money teaching remedial math to employees than all the grade schools, high schools, and colleges in the country combined spend on math education. One major American corporation spends $200 on each of its workers to train them in statistical process control. A Japanese company spends 47 cents to accomplish the same thing: The instruction manual is given to the worker; he reads and comprehends it.

"You can't be technologically literate," Benton exclaims, "if you can't read and understand written instructions or deal with even simple arithmetic concepts. Yet today, one in five adult Americans lacks such functional skills. Every fourth high-school student in this country now drops out before graduating; and, of those who graduate, many have been passed through the system without having mastered the basics."

In Japan, 99 percent of high-school students graduate with a diploma that's comparable to two years of college in the United States. The functional illiteracy rate in Japan is only about 5 percent. W. Edwards Deming relates "In a recent seminar I conducted in Minneapolis, I asked the audience for a show of hands of how many had calculus. Only a few hands went up. What I was trying to explain was so easy to anyone who understood calculus. In Japan, everybody in the audience would have had calculus." Don Petersen emphasizes, "The future competitiveness of this country will depend on our determination to raise the level of American education to the best in the world. This means we must motivate our young people to take hard subjects—math, technical courses, and the sciences—even at the rudimentary levels. If they don't, they will lack the skills for entry into the workplace of the future. Our school systems must reorganize and restructure to meet the competition, just as industry is doing—because the quality of our work force is a survival issue for America. Without a quality work force, we cannot hope to retain the competitive edge."

After a five-year period of prosperity, the U.S. market faces some difficult times. The total 1989 car and truck sales came in at an estimated 14.9 million units compared to 15.7 million units in 1988. Total sales are forecast to decline again, down to somewhere between 14.2 to 14.5 million in 1990. With an anticipated overproduction of cars and trucks coupled with the current level of 2.3 million Japanese imports (plus the increased capacity of the transports), the industry is going to be in for some difficult times as the last decade of the 20th century begins.

While Ford's string of record profits will come to an end, it is probably in the best shape of the Big Three to weather the oncoming storm. Its product line appears to be the most competitive in Detroit, and its management substantially slashed its break-even point during the early 1980s and has managed to keep its overhead low ever since.

Just how well a publicly owned corporation's stock performs is said to be one barometer of what to expect in the future. The value of Ford shares has dropped in 1989, hovering around five times earnings and yielding about 6.5 percent interest. As Petersen points out, "The analysts have been saying that the one thing that Ford has yet to prove since our turnaround in the early 1980s is whether we can weather a recession. You know, it's basically been one continuous recovery since 1983, so according to Wall Street, we haven't proven anything yet. Well, the upcoming 1990s are bound to test the mettle of every automaker."

FORD IN THE 1990s

T he Dearborn Hyatt Regency Hotel is due west of the Glass House on the other side of the cloverleaf where Michigan Avenue intersects with the Southfield Freeway. Like other real estate around Ford's world headquarters, including the Fairlane Shopping Center, the Ritz-Carlton Hotel, the Dearborn Inn, and a host of office buildings, the Hyatt is a Ford property. In 1975, shortly before ground was broken to construct the 14-story bronze glass building, Henry Ford had the construction company put up a crane to measure how high the hotel would stand.

"He just wanted to make sure it wouldn't overshadow world headquarters," Ford Motor Land Development chairman, Wayne Doran, explains. "Henry Ford loved real estate and was deeply involved in our development activities. He reviewed every building plan and would study its architecture, select the glass, the color, material—everything. In fact, on the day he died, September 29, 1987, we had an appointment for him to come to my office so he could give his approval for the interior plans of the Dearborn Ritz-Carlton."

"What I think he enjoyed most about real estate was the satisfaction of knowing his involvement could be felt immediately," Doran continues. "He could select the brick or the glass, and in a matter of weeks or months, see it go up. There were times when he became frustrated with the automobile business. I recall him once telling me, 'I can look at bumpers and hub caps and it takes five years before they come out. Hell, by that time, I don't even remember what I looked at, let alone understand it.' "

The automobile industry has traditionally been a business in which crucial decisions are made several years prior to the introduction of a new model. The business requires substantial lead time for such things as designing, engineering, and retooling.

However, as John Grant, the former director of the corporate strategy staff and now deputy chairman of Jaguar, points out, the automotive industry looked to the future with tunnel vision. "For years, this has been a very provincial industry," Grant explains. "Ford, for example, has been making cars since 1903, so automaking was a business we knew all about, and, as a matter of course, we plodded along doing things like we always did. Sure, we'd update and freshen up our models each year, but rarely was there anything in the way of new technology. We made a lot of money, and our customers thought they were happy with our products, so there never was any reason for us to think otherwise. As time passed by, we developed some bad habits, especially in the fifties, sixties, and into the seventies. Although the oil crises in the 1970s caused us to do a few things differently, we really didn't do much to widen our horizon.

"Yet, in contradiction to this provincial viewpoint," Grant continues, "Ford has an international history tracing back to 1908 when the company opened its first overseas branch in France. Then, three years later in 1911, Ford established its first national company and assembly plant outside North America in Britain. Within the automobile industry, these international activities were always a characteristic of Ford that set the company apart. Under the guidance of Henry Ford II, the company's presence around the world provided our management with a global perspective unlike most other American manufacturers. For example, Ford of Europe is an integrated European company that operates as a single organization, and yet its components are 15 different national companies doing business in the same number of countries. Each unit operates in a land that differs in such things as language, government, currency, and culture. In contrast to Ford's U.S. operations, the European organization was always forced to deal with a wide range of external circumstances. In the United States, the operating people did not have to get involved with external factors—they had so much support. There was always an abundance of specialists at world headquarters who made economic forecasts, talked to government agencies, dealt with environmental and safety issues, and so on. Consequently, few Ford managers in Dearborn ever had to pay much attention to the outside. To some degree, they became introverted, keeping themselves busy going about their business inside the company."

Grant points out that Ford's overseas earnings in the early 1980s became a major source of funding for the North American operations.

This revenue, combined with the European assignments of so many executives, broadened management's horizon. "Additionally, we went through an extended period of government intervention," Grant adds, "that forced us to pay more attention to what was going on outside the company. In the past, we were only concerned about what GM was going to do and how much it would cost. It was that simple and little else seemed to matter. When we began to see what was happening externally, we realized that it was now mandatory to look further into the future. Most important, it made us recognize the need to *anticipate change.* External factors such as oil shocks, government regulations, exchange rate changes, and the new competitive pressures by the Japanese could have too severe an impact on us to ignore. We concluded that more long-term planning was essential; no longer could we afford the luxury of taking a business-as-usual approach. This led us to develop a strategic plan with each of our major businesses. These plans, at present, are without a fixed time period. We do have the flexibility, however, to project as far as ten years. It should be noted that a strategic plan is only a starting point to provide a framework and, accordingly, is periodically subject to review."

The consensus among industry experts is that the changes occurring during the 1990s will be the most dramatic since the first cars rolled off the assembly line. Although auto sales in 1989 took a nosedive, profits were still made, unlike ten years ago, when the Big Three were hit with enormous losses. The industry has enjoyed record-breaking prosperity since the mid–1980s; the yen—not the dollar—is strong. But the upcoming battle promises to be a formidable one, especially given the likely impact of turmoil in the Middle East.

Most alarming are the gains made by the Japanese automakers in U.S. market share, which jumped from 20.4 percent in 1981 to 25.4 percent by the end of 1989. Of the U.S.-based automakers, only Ford realized a gain in its U.S. market share during this eight-year period, holding a 1989 share of 22.3 percent as compared to 16.6 percent in 1981. Chrysler lost ground, having a 1989 U.S. market share of 10.4 percent versus 11.9 percent in 1981. The biggest loser was General Motors, dropping from 44.6 percent in 1981 to 35.1 percent in 1989. While the other foreign automakers' U.S. market share increased from 6.5 percent in 1981 to 6.8 percent in 1989, the European automakers actually lost some ground, while the non-Japanese automakers from Asia had a slight gain.

When the combined car and truck sales for U.S. market share are compared for the years 1981 and 1989, the numbers look good for Ford:

In 1989 Ford had 24.5 percent versus 19.7 percent in 1981; General Motors had 34.7 percent versus 43 percent in 1981; Chrysler went to 13.5 percent from 11.7 percent in 1981; the Japanese automakers went to 21.6 percent from 18.8 percent in 1981, and the others had 5.7 percent versus 6.8 percent in 1981. Truck sales presently account for one-third of the entire units sold in the United States, but profits from trucks are less than those from cars. These combined figures also reveal that truck sales is the one area in which the Japanese have not made any headway.

As automakers engage in combat for each one-tenth of a percentage point of a market share, the consumer will be the ultimate beneficiary. The 1990s promise to bring advances in technology, and, according to John McTague, until recently Ford's vice-president of research but now in charge of all the company's technical affairs, "The manufacturing sector will realize better precision capability through the use of robotics. Robots have made and will continue to make a substantial contribution in reducing variability, thereby increasing productivity and improving the quality of the product. As automakers make great strides in manufacturing, capacity will increase, and, in turn, lower the cost of the product."

In addition to gains made on the plant floor, McTague says, "Changes in cars are occurring more rapidly today than at any time since Charles Kettering's introduction of the electric starter back in 1912. The biggest technology changes will be in the area of electronics, which will influence various types of control, affecting interactions of one system of the vehicle with another such as suspension with braking and braking with throttle control. There will even be electronic mufflers with antinoise devices to cancel out unpleasant sounds. Thus different systems in the car will impact on others because various sensors will share information pertaining to the operation of the vehicle. Through multiplexing systems, a control of power distribution coupled with electronic control will truly change the character of the car in the 1990s. Bear in mind that to the casual observer the vehicle won't seem much different. There won't be an appreciable alteration in the interior of the car, nor will the driver necessarily realize a significant difference in the ride of the car. What will have changed, however, is how he gets there, what he saves on fuel, and how much of an impact he makes on the environment.

"Also on the horizon in the 1990s," McTague continues, "is the introduction of flexible fuel vehicles. These cars will be able to run on gasoline, methanol, ethanol, or any mixture of the three—whatever is available from the nearest pump. Moreover, the driver won't have to 'inform the car' what's going into the cylinders. Instead, via electronics, the car will automatically adjust. This means the car of the 1990s will have the capacity to program itself to the correct air-fuel ratio to optimize performance for prevailing conditions.

"Also coming up in the not-too-distant future will be electric vehicles that can run for about 100 miles and require recharging for six to eight hours at night. Their pickup will be comparable to one of today's diesel cars and they'll hardly make a sound. At present, Ford is engaged in a joint research effort with General Electric and the U.S. Department of Energy to develop electric vehicles. The environmentalists will love these cars, particularly if the electricity is created by a source of energy, such as hydroelectric power, that doesn't produce environmental pollutants. These vehicles should do well in urban areas, especially for drivers with a regular daily route who drive a limited distance."

The mass production of the electric car is still on the drawing board, but its introduction couldn't come too soon, especially with the pending legislation to curb air pollution. The most stringent antipollution plans are those being considered by California's air-quality regulators, which, if passed, would be phased in starting in 1994. In the summer of 1989, California State regulators cut allowable hydrocarbon and carbon dioxide emissions by 36 and 51 percent, to be effective for those cars produced in 1993 and 1995, respectively. Most cars don't even come close to those standards now, and there is proposed legislation for another 50 to 84 percent reduction. The state wants the automakers to phase in three generations of new cars, each progressively cleaner. Up to 10 percent of new cars and light trucks sold in the Golden State in 1994 to 1996 would have to emit no more than 0.125 gram of polluting hydrocarbons per mile—the current limit is 0.39 gram. Then, by 1997, the hydrocarbon limit would be dropped to 0.075 gram per mile, with 25 percent of the cars sold in California having to meet this standard. By the year 2000, 98 percent of all cars sold in the state would be required to meet the 0.075 standard and 2 percent would be limited to 0.04 gram or less of hydrocarbons. This would require cars to run on alternative fuel such as methanol, natural gas, or electricity.

Although automakers say the California proposal is "fantasy," claiming existing technology cannot do it, it has caused considerable concern within the industry. At present, the California regulation is looked at as the bellwether for auto emissions standards because several other states traditionally follow its lead and adopt such legislation as their own. What's more, California accounts for 10 percent of the U.S. car market.

On the East Coast, more environmental legislation has already been passed that will affect the automobile industry. In Vermont, air-conditioners that use chlorofluorocarbons (CFCs) will be banned in new vehicles beginning in 1993. CFCs have caused a depletion of the ozone layer that protects the earth, contributing to global warming often referred to as the greenhouse effect. CFCs can be found in Freon, the trade name for the chemical made by DuPont, which is the chief cooling agent in automobile air-conditioners. A new product known as HFC-134a has been developed; it is less efficient but contains no environmentally harmful CFCs. To make the changeover to HFC-134a, auto air-conditioning units will have to be bigger, cost more, and probably won't perform as well the former ones. While Vermont's small 500,000 thousand population is only a fraction of 1 percent of the U.S. car market, environmentalists believe its new law will touch off a wave of similar moves by other states as well as the federal government. At present, Congress and more than 20 states are considering a ban similar to Vermont's.

Carbon dioxide emissions have also been linked to global warming. The only way to reduce carbon dioxide emission from automobiles (which is minor compared to that of utilities and manufacturing plants) is to decrease gasoline consumption. In the 1990s, there will be a continued push to get more miles per gallon. Recently, the head of the Environmental Protection Agency suggested that cars should average as much as 50 miles per gallon (MPG) by the year 2000, up from the present average of 26.5 MPG. As McTague asks, "We might be able to produce such a vehicle, but will it provide the ride the customer wants, have room for two or three children in the back, and be safe?"

Chances are that cars will be made smaller during the 1990s, which will require automakers to produce compact fuel-efficient engines that leave more room for passenger space. However, bigger air-conditioners may be required as well as bigger fuel tanks to contain the less-polluting methanol (which gets fewer miles per gallon than gasoline), making the downsizing of cars more complex. Technological solutions to these problems and the added expense of additional safety features will undoubtedly be reflected in higher sticker prices throughout the remainder of the 20th century.

One way to cut down on pollution might be to curb the number of drivers on the road. Los Angeles drivers have not forgotten the 1970s, when odd or even numbered licensed plates determined which days of the week those cars could be driven. For obvious reasons, restrictions of this nature are opposed by the automakers, oil companies, and general public. Helen Petrauskas, Ford's vice-president of environmental and safety engineering, says, "There is a real challenge out there to preserve mobility for the American public in congested areas such as Los Angeles and New York that are not meeting the health standards for air pollutants. As far as the gasoline-powered–internal-combustion engine is concerned, there isn't much more that can be done to clean up the air." A plaque on Petrauskas's desk reads, Perfect is the enemy of good. "I really believe that," she says, nodding at the plaque. "In the past, the government has written regulations in a way that requires industry to attain perfection, yet there are situations when achieving 90 percent of a goal versus 100 percent is better. The extra effort and expense to achieve 100 percent may not provide added value to the customer because it crosses the threshold where it fails to supply the customer with an additional benefit. Or due to technology, 100 percent simply isn't doable."

There are cynics who believe the automobile companies and the oil companies have conspired to keep the 100 MPG car off the road. "That myth has been around for years," Jack Eby notes. "As a kid, I remember reading an article in *Popular Mechanics* about such a conspiracy. Can you imagine during the oil shock when we were practically going out of business what it would have meant to put on the market a car with a 100 MPG carburetor or a car that ran on water?"

David Hagen, general manager of the Engine Division, concurs, "Just look at the struggles we had to add 0.01 MPG for CAFE. For years, we've battled the oil companies to get the lead out of the gasoline, and we've squabbled over various additives that caused problems with our catalyst systems. Believe me, the oil industry was not a friend of the auto industry.

"People are still predicting that the gasoline engine won't be around in ten years," Hagen adds. "This is consistent with what they were predicting in 1960 when I joined Ford in research. Well, during the 1990s, we'll likely see another form of hydrocarbon fuel on which the internal-combustion engine will run. So those predictions might come true after all—but a modified version. The new engines will probably be dependent upon gasoline as well as some other fuel."

Between 1986 and 1989, Ford invested nearly $11 billion in research and development. While this money will produce significant strides in products and technology, according to McTague, "There isn't likely to be any silver bullet. Instead, you'll see continuous improvement. These improvements, however, won't be the things that makes the front page of the newspapers."

McTague gives much of the credit to today's high standards for improved products to the Japanese automakers. "They showed us what we could do in the 1980s," he points out. "Do you remember when Roger

Bannister ran the four-minute mile? Prior to Bannister breaking the first four-minute mile, everybody thought it couldn't be done. People thought the human body couldn't endure such physical strain. When Bannister collapsed on the track, the spectators thought he was going to die. Now high-school kids do it and they don't collapse."

Bill Powers, director of product and manufacturing systems, stresses that while the Big Three lost ground to the Japanese automakers in the 1980s, by the year 2000, the U.S. automakers could again take the lead. "Remember back in 1960 when the Soviet Union launched *Sputnik*," Powers says. "At that time, many Americans felt that our space program could never beat theirs. The Russians were putting thousand-pound satellites into orbit while we were launching tiny 70-pound satellites. Then America set a goal to go to the moon by the end of the decade. Well, we did, and in the process, we took over the lead in space. We later learned that the reason the Russians put such big satellites into space was because they didn't have the technology to miniaturize their electronics. When America got its act together, government contracts were awarded to American computer companies, and through an all-out joint effort to develop our space program, the U.S. computer industry was born, which is the world's best. Although the Japanese are going to be a lot tougher to beat, I believe that with the proper commitment, the American automotive industry can beat them during the 1990s."

In the meantime, Ford's crosstown rival, General Motors, is still its number one competitor. With Ford's recent successes in the late 1980s, David McCammon, Ford's vice-president of finance and treasurer, comments, "The two questions most often asked to senior management at press conferences are 'When do you expect to pass General Motors in sales?' and 'How do you feel about beating General Motors in profits?' Our response to these questions is 'Neither is one of our goals. Our goal is to turn out quality products that the customer likes and wants to buy again.' "

This goal was accomplished during Ford's magnificent turnaround in the 1980s. The company had a series of successes, beginning in 1983 with the new Thunderbird and Ranger. Then there was the Escort's high-volume sales that dominated the small-car market. Later, with the introduction of such models as the Taurus and Sable, the Aerostar, and the Continental, Ford recaptured its lost market share. Equally important, customers liked Ford products enough to come back and buy them again. And they recommended them to their friends and relatives. As a low-cost manufacturer of popular quality products, Ford had back-to-back record earnings in 1986 and 1987, making more money than any automaker ever made in the history of the automobile industry. In fact, in 1987 Ford's earnings of $4.6 billion surpassed the combined earnings of General Motors and Chrysler. In 1988, Ford's net income of $5.3 billion was the first time ever that an automotive company had earned in excess of $5 billion.

Ford's immense success in the mid– and late–1980s is no assurance of a repeat performance during the 1990s. On the contrary, the competition from all fronts will be unyielding and is certain not to leave any room for complacency. Like Ford, General Motors and Chrysler have also made great strides in improving quality and productivity. As the world's largest industrial company, General Motors is certain to be an awesome presence in the 1990s. And the Japanese automakers have not been sleeping. They, too, remain dedicated to continuous improvement, which is clearly reflected in the quality of their early 1990 models.

It's been predicted that an estimated 14.5 million cars and trucks will be sold in the United States during the calendar year ending 1990, the lowest since 1983, and down nearly 2 million from the decade's peak year in 1986, when 16.3 million units were sold. An overproduction of 6 million units is being assembled throughout the world; a majority of these cars will find their way into the U.S. market. The havoc created by this mammoth automotive glut could set the stage for another automotive depression reminiscent of the early 1980s, testing the company's turnaround.

The company is doing some hedging by diversifying into related businesses, namely financial services. "A lot of people ask why we're leaning so heavily in this direction," says Kenneth Whipple, president of Ford Financial Services Group. "No matter how well we do in the automotive business, it will always be a cyclical business. So, we have asked ourselves, 'Is there some element that diversification can provide—a business less cyclical than the car and truck business with a faster inherent growth?' We know that the car business will grow at a slower rate than the GNP during the 1990s, so what is there that will grow at a faster rate? Second, because Ford is a big company, whatever we get into must be large enough in size so it can make a difference. And finally, it should certainly be a business that we know something about.

"Well, with these criteria, financial services is the best business for us to be in," Whipple continues. "With this in mind, our goal is for our financial services interests, in time, to provide 30 percent of Ford Motor Company's profits. Such diversification will enable us to better weather serious downturns in the automotive industry."

Essentially, though, Ford's style is to stick to the basics. "I believe every company should strive to be the low-cost producer," Poling reiterates. "This gives you the greatest opportunity to meet all of the challenges that you are going to face. In an extremely competitive environment, you are in control. You can then decide what to do with your cost advantage—you can maximize your profits, increase your market share by utilizing your low-cost base or you can provide more value to the customer. Or you can do a combination of all three."

There's no question a different Ford Motor Company exists today than the one that lost more than $3.3 billion back in the 1981–1983 depression. The 1990s' Ford is a strong, healthy company. The adversarial relationship between the company and the union is now history. There is open communication between management and labor; new ideas are listened to and when feasible, they are implemented. After several years of sharing in the company's successes in the form of large profit-sharing checks, Ford employees are highly motivated.

Ford workers and managers alike understand the cyclical nature of the automotive industry. Those who have been around for the last 25 years have lived through enough upswings and downswings to accept them as part of the business. However, as the automotive glut of the 1990s rolls in, Ford is a lean, well-managed organization.

As Allan Gilmour emphasizes, "Back in 1978, our U.S. break-even point was 4.2 million units and it's now down to 2.8 million. Even with another period like 1979 to 1982, with the lower overhead, it's probable Ford would still operate in the black. So if there is too much overproduction throughout the industry, by managing our capacity, we'll hold our own. The excess capacity will belong to some other automaker(s), so let them worry about how they manage with too many plants, too many cars, and too much dealer inventory."

Poling adds, "This business is a constant challenge. You can't relax for a moment because somebody out there is trying to beat you— always. It isn't just Japan. It's Korea, General Motors, and Chrysler, and you can count on there being somebody else tomorrow."

Red Poling was once told there seemed to be a paranoia among Ford people. In spite of the record earnings, there still seemed to be an uneasiness, as if they're still running scared.

"A paranoia?" Poling questioned. "Really?"

A broad smile then appeared on his face. "That's good. It means we've done our job well."

APPENDIX

CRUCIAL DATES IN FORD HISTORY

1863	July 30	Henry Ford is born on a Springwells Township farm, Wayne County, Michigan.
1889–1890		Henry Ford experiments on internal-combustion engines.
1896	June 4	Completion of first car at 58 Bagley Avenue in Detroit.
1903	June 16	Ford Motor Company files articles of incorporation in Lansing, Michigan. Henry Ford is named vice-president and chief engineer, receives 25.5 percent of stock.
	July 15	First production car, a two-cylinder Model A, is sold to Ernst Pfennig, a Chicago dentist.
1904	Jan. 12	Henry Ford sets world's speed record by driving "999" 91.37 MPH on frozen Lake St. Clair.
	Aug. 17	Ford Motor Company of Canada, Ltd. is incorporated near Windsor, Ontario.
1906	Oct. 22	Henry Ford succeeds John S. Gray as president of company; acquires 58.5 percent of stock.
1908		Ford opens a sales office in France.
	Oct. 1	Model T is introduced; first production model with left-side steering.

1909		Ford of Canada opens a branch in Australia.
		Ford opens a branch of U.S. parent company in England.
1911		Ford builds an assembly plant in England.
		Ford enters the Latin American market and begins selling cars in Venezuela.
1913		Ford opens an assembly line in France.
	Oct. 7	First moving automobile assembly line starts at Highland Park, Michigan.
1914	Jan. 5	Daily wage of $5 for eight hours of work is announced, replacing scale of $2.34 for nine-hour day.
1915	July	Rouge Plant property is acquired.
	Dec. 10	The 1 millionth Ford car is built.
1917		Henry Ford and Son, Ltd. is established in Cork, Ireland, the only Ford company bearing the full name of the founder.
	July 2	First Ford truck is introduced.
	Sept. 4	Henry Ford II is born.
	Oct. 1	Fordson, the world's first mass-produced tractor, is made in Dearborn.
1918	Jan. 4	First Rouge complex construction begins.
1919		Ford incorporates in Denmark.
		Ford establishes a sales office in Brazil and the following year begins to assemble cars there.
	Jan. 1	Edsel B. Ford succeeds Henry Ford as president.
	July 1	Ford Motor Company is incorporated in Delaware.
1920		Ford begins assembly plant operations in Cadiz, Spain.
1922		Ford builds an all-new automotive assembly plant in Argentina, the first in Latin America.
		Ford is incorporated in Belgium.
	Feb. 4	Lincoln Motor Company is purchased for $8 million.

1923		Ford establishes a national company in Italy.
1924		Ford forms a company in Sweden.
		Ford expands to the Netherlands.
	June 4	The 10 millionth Ford car is built.
	Aug. 5	First public tours of the Rouge are made.
1925		Ford establishes a national company in Mexico and the following year begins assembling cars there.
		Ford Werke AG is formed in 1925 in Germany and the following year begins operating an assembly plant in Berlin.
		Ford opens in Japan and begins to assemble cars in a waterfront warehouse in Yokohama.
1926		Ford establishes a sales office in Finland.
1927	Feb. 10	First radio-range system guides a Ford trimotor plane from Dearborn to Dayton, Ohio, through a snowstorm. System is later made available to air transport industry for free.
	Nov. 1	New 1928 Model A production begins at Rouge.
	Dec. 2	Model A is introduced to public.
1928	Nov. 1	Ford Motor Company becomes first mass producer to use safety glass as standard equipment.
1929	Mar. 28	Total Rouge employment climbs to 103,000.
1931		Ford opens an assembly plant and manufacturing facility in Cologne, Germany.
	Apr. 14	The 20 millionth Ford car is built.
1932		Ford expands to Portugal.
	Feb. 28	End of production of Model A passenger cars and trucks. A total of 4,813,617 were produced in the United States.
	Mar. 9	First V-8 Ford car is built.
1933	Jan. 8	Final Ford trimotor plane is completed; a total of 199 were built.
	June 12	Greenfield Village is opened to the public.

1936		Ford Motor Company of New Zealand Ltd. is formed.
	May	The Ford Foundation is established by Henry and Edsel Ford.
1937	Jan. 18	The 25 millionth Ford car is built.
1938	Oct. 8	First Mercury is produced.
	Dec. 19	Henry Ford II is elected a director of company.
1939	Apr. 30	New York World's Fair opens; Ford Exposition Building features ride on the "Road of Tomorrow."
	Oct.	Lincoln Continental is introduced.
1941	June 20	The company and UAW-CIO execute the first closed-shop contract with check-off dues; 123,000 employees were covered.
1942	Feb. 10	World War II halts civilian automobile production.
1943	May 26	Edsel B. Ford dies at age forty-nine.
	June 1	Henry Ford is reelected president.
	Dec. 15	Henry Ford II is elected vice-president.
1944	Jan. 23	Henry Ford II is elected executive vice-president.
	Aug. 31	Willow Run Plant hits peak monthly production of 432 B-24 Liberator bombers.
1945	June 28	Last B-24 Liberator bomber is assembled at Willow Run. Ford Motor Company completes World War II assignment after having manufactured 8,600 bombers; 250,000 jeeps; 93,000 military trucks; 27,000 tank engines; 4,300 gliders; 1,700 tanks and tank destroyers; 13,000 amphibians; 12,500 armored cars; and 57,000 aircraft engines.
	July 3	Ford passenger car production resumes.
	Sept. 21	Henry Ford II is named president.
1946	July 1	Ernest R. Breech is named executive vice-president.
	Dec. 31	After having lost $50 million during the first seven months of the year, a profit of $2,000 for the year is announced.
1947		Ford establishes a sales company in Austria.

	Apr. 7	Henry Ford, age eighty-three, dies at Fair Lane, his home in Dearborn.
	Apr. 18	Henry Ford's will is made public; nonvoting stock left to the Ford Foundation.
1948		Ford expands to Switzerland.
	Apr. 8	Production starts on 1949 Ford, the first new post-war design. It leads the way to the company's first 1 million car-sales year since 1929.
	June 4	William Clay Ford is elected a director of company.
1950	Sept. 7	Cost-of-living salary adjustment plan for hourly and salaried employees is announced.
1953	May 12	William Clay Ford is elected vice-president and general manager of Special Product Operations.
	June 16	Dedication of the Ford Research and Engineering Center.
	Sept. 9	The 40 millionth Ford vehicle (a Mercury convertible) is produced.
1954	Oct. 22	Thunderbird is announced.
1955	Jan. 25	Ernest R. Breech is named chairman of the board.
	Apr. 18	Separate Lincoln and Mercury divisions are established and a new Special Products Division is formed.
	Oct. 4	William Clay Ford introduces the new Continental Mark II.
1956	Jan. 17	Public sale of Ford Motor Company common stock begins.
	Mar. 27	Company's first public annual report proclaims a "Decade of Growth," announcing that Ford went from net loss in 1946 to record profits of $437 million in 1955.
	May 10	Aeronutronic Systems, Inc., a new company division, is established.
	July 21	The Lincoln and Continental divisions consolidate.
	Sept. 26	Ford's new 12-story central office building (the Glass House) is dedicated in Dearborn.

	Nov. 19	The Edsel is announced and the Special Products Division becomes the Edsel Division.
1957	Apr. 18	The 2.5 millionth Ford-built tractor is produced.
	Aug. 31	The Lincoln and Mercury divisions are combined.
	Sept. 4	The public introduction of the Edsel is made.
1958	Jan. 10	Ford Division announces its entry into the heavy- and extra-heavy-duty truck field.
1959		Ford creates a national company in Venezuela.
	Apr. 29	The company's 50 millionth vehicle, a Ford Galaxie Town Sedan, is produced at the Dearborn Assembly Plant.
	June 24	Aeronutronic Systems, Inc., becomes Aeronutronic, a division of Ford.
	Aug. 24	Ford Motor Credit Company is formed.
	Oct. 8	The Falcon is introduced to public.
	Nov. 19	The Edsel line is terminated.
1960		Ford expands to Norway.
	July 13	Ernest Breech resigns as chairman, and Henry Ford II is elected chairman in addition to being president of company.
	Sept. 27	Ford Division introduces new Econoline truck series, including van, pickup, and station wagon bus.
	Nov. 9	Robert S. McNamara is elected president of Ford.
	Dec. 12	McNamara is named secretary of defense by President-elect Kennedy and resigns as president of Ford effective January 1, 1961. Henry Ford II resumes duties of president.
1961	Apr. 12	John Dykstra is elected president of Ford.
	Apr. 16	Ford Parts Division is formed.
	Oct. 3	UAW calls first companywide strike against Ford Motor Company in the history of their 20-year relationship. Strike ends 17 days later.
	Nov. 16	Fairlane, a new intermediate-size Ford Division car, is introduced.

	Dec. 11	Philco Corporation is acquired.
1962	July 2	The 30 millionth V-8 engine is produced by Ford.
	Nov. 9	Ford Rotunda is destroyed by fire.
1963	Jan. 7	The 60 millionth Ford car is produced.
	May 1	Arjay Miller becomes Ford's seventh president.
	July 30	The 100th anniversary of birth of Henry Ford is celebrated.
1964	Apr. 17	The Mustang, a low-priced, four-passenger car, is introduced.
1965	Oct. 1	The new four-wheel drive Bronco utility vehicle is introduced.
1966	Mar. 2	The 1 millionth Mustang is built in less than two years of production.
	Sept. 30	The Mercury Cougar is introduced.
1967	Mar. 8	Two industry "firsts" are dedicated—Ford's Automotive Safety Research Center and the company's Service Research Center.
	May 3	Ford's 70 millionth U.S.-built vehicle is produced.
	Sept. 6	The UAW begins a companywide strike, which ends on October 22.
1968	Feb. 6	Semon E. Knudsen is elected president and Arjay Miller becomes vice-chairman of the board.
	Apr. 5	The Continental Mark III is introduced.
1969	Apr. 17	The Maverick, a new low-priced compact car, is introduced.
	Sept. 11	Lee A. Iacocca is named president of Ford North American Automotive Operations, Robert Stevenson is elected president of Ford International Automotive Operations, and Robert J. Hampson is elected president of Ford Non-Automotive Operations.
1970	Sept. 11	Ford Division introduces the Pinto, a new subcompact car.
	Dec. 10	Lee Iacocca is elected president of Ford Motor Company.

1971   Apr. 12   Ford Customer Service Division is formed.

1972   Ford establishes a company in Taiwan.

        May 22   Henry Ford II and architect John Portman announce
                   a major development project for Detroit's riverfront,
                   now known as the Renaissance Center.

1973   Jan. 12   Clifton R. Wharton, Jr., becomes the first black to
                   be elected to Ford's board of directors.

        Sept. 21   The Mustang II is introduced to the public.

1974   Jan. 7   Edsel Ford II joins company as a product analyst.

        July 29   The new 14-story Hyatt Regency Dearborn Hotel
                   has a "topping out" ceremony.

        Dec. 22   Ford Parts and Service Division is formed.

1976   Sept.   The new subcompact Fiesta is introduced to Euro-
                   pean market.

        Oct. 26   New manufacturing complex in Valencia, Spain, is
                   dedicated by Henry Ford II. King Juan Carlos is in
                   attendance.

1977   Apr. 15   Grand opening of Renaissance Center.

        Nov. 15   The 100 millionth U.S.-built vehicle is made—a 1978
                   Fairmont Futura off the assembly line in Mahwah,
                   New Jersey.

1978   June 16   Ford Motor Company celebrates its 75th anniversary.

        July 27   Benson Ford, director and vice-president, dies.

        Sept. 14   Philip Caldwell is elected president.

        Oct. 15   Lee Iacocca leaves Ford Motor Company.

        Dec. 14   The 150 millionth Ford vehicle is produced—a 1979
                   Mustang at Dearborn Assembly Plant.

1979   Oct. 1   Henry Ford retires as CEO and is replaced by Philip
                   Caldwell.

        Oct. 15   William Clay Ford, Jr., joins the company as a prod-
                   uct planning analyst.

        Nov. 1   Ford purchases 25 percent equity in Toyo Kogyo of
                   Japan, which is later to become Mazda Motor
                   Corporation.

1980	Feb. 7	The dedication of Engineering Computer Center in Dearborn, the largest concentration of automated design and engineering computers in the automotive industry.
	Mar. 13	Philip Caldwell succeeds Henry Ford as chairman of the board of directors. Donald Petersen is elected president and chief operating officer.
	Aug. 11	Launching of Ford's "world cars," the 1981 Ford Escort and Mercury Lynx.
1981	Apr. 9	Dedication of Diversified Products Technical Center in Dearborn.
	Sept.	The Escort sets world's record for the manufacture of the fastest-ever first-million sales of any new car, breaking a record formerly held by the 1918 Model A Ford.
	Dec. 10	The Rouge Steel Company subsidiary is formed.
1982	Feb. 13	Historic Ford-UAW agreement is reached featuring many innovative labor-management concepts.
	Mar. 12	The Ranger pickup truck is introduced.
	Sept. 28	The UAW-Ford National Development and Training Center is opened in Dearborn.
	Oct. 1	Henry Ford II retires as company officer and employee.
	Oct. 4	Asia-Pacific Testar is introduced.
	Dec. 2	Ford Robotics and Automation Applications Consulting Center is opened in Dearborn.
1983	Feb. 17	The aerodynamically designed Thunderbird and Cougar are introduced.
	Mar. 10	The Bronco II utility vehicle is introduced.
	May 26	The Tempo and Topaz are introduced.
	Aug. 25	The Escort Cabriolet, the first Ford convertible in Europe in 25 years, is introduced.
	Oct. 14	Ford acquires a 30 percent equity interest in Otosan, an automotive manufacturer in Turkey.
	Dec. 17	The Continental Mark VII is introduced.

1984	Jan. 16	Ford agrees to purchase the historic Dearborn Inn.
	Feb. 1	The 3 millionth Fiesta is built at Ford of Spain.
	Mar. 26	Ford Escort is heralded as the world's best-selling car for the third consecutive year.
1985	Feb. 1	Donald E. Petersen succeeds Philip Caldwell as chairman of the board; Harold A. Poling is elected president.
	Feb. 7	The first air bag–equipped Ford Tempo is delivered to the Department of Transportation as part of a 5,000 car experimental fleet.
	May 22	Merger of Ford and Amcar operations in South Africa is completed. The new company is called South African Motor Corporation (SAMCOR).
	July 17	The first Aerostar minivan rolls off the line at the St. Louis Assembly Plant.
	Sept. 7	A two-week strike occurs at Lorain Assembly Plant and ends an eight-year period in which not a single unit of production was lost by Ford due to work stoppage.
	Oct. 10	Ford pays $330 million to acquire Sperry New Holland, the world's largest manufacturer of speciality farm equipment and combines.
	Dec. 16	Ford completes the acquisition of First Nationwide Financial Corporation, operator of the ninth-largest U.S. savings and loan, for $493 million.
	Dec. 26	The Ford Taurus and the Mercury Sable go on sale after a five-year, $3 billion development.
1986	Dec.	Ford acquires a 10 percent equity interest in Kia Motor Company of South Korea.
1987		In a joint venture with Mazda, Ford creates the largest vehicle assembly plant in New Zealand, a company in which Ford owns a 74 percent equity interest.
	Sept. 27	Henry Ford II dies at age seventy.
	Oct. 21	Ford becomes majority shareholder with controlling interest of AC Cars, Ltd.

Nov. 18 Ford acquires United States Leasing International, Inc.

Dec. 26 The new front-wheel–drive Lincoln Continental is introduced.

Dec. 30 Hertz Corporation is acquired for $1.3 billion by Park Ridge Corporation, formed by Ford and certain members of Hertz senior management.

1988 Jan. 14 Edsel B. Ford II and William Clay Ford II are elected to the board of directors.

Feb. 18 Ford announces a record $4.6 billion net income for 1987—a world's all-time record for an automotive manufacturer.

Apr. 25 Ford completes its disinvestment from South Africa.

May 12 The Probe, a new front-wheel–drive sporty specialty car, is introduced.

May 23 The 3 millionth U.S. Ford Escort is built at the Wayne Assembly Plant.

Sept. 12 A joint program with Nissan is announced to design, engineer, and produce a minivan to be sold in North America.

Oct. 31 Ford agrees to provide approximately $300 million in financing for acquisition of Budget Rent A Car by Breech Holdings Corporation.

Dec. First Nationwide, an operation of Ford's Financial Services Group, acquires four savings and loans with combined assets of $8.2 billion and a total of 82 branches.

1989 Feb 10. Ford announces its earnings for 1988 are an all-time high of $5.3 billion —the third consecutive year of record profits and the highest ever for any automotive company.

Apr. 1 William Clay Ford retires.

Apr. 25 The 25th anniversary of the Mustang is celebrated.

Oct. 31 Associates First Capital Corporation, the nation's third largest independent finance company, is purchased for $3.355 million.

	Nov. 11	Ford acquires Jaguar PLC for $2.5 billion.
1990	Jan. 2	Harbour and Associates, Inc. reports that Ford achieved a 31 percent improvement in overall car and truck assembly efficiency in the 1980s. Chrysler's rate of improvement was 17 percent; GM's was 5 percent.
	Jan. 4	Lincoln Town Car is named car of the year by Motor Trend, marking the first time in 38 years that the honor went to a four-door luxury sedan. A Ford Motor Company car has been Motor Trend car of the year for an unprecedented four out of five years.
	Jan. 29	By a large margin, Ford is ranked number one by Fortune magazine as the most admired U.S. company in the motor vehicles and parts industry.
	Mar. 1	Donald Petersen retires. Harold Poling is named chief executive officer and chairman of the board. Philip Benton is named president and chief operating officer. Allan Gilmour is named president of Ford Automotive Group.

A NOTE FROM THE AUTHOR

I wrote two previous books about multinational billion-dollar corporations—two of the world's best: IBM (*The IBM Way*, 1986, with Buck Rodgers) and Honda Motor Company (*Honda: An American Success Story*, 1988). I was intrigued and impressed by both IBM and Honda, and this inspired me to write a third book about another company. My criteria were that it should be an exceptional American firm and one that would deliver a message to benefit American management.

The last decade of the twentieth century has arrived—a decade that I believe will be remembered as the era when the survival of a major corporation became dependent on its capacity to compete in a world market. I wanted to write about a company that was on the leading edge of this crucial transformation.

I investigated several companies, but none came close to fulfilling these criteria except Ford. First, I became fascinated with Ford's intriguing history, which, at times, read like a Hollywood script. Second, I was spellbound by the dramatic story of how its management had turned things around from near disaster to stupendous success. And third, many lessons that were revealed could be emulated by other U.S. firms. In fact, they must be.

I was delighted by the willingness of Ford managers to cooperate—with no strings attached. The company agreed to open its doors and assist me in attaining meetings with past and present Ford employees whom I asked to interview. Ford did not receive the right to change any of the content of my completed manuscript—I would tell the Ford story as I saw it. In effect, management was willing to risk that I might not deliver a positive message about the company. As I eventually discovered, after conducting scores of extensive interviews, there wasn't much of a risk after all.

Now for the part of a book I enjoy writing the most—the acknowledgments. I feel this way because (1) it's the last thing I do following a long and tedious effort to complete a manuscript, (2) it gives me an opportunity to thank those people who contributed to work for which I receive the credit (although much of it deserves to go to them), and (3) it's a good time to reflect on many new friends and acquaintances.

My first contact with Ford was with Jerry Sloan, executive director of public affairs. It was my good fortune to be put through to Jerry after making a single cold telephone call to the company. In the beginning, he mostly listened and remained noncommittal, but about two months later I was given carte blanche to carry on, virtually as I pleased, throughout the Ford organization. During the entire 12 months that I worked on the project, Jerry was supportive and absolutely delightful. He has become a dear friend.

Jerry's boss, David Scott, vice-president of external affairs, presented my proposal to Don Petersen and Red Poling, and they consented to open the right doors so I could have access to Ford employees, suppliers, dealers, and consultants, as well as receive hundreds of written documents, speeches, and articles from the company's archives. I am very grateful to David Scott, Don Petersen, and Red Poling.

Dick Routh, assistant manager of the corporate news department, was unbelievably cooperative. Dick was my liaison to the entire Ford Motor Company, and without him there is no doubt I would have been lost. Dick also served as a wonderful sounding board and as an excellent source of information. I deeply appreciate his advice, his follow-through, and above all else, his friendship.

Other people in public affairs to whom I am grateful are Ray Anderson, Linda Becker, Jim Bright, Al Chambers, Cheryl Crawford, Bob Day, Stanley Drall, Tom Foote, Beryl Goldsweig, Evelyn Hankins, Elaine Hopkins, John Jelinek, Mary Joseph, Dick Judy, Gene Koch, David Krupp, Jim McCraw, Gene McKelvey, Bill Peacock, Paul Preuss, Tom Rhoades, Bert Serre, Chuck Snearly, John Spelich, Joy Stinson, Larry Weis, Bud Williams, and Joy Wolfe.

Hundreds of hours for interviews were granted to me by top ranking Ford managers who juggled their busy schedules to give me their generous time. I deeply appreciate their cooperation. These people include Raymond Ablondi, Robert Adams, Nancy Badore, Edward M. Baker, James Bakken, Paul Banas, Edmund Baumgartner, Frank Benesh, Philip

Benton, John Betti, Jack Caldwell, Philip Caldwell, Louis Calloway, Daniel Coulson, Ken Dickinson, Wayne Doran, John Durstine, Jack Eby, William Clay Ford, Allan Gilmour, John Grant, Chuck Gumushian, E. Wray Haack, David Hagen, Edward Hagenlocker, Jack Hall, Robert Hefty, Renaldo Jensen, Frank Judge, Marty Kennedy, Joe Kordick, Clinton Lauer, Helen Love, David McCammon, Doug McClure, John McTague, John Martin, Roger Maugh, Hugh Merchant, Lee Miskowski, Henry Nichol, William Odom, Peter Pestillo, Donald Petersen, Helen Petrauskas, Harold Poling, William Powers, Robert Rewey, John Risk, Ross Roberts, Lou Ross, Julius Sabo, Marvin Sara, William Scollard, Susan Shackson, Jack Telnack, John Vanderzee, Lewis Veraldi, Daniel Vergari, Thomas Wagner, Ron Wallace, Kenneth Whipple, and Morgan Whitney.

Still more interviews included other members of the Ford family—suppliers, dealers, consultants, and friends. In this group, I thank Hank Aguirre, Henry Anzuini, William Brock, Jim Burke, David Crippen, W. Edwards Deming, Ari Deshe, Boyd Fackler, Philip Gardner, Martin Goldfarb, Carlton Guthrie, Henry Hansen, Harry Lum, Southwood Morcott, Patrick O'Daniel, Richard Strauss, Bob Tasca, and EJ Yancy. Their cooperation and candor provided the book with another dimension.

There are several people with the United Auto Workers to whom I am thankful. They include Ken Bannon; Joe D'Amico; Donald Ephlin; Doug Fraser; past UAW president, Frank Joyce; Daniel Vergari; and Stephen Yokich. These individuals provided valuable insight on the union's views of important issues.

During the dozen trips I made to Detroit, I always received warm hospitality at my "home away from home," the Hyatt Regency Dearborn. The entire staff was gracious; in particular, Klaus Peters, general manager, and his assistant, Debbie Levack.

My secretary, Mary Liff, had the tedious task of transcribing hundreds of audiotape cassettes, as well as typing, retyping, and photocopying what amounted to thousands of pages of manuscript. As usual, Mary did a fine job. Beverly Connors helped with some editing of the original manuscript, and she, too, did excellent work. This is the second book that I've had the pleasure to work on with Prentice Hall Press's Paul Aron. I feel fortunate to work with an editor of his talents. I also thank Paul's assistant, David Dunton, for his many contributions. And once again, my thanks to my agent, Al Zuckerman, who guided and advised me throughout the course of writing my manuscript. I feel quite fortunate to have so many wonderful people give their support to me; without them, this book could not have been written.

INDEX